BEHAVIORAL ACCOUNTING

Recent Titles from Quorum Books

BEHAVIORAL ACCOUNTING

The Research and Practical Issues

Ahmed Belkaoui

QUORUM BOOKS
New York · Westport, Connecticut · London

Library of Congress Cataloging-in-Publication Data

Belkaoui, Ahmed, 1943–
  Behavioral accounting.

  Bibliography: p.
  Includes index.
  1. Accounting—Psychological aspects—Research.
I. Title.
HF5630.B437 1989   657'.01'9   88–32147
ISBN 0–89930–341–2 (lib. bdg. : alk. paper)

British Library Cataloguing in Publication Data is available.

Library of Congress Catalog Card Number: 88–32147
ISBN: 0–89930–341–2

First published in 1989 by Quorum Books

Greenwood Press, Inc.
88 Post Road West, Westport, Connecticut   06881

Printed in the United States of America

The paper used in this book complies with the
Permanent Paper Standard issued by the National
Information Standards Organization (Z39.48–1984).

10 9 8 7 6 5 4 3 2 1

To the Nurturers: Habiba Zribi-Belkaoui *(Sousse, Tunisia)*
Elda Cameli-Monti *(Chicago Heights, Illinois)*
Ada Monti-Gasparetti *(Cento Buchi, Italy)*

CONTENTS

EXHIBITS

PREFACE

Most traditional approaches to the construction of an accounting theory have failed to take into account user and preparer behavior in particular, and behavioral assumptions in general. In 1960 Devine made the following criticism:

Let us now turn . . . to the psychological reactions of those who consume accounting output or are caught in its threads of control. On balance it seems fair to conclude that accountants seem to have waded through their relationships to the intricate psychological network of human activity with a heavy-handed crudity that is beyond belief. Some degree of crudity may be excused in a new discipline, but failure to recognize that much of what passes as accounting theory is hopelessly entwined with unsupported behavioral assumptions is unforgiveable. ("Research Methodology and Accounting Theory Formation," *Accounting Review* [July 1960]:394)

Behavioral accounting emphasizes the relevance of accounting information to decision making as well as the individual and group behavior caused by the communication of this information. Accounting is assumed to be action oriented; that is, its purpose is to influence action, or behavior, directly through the informational content of the message conveyed and indirectly through the behavior of accountants. Because accounting is considered a behavioral process, behavioral accounting can be described as the application of behavioral science to accounting. The overall objective of this approach is similar to that of behavioral science. The American Accounting Association's Committee on Behavioral Science Content of the Accounting Curriculum has provided the following view of the objective of behavioral science, a view that also can be applied to behavioral accounting:

The objective of behavioral science is to understand, explain and predict human behavior, that is, to establish generalizations about human behavior that are supported by empirical evidence collected in an impersonal way by procedures that are completely open to review and replication and capable of verification by other interested scholars. Behavioral science, thus, represents the purpose of experimentally confirming specific hypotheses by reference to observable changes in behavior. ("Report," supplement to *Accounting Review* [1971]:247)

Behavioral accounting concerns itself with human behavior as it relates to accounting information and problems. Its basic objective is to explain and predict human behavior in all possible accounting contexts.

Research studies in behavioral accounting have applied behavioral concepts and theories to accounting and have relied on experimental, field, and correlational techniques. The results of this research help to provide an understanding of the behavioral environment of accounting and aid in solving practical behavioral problems that result from the preparation and use of accounting information.

The objective of this book is to provide the reader with a thorough exposure to the various behavioral constructs under investigation in the field of behavioral accounting. Seven chapters examine the main behavioral constructs as follows:

1. Contingency Approaches to the Design of Accounting Systems
2. Functional and Data Fixation
3. The Practice of Slack: A Review
4. Accounting and Language
5. Goal Setting, Participative Budgeting, and Performance
6. Human Resource Considerations in Public Accounting Firms
7. Cultural Determinism in Accounting

The book should be of interest to a variety of reader groups, including researchers in the field of behavioral accounting, accounting practitioners interested in the implementation of behavioral accounting findings, and graduate and undergraduate students in behavioral accounting classes.

Many people helped in the development of this book. Todd Adkins and Eric Valentine of Greenwood Press are true professionals. They have my best gratitude. Finally, thanks to Hedi and Janice M. Belkaoui, whose sense of humor and perseverance made everything possible.

1

CONTINGENCY APPROACHES TO THE DESIGN OF ACCOUNTING SYSTEMS

A perfect match between specific contingencies and the various characteristics of accounting systems is the objective of the method of theoretical and empirical research generally known as the contingency approach to the design of accounting systems. Research of this type dismisses the notion that universality in the design of accounting systems can be reached to accommodate all situations through a search for the factors that can best ensure the effectiveness of the accounting systems. The purposes of this chapter are to explain the contingency approach and to elaborate on the various theoretical and empirical studies that have adopted it.

CONTINGENCY THEORY

The contingency theory approach to the design of accounting systems assumes that a general strategy applicable to all organizations does not exist. On the contrary, it assumes that the design of various components of accounting systems depends on specific contingencies that can create a perfect match. It is then the perfect link or match between the design of accounting systems and the specific contingencies that is the scope of contingency theory. To date, the contingency formulations have considered the effects of technology, organizational structure and theory, and the environment in attempting to explain how accounting systems differ in various situations. All of these formulations point to the accepted thesis that there is no universal, "best design" for a management accounting information system, and that "it all depends upon situational factors."[1]

These formulations adopt a general framework that links (1) some contingent variables (that is, variables that cannot be influenced by the organization) to (2) any components of an organizational control package (consisting of accounting

information design, other management information design, organizational design, or organizational control arrangements), and then through (3) some intervening variables provide a link to (4) a measure of organizational effectiveness.[2]
The formulations are either empirical or theoretical. In what follows, both types
will be covered.

THEORETICAL FORMULATIONS

Waterhouse and Tiessen's Framework

Waterhouse and Tiessen proposed an efficient design of a management accounting system and a choice of control mechanisms that depend on the structure
and context of an organization (see Exhibit 1.1).[3] The contextual variables that
shape the organizational structure are assumed to be technology and environment. Technology is conceptualized as variable, from routine to nonroutine,
based on the nature of raw materials and search processes. Environment is
mapped on a continuum from highly predictable to highly unpredictable. The
properties of the organizational structure that are shaped by technology and
environment are the distribution of authority and power, the question of centralization versus decentralization, and the issue of procedure specification. In
other words, the distribution of organizational authority and the extent to which
procedures can be specified depend on technology and environment. The type of
organizational structure, in turn, is assumed to affect management accounting
processes such as planning, resource allocation, and measures of performance.

Gordon and Miller's Framework

Gordon and Miller proposed a contingency framework for the design of accounting information systems that takes into account the environment, organizational attributes, and managerial decision-making styles (see Exhibit 1.2).[4] The
environment is characterized by three key dimensions: dynamism, heterogeneity,
and hostility. The organizational attributes include decentralization, differentiation, integration, bureaucratization, and resources. Finally, the decision-making
style of executives is characterized by the following six dimensions: analysis of
decisions, decision time horizons, multiplexity of decision making, adap-
tiveness, proactivity, and consciousness of strategies. These contextual factors
and their key dimensions are assumed to have an impact on such prerequisites of
the accounting information system as information load, centralization of reporting, cost allocation methods, frequency of reporting, method of reporting, time
element of information, performance evaluation, measurement of events, and
valuation methods. While the number of permutations of these variables may

Exhibit 1.1
Waterhouse and Tiessen's Contingency Model for the Design of a Management Accounting System

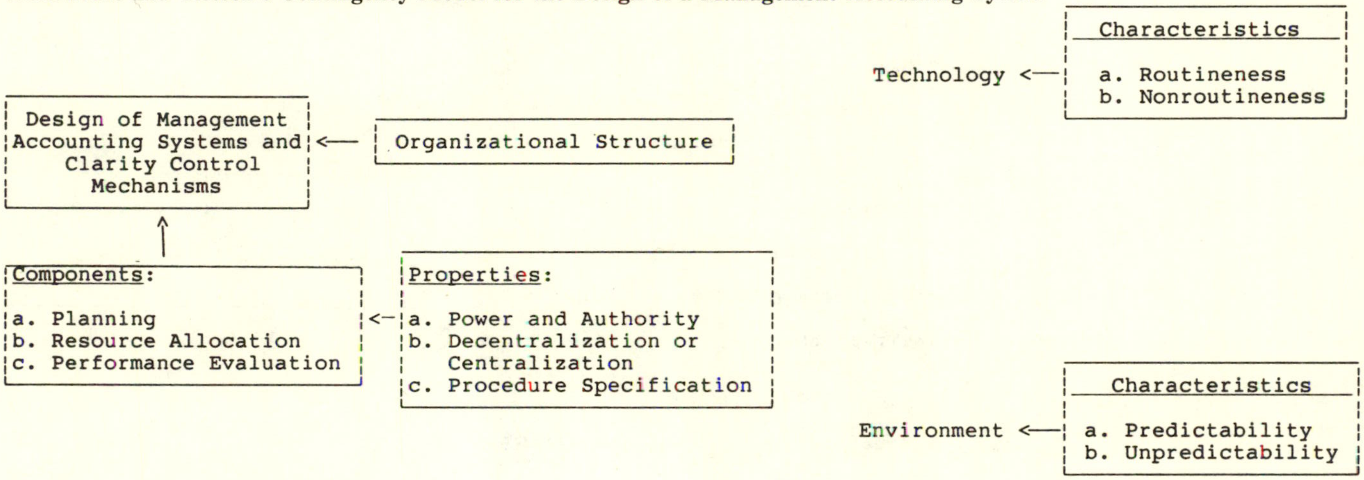

```
                              ┌─────────────────────┐
                              │ Characteristics     │
                              ├─────────────────────┤
                Technology <──│ a. Routineness      │
                              │ b. Nonroutineness   │
                              └─────────────────────┘


                              ┌─────────────────────┐
                              │ Characteristics     │
                              ├─────────────────────┤
               Environment <──│ a. Predictability   │
                              │ b. Unpredictability │
                              └─────────────────────┘


                    ┌──────────────────────────┐
                    │ Organizational Structure │
                    └──────────────────────────┘
                                  │
                                  v

     ┌──────────────────────┐        ┌─────────────────────────────┐
     │ Design of Management │        │ Properties:                 │
     │ Accounting Systems and│<──────│ a. Power and Authority      │
     │ Clarity Control      │        │ b. Decentralization or      │
     │ Mechanisms           │        │    Centralization           │
     └──────────────────────┘        │ c. Procedure Specification  │
              ^                       └─────────────────────────────┘
              │
     ┌──────────────────────┐
     │ Components:          │
     │ a. Planning          │
     │ b. Resource Allocation│
     │ c. Performance Evaluation│
     └──────────────────────┘
```

Exhibit 1.2
Gordon and Miller's Contingency Model for the Design of an Accounting Information System

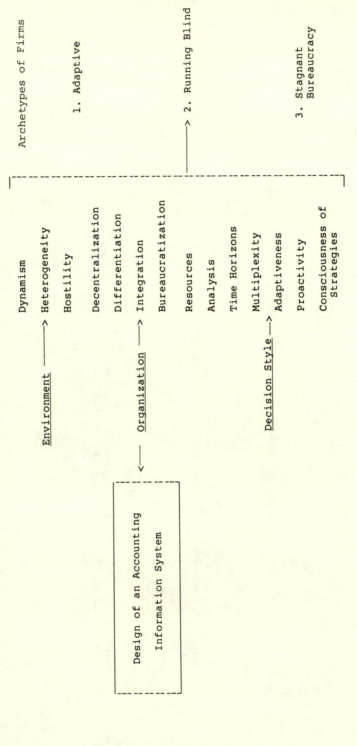

suggest an unmanageable number of situations, Gordon and Miller suggested, in fact, that "it seems that environmental, organizational, and decision style traits are not distributed randomly but actually cluster together to form commonly accruing configurations."[5] Three archetypes—the adaptive firm, the firm running blind, and the stagnant bureaucracy—are presented as evidence of the need for a contingency approach in the design of an accounting information system.

MacIntosh and Daft's Framework

MacIntosh and Daft investigated the relationship between one characteristic of the organization and the control system design.[6] By interdependence they meant the extent to which departments depend on each other and exchange information and resources to accomplish a task. It is also a variable relevant to control systems. Interdependence can be (1) *pooled* when the departments are relatively autonomous and little work flows between them, (2) *sequential* when the departments are linked in a serial fashion, with the output of one department used as the input of the next department, and (3) *reciprocal* when the departments work jointly on a project and work flows back and forth between them.[7] The management control system is viewed in terms of three control subsystems: operating budgets, statistical reports, and standard operating procedures and policies. The hypothesized relationships and the use of management control systems are as follows:

1. In the case of pooled departmental interdependency, the preferred means of control is standardization and a greater reliance on standard operating procedures than on either operating budgets or statistical reports.
2. In the case of sequential departmental interdependency, the preferred means of control are planning and measurement, with more reliance on operating budgets and statistical reports than on standard operating procedures.
3. In the case of reciprocal departmental interdependency, the preferred means of control is mutual adjustment; less reliance is put on operating budgets, statistical reports, and standard operating procedures.

The results of MacIntosh and Daft's field study showed that when interdependence is low, control is focused on the use of standard operating procedures; when it is moderate, control rests on budgets and statistical reports; and when it is high, the role of the three control systems diminishes.

MacIntosh's Framework

MacIntosh proposed a contextual model of information systems that embraces both a macro-organizational concept—technology and a human information pro-

Exhibit 1.3
A Contextual Model of Information Systems

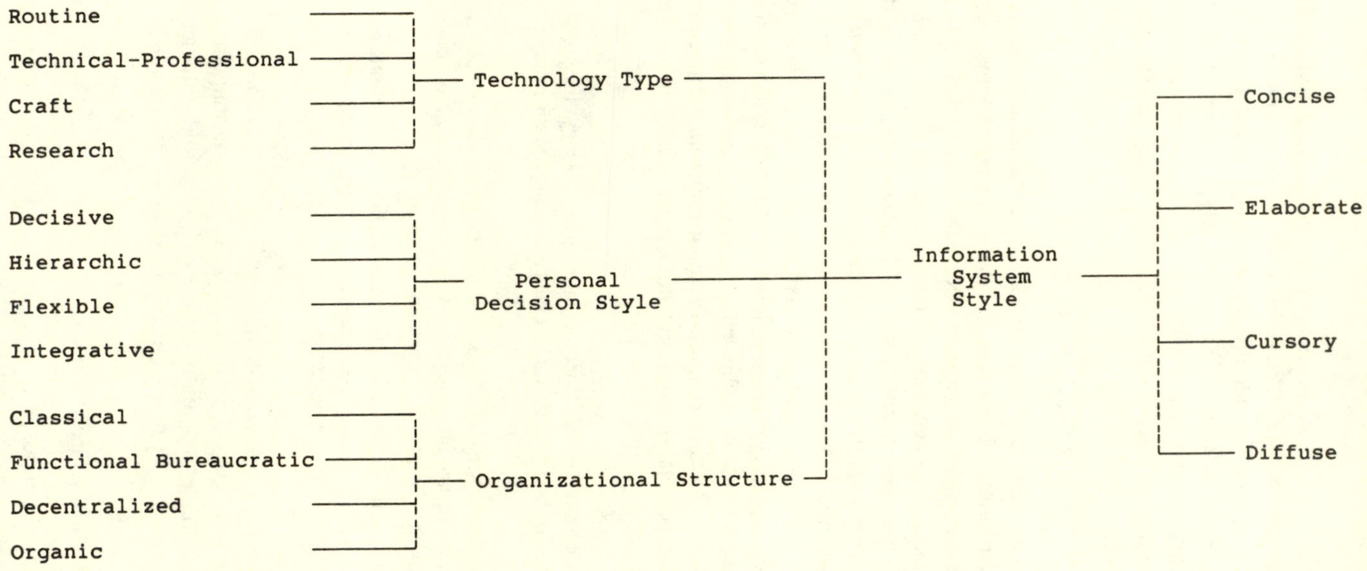

```
                                                        ┌── Concise
                                  ┌── Technology Type ───┤
                                  │                      └── Elaborate
                                  │
  Routine ──────┐                 │     Information      ┌── Cursory
  Technical-Professional ─┤       │──── System ─────────┤
  Craft ────────┤                 │       Style          └── Diffuse
  Research ─────┘                 │
                                  │
  Decisive ─────┐                 │
  Hierarchic ───┤── Personal ─────┤
  Flexible ─────┤   Decision Style
  Integrative ──┘

  Classical ────────────┐
  Functional Bureaucratic ── Organizational Structure
  Decentralized ────────┤
  Organic ──────────────┘
```

cessing system construct—and personal decision style.[8] Basically, the model combines personal decision style, technology type, and organizational structure to derive an information system style (see Exhibit 1.3). These variables are defined as follows:

1. Driver and Mock's decision-style model is used to define the decision-style variables.[9] The model assumes two dimensions of information processing: amount of information used (from minimum to maximum) and degree of focus in the use of data (from one solution to multiple solutions). These two dimensions are combined to derive four distinctive styles: decisive, flexible, hierarchic, and integrative.

The *decisive* style assumes the use of a minimum amount of data to generate different meanings at different times. Decisive individuals look for efficiency, speed, and consistency in the information to be used. They prefer brief communications and summary reports focusing on one solution, results, and action. They like to be in hierarchic organizations with a short, clear span of control and clear rules.

The *flexible* style assumes the use of a minimum amount of data to generate different meanings at different times. Flexible individuals look for speed, adaptability, and intuition rather than developing and operating in accordance to a plan. They prefer brief communications that focus on a variety of solutions. They favor loose and fluid organizational patterns.

The *hierarchic* style assumes the use of masses of data to generate one firm opinion. Hierarchic individuals look for thoroughness, precision, and perfectionism. They prefer long, formal, thorough reports that present problems, methods, and data and generate one best solution. They like to be in a classic organization with a broad span and control as well as elaborate procedures.

The *integrative* style assumes the use of masses of data to generate a multitude of possible solutions. Integrative individuals look for the creative use of information in experiments, simulations, and games. They prefer complex and fluid communication that emphasizes discussion rather than reports. They like to work in nonautocratic teams and in nonhierarchic organizations of the matrix type.[10]

2. Perrow's categories of technology are used to define the technology variable.[11] The model assumes two dimensions of technology: task knowledge (from analyzable to unanalyzable) and task variety (from low to high). These two dimensions derive from distinctive categories of knowledge: (*a*) craft technology (analyzable task knowledge and low craft technology task variety); (*b*) routine technology (analyzable task knowledge and low task variety); (*c*) research technology (unanalyzable task knowledge and high task variety); and (*d*) technical-professional technology (analyzable task knowledge and high task variety). Each of these categories of knowledge is assumed to be best served by a distinctive organizational structure that fits the special needs of the task.

3.   Finally, four information styles are differentiated in terms of two dimensions: amount and ambiguity. MacIntosh defined them in the following manner:

The concise information system. Small to moderate amounts of information that are precise and unambiguous, and are used in a quick and decisive way.

The elaborate information system. Large amounts of information, frequently in the form of data bases or simulation models, which tend to be detailed and precise; recipients normally use such information in a slow and deliberate manner.

The cursory information system. Small amounts of information, neither precise nor detailed and frequently superficial, that are used in a causal yet decisive way.

The diffuse information system. Moderate to large amounts of information, covering a wide range of material, frequently ill-defined and imprecise, that typically are used in a slow, deliberate manner.[12]

Ewusi-Mensah's Framework

Ewusi-Mensah investigated the impact of the external organizational environment on management information systems.[13] The organizational environment was classified as either static or dynamic, and as controllable, partially controllable, or uncontrollable. Variations in organizational environments are assumed to require different decision processes and, consequently, different information characteristics, including information quality, information availability, information value, impact on decision making, organizational interaction, organizational search, response time, time horizon, information source, and information type (see Exhibit 1.4).

EMPIRICAL STUDIES IN CONTINGENCY THEORY

Use of Capital Budgeting Techniques

The use of discounted cash-flow techniques has been touted in the corporate finance literature as superior to nondiscounting techniques as tools for the selection of capital investments. Several empirical studies have attempted to confirm the thesis that a firm should not perform better if it uses naive techniques.[14] Their results, however, have been mixed. To correct for a variety of theoretical and methodological limitations, Haka, Gordon, and Pincher used a theoretical model, derived from financial economic theory, which showed that improved firm performance (a measurement of stock market data) was not significantly associated with discounted cash-flow techniques.[15] The relationship between the use of capital budgeting techniques and firm performance is obviously mitigated by contingent, firm-specific characteristics. Using such a perspective Haka developed and tested a contingency theory that could predict which firms were

Exhibit 1.4
Impact of the External Organizational Environment on Management Information Systems

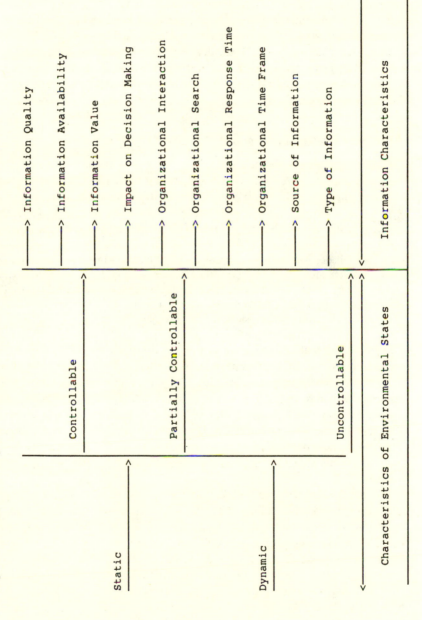

most likely to benefit from using sophisticated capital budgeting techniques.[16] The external characteristics used in the model were (1) the strategy of the firm (defender or prospector), (2) environmental predictability (stable or dynamic), and (3) environmental diversity (homogeneous or heterogeneous). The internal characteristics were (1) the information system (supportive or nonsupportive), (2) the reward structure, and (3) the degree of decentralization. The results of the survey study provided evidence of a positive relationship between the effectiveness of the sophisticated capital budgeting techniques and a predictable environment, the use of long-term reward systems, and the degree of decentralization.

Business Strategy and Control Systems

Business strategy is another source of contingency in the design of organizations and control systems.[17] Govindarajan and Gupta examined the linkages between strategy, incentive bonus systems, and effectiveness at the strategic business unit level within diversified firms.[18] A survey of general managers of strategic business units (SBUs) in diversified firms yielded the following results:

(1) greater reliance on long-run criteria as well as greater reliance on subjective (nonformula) approaches for determining the SBU general managers' bonus contributes to effectiveness in the case of built SBUs but hampers it in the case of harvest SBUs, and (2) the relationship between the extent of bonus system's reliance on short-run criteria and SBU effectiveness is virtually independent of SBU strategy.[19]

The first result stands to reason given the expectation that built units will face greater environmental uncertainty than will harvest units. Built strategies take place in the growth stage of the product life cycle, whereas harvest strategies take place in the mature and decline stages of the product life cycle. This explains the greater changes and unpredictability in factors such as technology, product design, process design, market demand, number of completions, and competitive structure in the growth stage of the product life cycle.[20] Subjective bonus determinations may alleviate the burden of the dependencies that face the build manager.

The relationship between business strategy and accounting-based control system attributes was also examined by Simons.[21] This study was motivated, first, by the inconclusive attempts to test Burns and Stalker's findings that unstructured, organic organizations with minimal formal controls were best suited to a strategy of innovation, and, second, by Miller and Friesen's conclusion that controlling for the strategy of the firm is critical to understanding the relationship between control and innovation.[22] Using interviews and a derived questionnaire, Simons expressed the attributes of control systems in terms of tightness of budget goals, use of control, frequency of reporting, and intensity of the monitoring of performance results. Using Miles and Snow's typology, strategies were classified with reference to defenders, prospectors, and analyzers.[23] These types were defined as follows:

Defenders operate in relatively stable product areas, offer more limited products than competitors, and compete through cost leadership, quality, and service. They engage in little product/market developments. Prospectors, on the other hand, compete through new products and market development. Product lines change over time and this type of firm is constantly seeking new market opportunities. Analyzers are an intermediate hybrid, combining both Defender and Prospector strategies.[24]

The results of the study verified the proposition that firms that rely on different strategies use accounting control systems in different ways.

Perceived Importance and Use of Budget Control

The empirical literature in contingency theory attempted to explain variations in the perceived importance and/or use of budget control on various contingency variables. Khandwalla reported that managers' perceived use of flexible budget control is a positive function of the competition that confronts their organization.[25] He concluded in the following manner:

This implies that as competition intensifies, the expected benefits from the application of these controls tend to outweigh their costs. Thus, for those entrusted with the planning of control systems, it is important to know the degree of competition faced by the firm. Other things being equal, an elaborate control system for a firm not facing serious competition may also do more harm than good.[26]

Burns and Waterhouse found that the importance and use of budget control is higher in larger, decentralized, more technologically sophisticated organizations in which there are formal and standard operating procedures.[27] They observed that

those in highly structured organizations tend to perceive themselves as having more influence, they participate more in budget planning, and they appear to be satisfied with budget-related activities. Managers in organizations where authority is concentrated are generally held accountable for fewer financial variables, they experience superior-initiated pressure, they see budgets as being less useful and limiting their flexibility, but they appear to be satisfied with the use of budgets by their superiors.[28]

Merchant found, furthermore, that the use and importance of budget control is higher in larger, more differentiated, decentralized organizations that have automated technology.[29] Smaller firms were found to rely more on social controls, that is to say, vigorous personnel selection policies, hazing, direct supervision, oral communication, personal interaction, and professional membership.

Finally, Rockness and Shields analyzed differences in the perceived importance of expenditure budget control in research and development work groups that were due to the organizational context (organizational size, expenditure budget size, source of funds) and the management control system (importance of social control, steps in the control process).[30] The results were significant and supportive of previous research, in that they provided additional evidence of a contingency relationship between budget control and organizational context.

Choice of Control Actions and Systems

The effectiveness of organizations depends to a large extent on the achievement of organizational control and the maintenance of overall organizational integrity. The ability of the organization's members to design and maintain control systems appropriate with the overall structure may also be contingent on other various factors. Das, for example, using a simulated setting, found that persons working in organic organizations are more likely to choose intrinsically motivating control strategies, and that those who work in mechanistic organizations are more likely to choose extrinsically motivating control strategies.[31] Das concluded:

Based on the current research evidence, it would appear that major changes in managerial styles (especially in the context of the control process) cannot be expected to emerge until some important changes in the perceptions of organizational characteristics and climate have occurred. Thus, a mere introduction of sophisticated training programs in leadership practices may not bring about the desired effects in the control behaviors of managers if they do not perceive the organizational characteristics and climate to be consistent with these new practices. In this sense, organizational socialization and prevailing organizational norms about appropriate managerial behavior may have greater effects on control behaviors of managers than has hitherto been suspected.[32]

Belkaoui also investigated the relationship between self-disclosure and attitudes to responsibility accounting.[33] Because a responsibility accounting system requires making public one's performance and implies an implicit trust between those controlled and their managers, reported self-disclosure can be related to the attitudes to responsibility accounting system. A field study involving 55 purchasing managers from the Department of Supply and Services in the Canadian government and based on the use of a self-disclosure instrument showed that the attitudes to responsibility accounting were positively related to the amount and control depth factors of self-disclosure and negatively related to the positive-negative, honesty-accuracy, and intended disclosures. Belkaoui concluded as follows:

The first result implies that those subjects willing to talk openly about themselves are more likely to accept one of the conditions of a responsibility accounting system which is responsibility over the controllable costs. The second result implies that the same subjects will be less willing to accept the above condition of a responsibility accounting system if the intended disclosure is to reveal negative versus positive things about themselves, or to assess the sincerity of their statements. Both results may be interpreted to imply the creation of both an open atmosphere and a trust between those controlled toward the acceptance of responsibility within a responsibility accounting system.[34]

Contingency Approach to Performance Assessment

A contingency approach to performance assessment was demonstrated by Hayes's study.[35] His results indicated that (1) internal factors are the major explanations for the performance of production departments, and (2) environmental as well as interdependency variables provide approximately equal contributions to the explanation of performance by marketing departments. Govindarajan examined the contingency relationship between environmental uncertainty and performance evaluation style.[36] Performance evaluation style was defined as "the degree of reliance superiors place on formula vs. subjective (nonformula) approaches towards the evaluation of the subordinate's performance and in deciding the subordinate's rewards (such as incentive bonus).[37] The results supported the following propositions: (1) superiors of business units that face higher environmental uncertainty will use a more subjective performance appraisal approach, whereas superiors of business units that face lower environmental uncertainty will use a more formula-based performance evaluation approach; and (2) a stronger fit between environmental uncertainty and performance evaluation style is associated with higher business unit performance. These results were used to reconcile Hopwood's dysfunctional effects of the budget constraint style with Otley's opposite findings by arguing that Otley studied units that might have operated in relatively stable environmental conditions while Hopwood may have examined units that might have operated in relatively uncertain environmental conditions.[38]

Determinants of Accounting Information Systems

Technology was examined as a major explanatory variable of an effective accounting information system by Daft and MacIntosh.[39] Their study, based on questionnaires sent to 253 individuals in 24 different work units, produced high correlations between four types of technology and four categories of information systems.

Perceived environmental uncertainty and organizational structures were also examined as to how they related to the information system by Gordon and Narayanan.[40] Their study indicated that the characteristics of information perceived to be important by decision makers are related to perceived environmental uncertainty, but that their relationships to organizational structure are a result of both sets of variables (that is, characteristics of information and structure) being related to perceived environmental uncertainty.

Pijer found that the financial control structure of an organization depends on the complexity of the task it faces (as defined by, for example, the range of products sold, the diversity of the range, seasonal variations, and variations in type of outlet). He also learned that task complexity depends on the financial control structure by way of the intervening variable of organizational structure.[41]

CONCLUSION

Various theoretical and empirical formulations have been proposed in the literature to illustrate the contingency theory approach to the design of accounting systems. Surveys and interviews have been used in the empirical studies. Much, however, remains to be done. For instance, contingent variables need to be better motivated theoretically and empirically. In addition, explicit recognition of the impact on organizational effectiveness is necessary to ensure the success of the match between the contingency variables and the accounting system.

NOTES

1. D. T. Otley, "The Contingency Theory of Management Accounting: Achievement and Prognosis," *Accounting, Organizations and Society* (December 1980): 413–428.

2. Ibid., pp. 420–421.

3. J. H. Waterhouse and P. Tiessen, "A Contingency Framework for Management Accounting Systems Research," *Accounting, Organizations and Society* (August 1978): 65–76.

4. L. A. Gordon and D. Miller, "Design of Accounting Information Systems," *Accounting, Organizations and Society* (June 1976): 59–69.

5. Ibid., p. 65.

6. N. B. MacIntosh and R. L. Daft, "Management Control Systems and Departmental Interdependencies: An Empirical Study," *Accounting, Organizations and Society* (January 1987): 49–61.

7. J. D. Thompson, *Organizations in Action* (New York: McGraw-Hill, 1967).

8. N. B. MacIntosh, "A Contextual Model of Information Systems," *Accounting, Organizations and Society* (February 1981): 39–52.

9. M. J. Driver and T. J. Mock, "Human Information Processing: Decision Style Theory and Accounting Information System," *Accounting Review* (July 1975): 497.

10. In spite of more critical doubts cast on the empirical support for the decision-style model, Driver and Mock argued for a relationship between decision style and the amount of information used. For a criticism of their results, see P. A. Tiessen and D. M. Baker, "Human Information Processing, Decision Style Theory, and Accounting Information Systems: A Comment," *Accounting Review* (October 1977): 984–987.

11. C. Perrow, *Organizational Analysis: A Sociological Review* (Belmont, Calif.: Wadsworth Publishing, 1970).

12. MacIntosh, "A Contextual Model," p. 47.

13. K. Ewusi-Mensah, "The External Environment and Its Impact on Management Information Systems," *Accounting, Organizations and Society* (December 1981): 301–316.

14. G. A. Christy, *Capital Budgeting—Current Practices and Their Efficiency* (Eugene: University of Oregon, Bureau of Business and Economic Research, 1966); T. P. Klammer, "The Association of Capital Budgeting Techniques with Firm Performance," *Accounting Review* (April 1973): 353–364; G. L. Sundem, "Evaluating Simplified Capital Budgeting Models Using a Time-State Performance Matrix," *Accounting Review* (April 1974): 306–320; G. L. Sundem, "Evaluating Capital Budgeting Models in Simulated Environments," *Journal of Finance* (September 1975): 977–992; S. H. Kim, "An Empirical Study on the Relationship between Capital Budgeting Practices and Earnings Performance," *Engineering Economist* (Spring 1982): 185–196.

15. S. F. Haka, L. A. Gordon, and G. E. Pincher, "Sophisticated Capital Budgeting Selection Techniques and Firm Performance," *Accounting Review* (October 1985): 651–669.

16. S. F. Haka, "Capital Budgeting Techniques and Firm Specific Contingencies: A Conditional Analysis," *Accounting, Organizations and Society* (January 1987): 31–48.

17. A. K. Gupta and V. Govindarajan, "Business Unit Strategy, Management Characteristics and Business Unit Effectiveness at Strategy Implementation," *Academy of Management Journal* (March 1984): 221–233.

18. V. Govindarajan and A. K. Gupta, "Linking Control Systems to Business Unit Strategy: Impact on Performance," *Accounting, Organizations and Society* (January 1985): 51–66.

19. Ibid.

20. C. W. Hofer and D. E. Schendel, *Strategy Formulation: Analytical Concepts* (St. Paul, Minn.: West Publishing, 1978); D. C. Hambrick, I. C. MacMillan, and D. I. Day, "Strategic Attributes and Performance in the Four Cells of the BCG-matrix: A PIMS-based Analysis of Industrial-Product Business," *Academy of Management Journal* (January 1982): 510–531.

21. R. Simons, "Accounting Control Systems and Business Strategy: An Empirical Analysis," *Accounting, Organizations and Society* (July 1987): 357–374.

22. T. Burns and G. H. Stalker, *The Management of Innovation* (London: Tavistock, 1961); D. Miller and P. H. Friesen, "Innovation in Conservation and Entrepreneurial Firms," *Strategic Management Journal* (February 1982): 1–27.

23. R. E. Miles and C. C. Snow, *Organizational Strategy, Structure, and Process* (New York: McGraw-Hill, 1978).

24. Simons, "Accounting Control Systems," p. 359.

25. P. N. Khandwalla, "The Effects of Different Types of Competition in the Use of Management Controls," *Journal of Accounting Research* (Autumn 1982): 275–285.

26. Ibid., p. 282.

27. W. J. Burns and J. H. Waterhouse, "Budgetary Control and Organizational Structure," *Journal of Accounting Research* (Autumn 1975): 177–203.

28. Ibid., p. 179.

29. Kenneth A. Merchant, "The Design of the Corporate Budgeting System: Influences on Managerial Behavior and Performance," *Accounting Review* (October 1981): 813–829; idem, "Influences on Departmental Budgeting: An Empirical Examination of a

Contingency Model," *Accounting, Organizations and Society* (June 1984): 291–307.

30. H. O. Rockness and M. D. Shields, "An Empirical Analysis of the Expenditure Budget in Research and Development," *Contemporary Accounting Research* (Spring 1988): 568–581.

31. H. Das, "Organizational and Decision Characteristics and Personality as Determinants of Control Actions: A Laboratory Experiment," *Accounting, Organizations and Society* (May 1986): 215–231.

32. Ibid., p. 226.

33. A. Belkaoui, "The Relationship between Self-Disclosure Style and Attitudes to Responsibility Accounting," *Accounting, Organizations and Society* 6, no. 4 (1981): 281–290.

34. Ibid., p. 287.

35. D. C. Hayes, "The Contingency Theory of Management Accounting," *Accounting Review* (January 1977): 22–39.

36. V. Govindarajan, "Appropriateness of Accounting Data in Performance Evaluation: An Empirical Examination of Environmental Uncertainty as an Intervening Variable," *Accounting, Organizations and Society* (February 1984): 125–135.

37. Ibid., 130.

38. A. G. Hopwood, "An Empirical Study of the Role of Accounting Data in Performance Evaluation," supplement to *Journal of Accounting Research* (1972): 156–182; David T. Otley, "Budget Use and Managerial Performance," *Journal of Accounting Research* (Spring 1978): 122–149.

39. R. L. Daft and N. B. MacIntosh, "A New Approach to Design and Use of Management Information," *California Management Review* (Fall 1978): 82–92.

40. L. A. Gordon and V. K. Narayanan, "Management Accounting Systems, Perceived Environmental Uncertainty and Organizational Structures: An Empirical Investigation," *Accounting, Organizations and Society* (December 1983): 33–47.

41. J. Pijer, "Determinants of Financial Control Systems for Multiple Retailers—Some Case Study Evidence" (Unpublished paper, University of Loughborough, 1978).

SELECT BIBLIOGRAPHY

Belkaoui, A. "The Relationship between Self-Disclosure Style and Attitudes to Responsibility Accounting." *Accounting, Organizations and Society*, 6, no. 4 (1981): 281–285.

Burns, T., and G. H. Stalker. *The Management of Innovation*. London: Tavistock, 1961.

Burns, W. J., and J. H. Waterhouse. "Budgetary Control and Organizational Structure." *Journal of Accounting Research* (Autumn 1975): 177–203.

Christy, G. A. *Capital Budgeting—Current Practices and Their Efficiency*. Eugene: University of Oregon, Bureau of Business and Economic Research, 1966.

Daft, R. L., and N. B. MacIntosh. "A New Approach to Design and Use of Management Information." *California Management Review* (Fall 1978): 82–92.

Das, H. "Organizational and Decision Characteristics and Personality as Determinants of Control Actions: A Laboratory Experiment." *Accounting, Organizations and Society* (May 1986): 215–221.

Driver, M. J., and T. J. Mock. "Human Information Processing: Decision Style Theory and Accounting Information System." *Accounting Review* (July 1975): 497.

Ewusi-Mensah, K. "The External Environment and Its Impact on Management Information Systems." *Accounting, Organizations and Society* (December 1981): 301–316.

Gordon, L. A., and D. Miller. "Design of Accounting Information Systems." *Accounting, Organizations and Society* (June 1976): 59–69.

Gordon, L. A., and V. K. Narayanan. "Management Accounting Systems, Perceived Environmental Uncertainty and Organizational Structures: An Empirical Investigation." *Accounting, Organizations and Society* (December 1983): 33–47.

Govindarajan, V. "Appropriateness of Accounting Data in Performance Evaluation: An Empirical Examination of Environmental Uncertainty as an Intervening Variable." *Accounting, Organizations and Society* (February 1984): 125–135.

Govindarajan, V., and A. K. Gupta. "Linking Control Systems to Business Unit Strategy: Impact on Performance." *Accounting, Organizations and Society* (January 1985): 51–66.

Gupta, A. K., and V. Govindarajan. "Business Unit Strategy, Management Characteristics and Business Unit Effectiveness at Strategy Implementation." *Academy of Management Journal* (March 1984): 221–233.

Haka, S. F. "Capital Budgeting Techniques and Firm Specific Contingencies: A Conditional Analysis." *Accounting, Organizations and Society* (January 1987): 31–48.

Haka, S. F., L. A. Gordon and G. E. Pincher. "Sophisticated Capital Budgeting Selection Techniques and Firm Performance." *Accounting Review* (October 1985): 651–669.

Hambrick, D. C., I. C. MacMillan, and D. I. Day. "Strategic Attributes and Performance in the Four Cells of the BCG-matrix: A PIMS-based Analysis of Industrial-Product Business." *Academy of Management Journal* (January 1982): 510–531.

Hayes, D. C. "The Contingency Theory of Management Accounting." *Accounting Review* (January 1977): 22–39.

Hofer, C. W., and D. E. Schendel. *Strategy Formulation: Analytical Concepts.* St. Paul, Minn.: West Publishing, 1978.

Hopwood, A. G. "An Empirical Study of the Role of Accounting Data in Performance Evaluation." Supplement to *Journal of Accounting Research* (1972): 156–182.

Khandwalla, P. N. "The Effects of Different Types of Competition in the Use of Management Controls." *Journal of Accounting Research* (Autumn 1982): 275–285.

Kim, S. H. "An Empirical Study on the Relationship between Capital Budgeting Practices and Earnings Performance." *Engineering Economist* (Spring 1982): 185–196.

Klammer, T. P. "The Association of Capital Budgeting Techniques with Firm Performance." *Accounting Review* (April 1973): 353–364.

MacIntosh, N. B. "A Contextual Model of Information Systems." *Accounting, Organizations and Society* (February 1981): 39–52.

MacIntosh, N. B., and R. L. Daft. "Management Control Systems and Departmental Interdependencies: An Empirical Study." *Accounting, Organizations and Society* (January 1987): 49–61.

Merchant, Kenneth A. "The Design of the Corporate Budgeting System: Influences on Managerial Behavior and Performance." *Accounting Review* (October 1981): 813–829.

————. "Influences on Departmental Budgeting: An Empirical Examination of a Contingency Model." *Accounting, Organizations and Society* (June 1984): 291–307.

Miles, R. E., and C. C. Snow. *Organizational Strategy, Structure, and Process.* New York: McGraw-Hill, 1978.

Miller, D., and P. H. Friesen. "Innovation in Conservation and Entrepreneurial Firms." *Strategic Management Journal* (February 1982): 1–27.

Otley, David T. "Budget Use and Managerial Performance." *Journal of Accounting Research* (Spring 1978): 122–149.

————. "The Contingency Theory of Management Accounting: Achievement and Prognosis." *Accounting, Organizations and Society* (December 1980): 413–428.

Perrow, C. *Organizational Analysis: A Sociological Review.* Belmont, Calif.: Wadsworth Publishing, 1970.

Pijer, J. "Determinants of Financial Control Systems for Multiple Retailers—Some Case Study Evidence." Unpublished paper, University of Loughborough, 1978.

Rockness, H. O., and M. D. Shields. "An Empirical Analysis of the Expenditure Budget in Research and Development." *Contemporary Accounting Research* (Spring 1988): 568–581.

Simons, R. "Accounting Control Systems and Business Strategy: An Empirical Analysis." *Accounting, Organizations and Society* (July 1987): 357–374.

Sundem, G. L. "Evaluating Capital Budgeting Models in Simulated Environments." *Journal of Finance* (September 1975): 977–992.

————. "Evaluating Simplified Capital Budgeting Models Using a Time-State Performance Matrix." *Accounting Review* (April 1974): 306–320.

Thompson, J. D. *Organizations in Action.* New York: McGraw-Hill, 1967.

Tiessen, P. A., and D. M. Baker. "Human Information Processing, Decision Style Theory, and Accounting Information Systems: A Comment." *Accounting Review* (October 1977): 984–987.

Waterhouse, J. H., and P. Tiessen. "A Contingency Framework for Management Accounting Systems Research." *Accounting, Organizations and Society* (August 1978): 65–76.

2

FUNCTIONAL AND DATA FIXATION

Functional fixation, as it is used in accounting, suggests that under certain circumstances a decision maker might be unable to adjust his or her decision process to a change in the accounting process that supplied him or her with input data. Borrowed from the literature of psychology, the phenomenon has been used in a slightly different way by accounting researchers. The purposes of this chapter are, first, to differentiate between the functional-fixation phenomenon as it is understood in psychology and the data-fixation phenomenon as it is used in accounting; second, to examine the results of the various experimental studies in the area; and third, to provide possible theoretical explanations of the phenomenon and to suggest better methodologies for studying the phenomenon in accounting.

NATURE OF FUNCTIONAL FIXATION

Functional Fixation in Psychology

Functional fixation originated as a concept in psychology, arising from an investigation of the impact of past experience on human behavior. In his examination of the relation between stimulus equivalence and reasoning, Maier identified several ways in which past experience can affect the problem-solving process.[1] He viewed past experience as a salient factor in problem solving, in that problem solving can be facilitated by equivalences that exist in immediate problem situations and in past experiences. In addition, the background of past learning is an essential repertoire of behavior that is available for restructuring when it is needed for new situations. Not all psychologists, however, have viewed past experience as a positive factor. Some have seen it as an obstacle that prevents protective thinking. Duncker introduced the concept of functional fixation to illustrate the negative role of past experiences.[2] He investigated the hypothesis that an individual's prior use of an object in a function dissimilar to that required in a present problem would serve to inhibit the discovery of an appropriate, novel use for the object. His results supported the functional-fixation hypothesis with regard to several common objects, for example, boxes, pliers, weights, and paper clips. Birch and Rabinowitz criticized Duncker's experiments, showing that an individual can also learn about an object's versatility and therefore display a relatively low degree of fixation even if learning about one function of an object restricts the number of ways in which it is used.[3] A series of experiments by Flavell, Cooper, and Loisell supported this conclusion.[4]

Others who have refined Duncker's experiments nevertheless have supported the functional-fixation hypothesis. Adamson, in his box experiment, gave subjects the task of attaching three small candles to a screen, at a height of about five feet, using to accomplish the task any of a large number of objects that were lying on the table, namely three pasteboard boxes, five matches, and five thumbtacks.[5] The solution consisted of putting one candle on each box by melting wax on the box, sticking the candle to the box, and then tacking the boxes to the screen. The idea was to have the box be used as a platform on which to attach the candle, a novel function for boxes. Two groups were used. The experimental one was presented with the objects inside the box, the control group had the objects on the table. ''Hence, the boxes had their initial function, that of containing, whereas in their solution function, they had to be used as supports or platforms.''[6] The results showed that the control group outperformed the experimental group in terms of both the number of solutions and the time required to reach the solutions. This suggested that the subjects in the experimental group were functionally fixated on using boxes as containers rather than as platforms.

In the two-string experiments, Adamson and Taylor asked their subjects to tie together the free ends of strings hanging from the ceiling.[7] Because the strings were placed so far apart, the problem could be solved only by tying a weight to one string, swinging it like a pendulum, and catching it while holding the other string. The task then could be completed by tying the two strings together. Of the various objects provided to the subjects, only two—an electrical switch and an electrical relay—were sufficiently heavy to serve as weights. Half of the subjects were trained before the experiment to use the switch to complete an electrical circuit, while the other half were trained to use a relay for the same task. The results of the experiment supported the functional-fixation hypothesis for the reason that the subjects trained to use the switch to complete the circuit used the relay to solve the two-string task, while those who had been trained to use the relay to complete the circuit used the switch as a pendulum weight. This fixation phenomenon was reported in a series of other experiments.[8] The degree of fixity also was found to depend on some mediating factors, such as the span of time since the object was previously used,[9] the necessity of using the object in a novel way to solve the problem,[10] hints,[11] and intelligence.[12]

Data Fixation in Accounting

Ijiri, Jaedicke, and Knight viewed the decision process as being characterized by three factors: decision inputs, decision outputs, and decision rules. They then introduced the conditions under which a decision maker cannot adjust his or her decision process to a change in the accounting process. For example, changes in depreciation methods or inventory techniques lead to different profit figures. Ijiri, Jaedicke, and Knight attributed the inability to adjust, if it existed, to the psychological factor of functional fixation.[13] They stated:

Psychologists have found that there appears to be functional fixation in most human behavior in which the person attaches a meaning to a title or object (e.g., manufacturing cost) and is unable to see alternative meanings or uses. People intuitively associate a value with an item through past experience, and often do not recognize that the value of the item depends, in fact, upon the particular moment in time and may be significantly different from what it was in the past. Therefore, when a person is placed in a new situation, he views the object or term as used previously.[14]

To link the psychological concept of functional fixation to accounting, they merely stated the following:

If the outputs from different accounting methods are called by the same name, such as profit, costs, etc., people who do understand accounting well tend to neglect the fact that alternative methods may have been used to prepare the outputs. In such cases, a change in the accounting process clearly influences the decisions.[15]

This extrapolation of a psychological concept to accounting is welcome if it is interpreted correctly. The literature now recognizes the point that the focus in psychology is on *functions,* whereas Ijiri, Jaedicke, and Knight focused on *outputs.* If we go back to the example of a change in inventory techniques, functional fixation in psychology implies that the decision makers are accustomed to using the data for one function (such as price decisions) and now fail to see its potential use for another function (for example, production decisions). As introduced by Ijiri, Jaedicke, and Knight, functional fixation implies that decision makers are fixated on the accounting output (for example, the profit output) and are unable to adjust to see that the change in output is due to the change in inventory techniques. Thus, while psychologists are interested in functional fixation involving functions or objects, accounting research, influenced by Ijiri, Jaedicke, and Knight's extrapolation, is interested in functional fixation involving data. One might assume correctly that most of the interest in psychology has been on functional fixation. The exceptions to this assumption are a psychological data-fixation study by Knight and a mixed data-fixation/functional-fixation study in accounting by Barnes and Webb.[16] Ashton also has recognized the difference between the two views of functional fixation in accounting and psychology.[17] He came to a peculiar conclusion, however, when he stated:

We should recognize that the functional fixation hypothesis in accounting is a modified form (or forms) of the hypothesis in psychology. The modified functional hypothesis should be subjected to research in accounting contexts, rather than relying entirely on the original functional fixation research as Ijiri, Jaedicke, Knight, and subsequent researchers appear to have done.[18]

The approach should consider two forms of the functional-fixation hypothesis, one focusing on function and one focusing on output or data. There lies the main difference: in the case of functional fixation, psychologists used objects such as medallions, string, and boxes to solve relatively simple tasks, whereas the data-fixation experiments all used data to solve unstructured problems.

DATA-FIXATION RESEARCH IN ACCOUNTING

Data-Fixation Research Based on the Ijiri-Jaedicke-Knight Paradigm

Functional-fixation research in accounting generally has followed Ijiri, Jaedicke, and Knight's prescriptions, focusing on data rather than function, and has led to a series of data-fixation experiments. Ashton used M.B.A. students to assess the extent to which individual decision makers alter their decision processes after the occurrence of an accounting change, from full-cost to variable-cost data, as evidenced by the effect of this cognitive change on subsequent decisions.[19] Ashton not only discussed the accounting change with the subjects but also mentioned whether it reflected more or less important informational content, and consequently may have dictated a change in the decision behavior of the subjects. This result suggests that a large proportion of subjects in the experimental groups failed to adjust significantly their decision process in response to the accounting change, thereby providing evidence of the existence of functional fixation in accounting. The study was not met with complete approval. First, Libby criticized it for an experimental design that might have become confounded with the effects of the accounting change.[20] He concluded that

serious questions concerning the way in which the conceptual network was operationalized, coupled with methodology deficiencies, question whether any conclusions can be drawn from the results. The major problems relate to the presentation of the accounting change to the subjects, the manipulation of the moderating variables information and importance, and the method of measuring the change in the subject's decision process.[21]

Second, Pearson, a practitioner, simply rejected the study's objectives and results as irrelevant to accounting.[22] These criticisms, as might be expected, motivated further empirical research.

Swieringa, Dyckman, and Hoskin looked into Libby's criticisms and found that subjects tended to adjust their information processing as a result of the accounting change even though the significance of these adjustments differed depending on how they were measured.[23] The amount of information provided was found to influence the subject's adjustments of their information processing. Swieringa, Dyckman, and Hoskin had made two modifications in Ashton's experimental design. One modification was to isolate the effects of the amount and form of the information about the accounting change. The second modification was to have the data received by the control groups be equivalent to the data received by the experimental groups.

A second study by Dyckman, Hoskin, and Swieringa merely replicated the earlier study by Swieringa, Dyckman, and Hoskin with subjects who, on average, were older and had more exposure to accounting and business matters.[24] The students used in the first study were enrolled in an introductory accounting course in a college of agriculture and life sciences and did not know what direct costing meant. In addition, the second study relied on a cross-sectional approach instead of a time-series approach to analyze the effects of the experimental conditions and demographic variables on the prices set by the subjects for each product. The results of the second study were found to be similar to those of the first one.

In their experiment, Chang and Birnberg provided M.B.A. students with a cost-variance report and a cost standard.[25] The subjects were required to indicate (1) whether they would investigate the production process, and (2) how large a variance would be necessary to justify an investigation. Their results pointed to the existence of a ''weak form'' of data fixity when a change in the variance amount was introduced. The ''weak form'' label was used to characterize a slight change in behavior; no change in behavior was evidence of the ''strong form'' of fixity. Two significant findings were noted by the authors:

First, fixity is not a phenomenon that is unavoidable. Research indicates that once we are aware of its presence, we can take steps to cope with it. The real question becomes one of finding the manner in which it can be reduced and efficient ways of doing so. Second, unfortunately, once alerted to the problem, there is reason to believe that the subject's behavior will continue to reflect elements of past behavior—behavior which should have been forgotten along with the superseded data set. This then suggests two topics for future research. One is how past experience affects the subject's behavior. The other is how to extinguish the older, now unnecessary patterns of behavior.[26]

Abdel-Khalik and Keller used bank investment officers and security analysts in their investigation of functional fixation.[27] They articulated their research problems as follows:

If investors are functionally fixated on the use of reported accounting earnings, then they will tend to ignore other accounting information which is not consistent with accounting numbers. The accounting signal which we chose to be inconsistent with reported earnings is the decision of management to switch the method of inventory valuation from First-in, First-out (FIFO) or from average cost to Last-in, First-out (LIFO) for both accounting and tax purposes.[28]

Because of the higher cash flows that result from change to LIFO in a period of rising prices, the investor using a cash-flow discounted model would value the firm higher, while another relying and fixated on earnings would value it lower. The results of the experiment showed evidence of functional fixation, as the subjects relied on the adjusted net income rather than cash flows in evaluating the securities. One problem with Abdel-Khalik and Keller's study is the fact that the firms that switched to LIFO received qualified audit opinions, while those on FIFO obtained unqualified opinions. This could explain why the LIFO firms generally were viewed as having lower expected returns.

Bloom, Elgers, and Murray extended the Ashton study by examining both individual and group decisions in response to a fully disclosed, cosmetic change in depreciation method.[29] The results of the study showed a moderate shift in the decision behavior of individuals, a phenomenon similar to what Chang and Birnberg called the weak form of fixation. In addition, they found that groups exhibited a higher degree of fixation than did individuals. Among the reasons given for this difference were the following: "One explanation is that the group process inhibited the collective or individual intellectual functioning of its members; yet another is that the groups incurred a higher cost in developing a new decision rule in response to the accounting change than did the individuals."[30] Another explanation was that the difference could be a reflection of the nature of the task, which consisted of the need both to reach a decision within the group on a decision rule and to make a decision on the task.[31]

Another accounting study provided evidence of functional fixation without being based on Ashton's and Ijiri, Jaedicke, and Knight's paradigms. A National Association of Accountants (NAA) research study on the effects of software accounting policies on bank lending decisions and stock prices showed clear evidence of fixation by loan officers making a decision on a loan to two fictional firms: the Campbell Corporation, which capitalized software expenditures; and the Edwards Corporation, which expensed all software costs.[32] Without mentioning data fixation per se, the results are indicative of the presence of the phenomenon. Witness the following:

Campbell was favored over Edwards by 62.2% of the respondents; Edwards was favored by 11.1%; 13.3% would treat the companies equally, but did not give any reason for the equal treatment; and 13.3% would treat the companies equally because a company's software policy would not influence the lending decision. Only 27.3% of the bankers would grant a $3 million, five year unsecured loan to Edwards; compare with 61.4% for Campbell. Of those respondents that gave an interest rate for both companies, 55% would charge Campbell a lower rate, 5% would charge Edwards a lower rate, and 40% would charge the same rate to both companies.[33]

A similar finding was made in another study. Belkaoui conducted an experiment in which bank loan officers evaluated a loan application that was accompanied by financial statements based on either accrual or modified cash accounting.[34] The loan officers in the experiment believed that the loan applicant presenting accrual accounting financial statements (1) was more likely to repay the loan, (2) was more likely to be granted the loan, (3) was given a different interest rate premium, and (4) had statements that were more reliable and freer of clerical errors.

Other Data-Fixation Research

Other accounting research studies have used the Ijiri-Jaedicke-Knight paradigm to explain their own results. This strategy has taken place both in the research of investor decisions and in capital market research.

In the research of investor decisions, a cross-sectional orientation was given to functional fixation as it was applied to alternative accounting methods rather than to changes in accounting methods over time. Jensen examined the impact of alternative depreciation and inventory costing methods on investor decisions.[35] To explain his findings that alternative accounting techniques affected decision making, he suggested that his subjects might be functionally fixated on net earnings. Livingstone examined the effects of alternative, interperiod tax-allocation methods on regulatory rate-of-return decisions affecting the electric utility industry.[36] In light of his findings that some rate-making books focus on "raw" rates of return and ignore the effects of alternative tax-allocation methods, he offered the explanation that some predictions might be functionally fixated on net operating revenue. Livingstone stated the following:

It is therefore hypothesized that the reason that original-cost jurisdictions have been so much slower to adjust for alternative treatments of deferred taxes is that they are functionally fixated with respect to financial statement data. Since normalizing changes the amount but not the name of net operating revenue, it is intended that original-cost jurisdictions tend to view net operating revenue under normalizing as being the same as without it.[37]

He also suggested that users of accounting information could have formed a *learning set* after having experience with a significant number of different problems, all of which can be solved in the same manner. One solution went as follows: "If the hypothesis of a learning set with respect to alternative accounting methods is valid, multi-informational accounting statements would tend to stimulate learning and reduce functional fixation by providing users with information on accounting alternatives."[38] Mlynarczyk examined the effect of alternative tax-accounting methods on common-stock prices of electric utility companies and related functional fixation to his work.[39]

In capital market research, the functional-fixation hypothesis has been used to explain the lack of efficiency in the capital market. Beaver argued, however, that the market is not functionally fixated.[40] He stated the following:

In essence, the implication of the functional fixation hypothesis is that two firms (securities) could be alike in all "real" economic respects and yet sell for different prices, simply because of the way the accountant reported the results of operations. The implication is that the market ignores the fact that observed signals are generated from different information systems. Hence, it does not distinguish between numbers generated by different accounting methods either over time or across firms. Needless to say, this implies market inefficiency. . . . The functional fixation hypothesis as described above is a rather extreme form of the market inefficiency argument, in that it implies that disequilibrium could exist indefinitely and presumably permanently.[41]

DATA FIXATION AND FUNCTIONAL FIXATION IN ACCOUNTING AND PSYCHOLOGY

As stated earlier, most accounting research has focused on data fixation, while psychological research has focused on functional fixation. The exceptions to this are a data-fixation study in psychology by Knight and a mixed data-fixation/functional-fixation study in accounting by Barnes and Webb.[42]

Knight conducted an experiment to investigate the impact of the successful solving of *n* water jug problems on the problem-solving techniques used in trial *n* + 1. The results showed that a series of successes caused the subject to persist in his early behavior, making it difficult for him to see the alternative (correct) approach. Furthermore, the subject would give complex, correct solutions to even trivial problems in cases where the complex solutions had led to successful results in the previous *n* trials.

Barnes and Webb were interested in the investigation of both the data-fixation and the functional-fixation hypothesis in accounting. Actual managers were asked to make price decisions based on real-life case studies that differed in their method of inventory valuation (full-costing versus direct-costing). The data-fixation hypothesis was confirmed in that the subjects were fixated by the total costs figure, altering their project price in response to the changes in reported costs caused by the measurement change. However, the functional-fixation hypothesis was not confirmed because the subjects did not try to recover overhead costs, even though they were instructed that this was unnecessary, simply because they were not used to doing so. The lack of evidence for the functional-fixity hypothesis, a phenomenon widely observed in psychology, was attributed to the use of highly experienced and intelligent scientists. This is not surprising since intelligence has been found to mitigate fixity.[43]

DETERMINANTS OF FUNCTIONAL FIXATION IN ACCOUNTING

The Conditioning Hypothesis

The impact of accounting data on users and their behavior has always been a subject of interest for social scientists. One extreme concern, expressed by Schumpeter, goes as follows:

Capitalist practice turns the unit of money into a tool of rational cost-profit calculations, of which the towering monument is double-entry bookkeeping. . . . Primarily a product of the evolution of economic rationality, the cost-profit calculus in turn reacts upon that rationality; by crystallizing and defining numerically, it powerfully propels the logic of enterprise. . . . This type of logic or attitude or method then starts upon its conqueror's career subjugating—rationalizing—man's tools and philosophies, his medical practice, his picture of the cosmos, his outlook on life, everything in fact including his concepts of beauty and justice and his spiritual ambitions.[44]

Accounting researchers have not reached the point of Schumpeter's consensus, but they also have stressed the notion that the socialization of accountants, with its emphasis on particular cost and income considerations, can lead to a form of conditioning and might explain some of the empirically observed decision processes. The argument is that users, individually or in aggregate, react because they have been conditioned to react to accounting data rather than because the data have any informational content. For example, Sterling contends that

if the response of receivers to accounting stimuli is to be taken as evidence that certain kinds of accounting practices are justified, then we must not overlook the possibility that those responses were conditioned. Accounting reports have been issued for a long time, and their issuance has been accompanied by a rather impressive ceremony performed by the managers and accountants who issue them. The receivers are likely to have gained the impression that they ought to react and have noted that others react, and thereby have become conditioned to react.[45]

It may also be argued that the recipients of accounting information react when they should not react or should not react the way they do. The conditioning hypothesis has also been advanced by Revsine as follows:

The process by which users may be conditioned to the data they receive could occur in at least two ways. First, as students in business training curricula, the prospective users are introduced to generally accepted accounting principles and the financial statements that result from the applications of these principles and their derivative procedures. Furthermore, they are taught manipulative operations and techniques such as ratio and funds flow analysis that utilize accounting data as a means for evaluating enterprise performance and prospects. In short, users are generally indoctrinated concerning the relevance and utility of traditionally disseminated information. Second, this formal conditioning is continually reinforced by each external report that users receive.[46]

One explanation of the data-fixation findings may be that the subjects of the experiments, mostly accounting students, have been conditioned to react to some form of accounting outputs (for instance, cost or income outputs), and have failed to adjust their decision processes in response to a "well-disclosed" accounting change. The conditioning phenomenon inhibits the subjects from adopting the correct behavior, which is to adjust to the accounting change, and has led them to act as they have been conditioned to act in their previous behaviors or socialization sessions. Thus, the conditioning phenomenon is a form of functional fixation, as the subjects no longer are able to discriminate.

Prospect Theory and the Framing Hypothesis

Kahneman and Tversky's prospect theory states that potential gains and losses are evaluated by an S-shaped value function, one that is convex (indicating a risk-averse orientation) for losses.[47] Four effects are observable in the process of choosing among bets:

1. *Certainty effect:* "People overweigh outcomes that are considered certain relative to outcomes which are merely probable."[48]
2. *Reflection effect:* "The selection of prospects around 0 reverses the preference order."[49]
3. *Aversion to probabilistic insurance:* Subjects do not like the idea of probabilistic insurance because it pays off with a probability of less-than-one but diminishes the premium.
4. *Isolation effect:* "In order to simplify the choice between alternatives, people often disregard components that distinguish them."[50]

The concept of framing options adds the key idea that the frame of the decision is simply the decision maker's concept of the decision problem or its structure. The *frame* is defined as follows: "The decision-maker's conception of the acts, outcomes and contingencies associated with a particular choice. The frame that a decision-maker adopts is controlled partly by the formulation of the problem and partly by the norms, habits and personal characteristics of the decision-maker."[51]

Framing occurs because the wording of a question has the potential to alter a subject's response. Functional fixation may be viewed as a result of the particular choice of framing options made by the subjects in the experiments. The formulation of the decision tasks as well as the norms, habits, and personal characteristics of the subjects affect the framing of the decision and lead to the functional- or data-fixation results.

Interference Theory: Stimulus Encoding versus Retroactive Intuition

The *learning theory* holds that prior knowledge can either interfere with or facilitate effective decision making. The *interference theory* emerged from the two possible outcomes of the *transfer-of-training hypothesis*. According to the latter hypothesis, the transfer of training may have either facilitating or inhibitory effects. When a subject learns two tasks, task 1 and task 2, then is asked to perform task 1, the effects of the transfer of training are as follows: "Transfer may facilitate the learning of the second task, or conceivably have an inhibitory effect and interfere with the second learning and the mastery of the second task may help or hinder the subsequent performance of the first task."[52] What results, then, are two possible effects:

1. A negative transfer is labeled *retroactive inhibition or retroactive interference*.[53] In such a case the learning of task 2 affects the performance of the first task. The design used for the study of *retroactive interference* is as follows:[54]

Experimental group:	Learn Task 1	Learn Task 2	Test Task 1
Control group:	Learn Task 1		Test Task 1

   Functional fixity has been viewed as "a classic case of negative transfer."[55]

2. A positive or facilitator effect is labeled *retroactive facilitation*. This positive transfer motivates the *stimulus-encoding hypothesis*, whereby a distinction is made between the nominal stimulus provided by the experiments and the functional stimulus perceived by the subject. No functional fixity would result from the stimulus-encoding process.

Haka, Friedman, and Jones used the above interference theory to test the hypothesis that exposure to cost and income measures causes fixated responses in a decision-making setting where market value is the appropriate response.[56] If subjects are presented with two stimulus-response pairs for market price ($A-B$) and one for cost or income ($C-D$), with separate stimulus and responses for each, and if C is confused with A, resulting in an $A-B$, $C-B$ paradigm, then response B becomes the fixated response because of retroactive interference. In other words:

The hypothesis posited that prevalence of cost and profit information interferes with (that is, causes fixation) or facilitates appropriate market-based decision models. In particular, if stimulus encoding is dominant, then subjects with more cost and profit exposure should be more likely to use the market price data than those with less exposure. If retroactive inhibition dominates, then the opposite effect should be discerned.[57]

The results of the study did not support the proposition that exposure to accounting concepts in accounting courses interferes with decision processes. In addition, only some moderate support was found for the theory that stimulus encoding causes some retroactive facilitation.

Primacy versus Recency and Ego Involvement

The findings on data fixation in accounting for the most part have been obtained by having students placed in a stressful situation make a given choice (for example, a price decision) before and after an accounting change. The students know the nature of the accounting change (such as from full costing to variable costing) from their courses and the learning process preceding the experiment. A relevant research question would be the impact of this learning order on the acceptance of accounting techniques and on the results observed in data-fixation research. The impact should be more obvious if the students are placed under stress. This is related to a general hypothesis in psychology which specifies that under stress an organism will respond with the behavior appropriate to the situation that was learned first.[58] Consequently, Belkaoui tested the specific hypothesis that if a student learns two alternative responses to an accounting problem or stimulus and is placed under stress unrelated to the behavior being observed, he or she will respond to the stimulus with the first-learned method.[59] The results supported the hypothesis. Few implications of importance to the data-fixation hypothesis were made:

1. The appraisal of the usefulness of accounting technique cannot be ascertained when subjects are exposed to a stressful situation.

2. Given that stressful situations are likely to be present in both classroom and professional situations, there will be a predisposition to the use of the first learned accounting method.

3. Finally, the theoretical justifications pertaining to the choice of the appropriate accounting procedure by the firms can be reinforced by the learning order and the learning techniques to which the accountants have been exposed in their schools.[60]

The communication literature has addressed extensively the problem of the effects of order of presentation.[61] Known as the primacy-recency question, it is expressed by the following question: When both sides of a problem are presented successively, does the first-presented side (primacy) or the last-presented side (recency) have the advantage?

Different studies have supported the principle of primacy,[62] while other studies have created a controversy by reporting primacy effects under some conditions[63] and recency effects under others.[64] Consequently, Hovland, Jarvis, and Kelly recommended conducting research on the factors leading to the inconsistent effects of primacy and recency in the various experiments.[65] Examples of these factors include reinforcement, strength, involvement, and commitment. Ego involvement is also believed to be a variable that affects primacy and recency. Morteson noted:

Despite an absence of research, there is reason to believe that ego involvement may work against either primacy or recency, and often in a brutal way. Stated as a hypothesis, we may say that the more highly involved one is on a belief-discrepant topic, the less is the chance for either a primacy or recency effect.[66]

Belkaoui investigated the impact on the primacy and recency effects of ego involvement or commitment to one's stand on an accounting topic.[67] He reasoned that under conditions of ego involvement, the forces for reinforcement were likely to be particularly active and the impact of primacy or recency to be particularly passive. Subjects coming in contact with a stressful situation, in the form of resolving an accounting problem, would revert to the technique or the side of the message that was more clear or basic to them. The results of his experiments, which used accounting students, showed that the students under stress responded with the ''accounting behavior'' that was more clear or basic to them. In other words, in matters of ego involvement with an accounting technique just learned, subjects will give importance to what is perceived as relevant, significant, or meaningful. This could explain some of the data-fixation findings where the subjects have reverted to either the use of the first-learned method (primacy) or the second-learned method (recency), or to the method more clear or basic to their ego involvement.

PROBLEMS IN DATA-FIXATION RESEARCH

Several problems exist in the present state of data-fixation research.

1.   Most studies have not distinguished between data fixation, with its focus on output, and functional fixation, with its focus on function. Research is needed on both concepts, as they provide insight into and represent different aspects of the behavior of decision makers.

2.   Extrapolations made by accounting researchers could contain serious flaws if the simple fact of ignorance is confused with the psychological phenomenon of functional fixation, especially since most of the subjects used have been students rather than actual decision makers. This was Pearson's main criticism of Ashton's study; Pearson claimed that the inability of the subjects to adjust their decision process was entirely due to ignorance.[68] This fact was

explicitly recognized by Barnes and Webb when they stated: "It is our view that functional fixity and ignorance are separate phenomenon and that in order to identify the former empirically, the absence of the latter needs to be insured."[69]

3.   Fundamental evidence points to the fact that intelligence mitigates fixity. The point has been recognized both in the psychological[70] and the accounting experiments.[71] Again, Barnes and Webb have stated:

It would appear that those who were not fixated were less concerned with financial matters than their colleagues, as they were more concerned with providing an intellectual stimulus for their staff. Two groups appear therefore: those who can see around "trivial" financial matters and are concerned with "high matters" and those who are not. The implication again is that intelligence mitigates fixity.[72]

4.   There are two methodologies in the functional-fixation research: (a) The "one-object" approach, where subjects are given an experimental task to perform and a novel or new way can be used in the solution. Fixity occurs when only a small number of solutions emerge from the group of subjects, for whom the usual function of an object is accentuated. (b) The "two-objects" approach, where subjects are given two objects and a control group is given the use of one of the objects. Functional fixation results from the tendency of the subjects to use that object in the critical problem whose function has not been accentuated. All the accounting studies have used the "one-object" approach, and therein lies a problem, which has been expressed by Flavell, Cooper, and Loisell:

While functional fixedness in the first case is a matter of solution vs. non-solution . . . , it is, in the second case a matter of choice of objects or means for the solution of a comparatively simple problem. It is to be expected that the last method is the one that gives the purest measure of functional fixedness. In the first method a difficult problem is used and the non-solution of this problem may very well be attributed to other factors than functional fixation.[73]

Thus, there is a need for evidence from accounting research that uses the "two-object" approach.

5.   Most accounting research on data fixation has been concerned with whether fixity exists rather than why it exists. With the exception of the study by Haka, Friedman, and Jones, none of the accounting experiments has offered explanations about why fixity exists or has provided ways to remove it. In contrast, the psychological literature began to focus on its causes immediately after discovering the phenomenon. Removing fixation became the objective as experiments investigated factors such as time and the number of "other functions" shown for the fixated objects that affect the degree of fixity.[74] Later studies focused on the various ways of providing hints and cues to overcome fixation.[75] Needless to say, accounting research should now deal with the question of why fixity exists and how it can be mitigated. Wilner and Birnberg have stated the following to that effect:

Despite the popularity among accounting researchers of the question of whether decision makers are fixated, the critical question would appear to be why at least a portion of decision makers exhibit fixation. Given that we know from various non-accounting studies that certain factors do inhibit creative problem analysis and solving, the role of accounting research should be to ascertain which of these inhibiting factors operate in the domain of accounting and to ascertain how we can reduce their detrimental effect.[76]

6.   Wilner and Birnberg have pointed to the following problems in the design of existing studies on fixation:

1. The studies used an input-output methodology and the divergence between the inputs and the expected outputs were attributed to functional fixation while in fact there may be other reasons why a subject fails to alter his information processing after an accounting change.

2. While random assignment of subjects to tasks is used to lessen the effects of individual differences, it still remains that it cannot overcome the systematic characteristics which prevent all subjects from understanding the task.

3. Most of the subjects used in these experiments are not sophisticated enough for the risks which suggests that they were not fixated but rather naive or ignorant.

4. Unlike the psychological experiments which provided feedback to subjects, the accounting experiments not only did not provide any feedback, but used experimental tasks that were judgmental rather than optimal (right or wrong), which suggests that the subjects in the accounting experiments never knew if their behavior was appropriate.

5. Some knowledgeable subjects may have resisted changing their decision (model) following the accounting change for reasons other than fixation if a) he/she viewed the change as irrelevant, b) if he/she viewed changing his decision process as not worthwhile in that it leads to a different action than that already performed, c) if he/she viewed the benefits of "better decisions" as not outweighing the costs of learning how to process the change, d) if he/she thought it beneficial for him to act in a fixated manner because of his double role as an information sender as well as an information user, and e) if possibly he/she formed a set which he/she cannot overcome.[77]

ALTERNATIVE METHODOLOGY FOR DATA-FIXATION RESEARCH

Most of the empirical studies in data-fixation research have been based on laboratory or field experiments, with the exception of one single case based on a survey. In addition, with few exceptions, these experiments have used students as subjects, thereby raising problems of external validity. The tasks have not been realistic or motivating and have required judgmental rather than optimal behavior. What stands out upon review of the accountancy and psychological literature on the phenomenon is the urgent need for a better methodology, one that will allow direct observation of the process by which a decision is made. An appropriate methodology would be some form of protocol analysis, in which the subjects are asked to think aloud while solving the requirements of an experimental task. Such an approach would answer some very important questions:

1. Did the subject note the change?
2. Did the subject give any indication of appreciating its relevance?
3. Was the change understood?
4. Was the change ignored on grounds of its materiality, etc.?[78]

Better insights on the phenomenon of functional fixation may be possible through the use of protocol analysis, as the experiments use richer tasks, smaller pools of subjects, and better debriefing.

CONCLUSION

Functional fixation as observed in psychology, functional fixation, and data fixation as observed in accounting need to be explained. Future research should provide theoretical as well as empirical explanations of the reasons why subjects in accounting experiments persist in failing to adjust their decision process in response to accounting changes. In addition, richer and more realistic experimental tasks, sophisticated subjects, as well as protocol analysis ought to be used to provide better explanations of the phenomenon if it exists.

NOTES

1. N. R. F. Maier, "Reasoning in Humans: The Mechanisms of Equivalent Stimuli and Reasoning," *Journal of Experimental Psychology* (April 1945): 349–360.

2. K. Duncker, "On Problem Solving," *Psychological Monographs* 58, no. 5 (1945).

3. H. G. Birch and H. S. Rabinowitz, "The Negative Effect of Previous Experience on Productive Thinking," *Journal of Experimental Psychology* (February 1951): 121–125.

4. J. H. Flavell, A. Cooper, and R. H. Loisell, "Effect of the Number of Pre-utilization Functions on Functional Fixedness in Problem Solving," *Psychological Reports* (June 1958): 343–350.

5. R. E. Adamson, "Functional Fixedness as Related to Problem Solving: A Repetition of Three Experiments," *Journal of Experimental Psychology* (October 1952): 288–291.

6. Ibid., p. 288.

7. R. E. Adamson and D. W. Taylor, "Functional Fixedness as Related to Elapsed Time and to Set," *Journal of Experimental Psychology* (February 1954): 122–126.

8. S. Glucksberg and J. H. Danks, "Functional Fixedness: Stimulus Equivalence Mediated by Semantic-Acoustic Similarity," *Journal of Experimental Psychology* (July

1967): 400–405; J. Jensen, "On Functional Fixedness: Some Critical Remarks," *Scandinavian Journal of Psychology* (Winter 1960): 157–162.

9. Adamson and Taylor, "Functional Fixedness."

10. Duncker, "On Problem Solving."

11. P. Saugstad and K. Raaheim, "Problem Solving, Past Experience and Availability of Functions," *British Journal of Psychology* (May 1960): 97–104.

12. A. S. Luchins and E. H. Luchins, "New Experimental Attempts at Presenting Mechanization in Problem Solving," in P. C. Watson and P. N. Johnson Laird, eds., *Thinking and Reasoning: Selected Readings* (Hammondsworth, Eng.: Penguin, 1968), pp. 42–44.

13. Y. Ijiri, R. K. Jaedicke, and K. E. Knight, "The Effects of Accounting Alternatives on Management Decisions," in R. K. Jaedicke, Y. Ijiri, and O. Nielsen, eds., *Research in Accounting Measurement* (Sarasota, Fla.: American Accounting Association, 1966), pp. 186–199.

14. Ibid., p. 194.

15. Ibid., p. 194.

16. K. E. Knight, "Effect of Effort on Behavioral Rigidity in Luchins' Water Jar Task," *Journal of Abnormal and Social Psychology* (1960): 192–194; Paul Barnes and John Webb, "Management Information Changes and Functional Fixation: Some Experimental Evidence from the Public Sector," *Accounting, Organizations and Society* (February 1986): 1–18.

17. R. H. Ashton, "Cognitive Changes Induced by Accounting Changes: Experimental Evidence on the Functional Fixation Hypothesis," supplement to *Journal of Accounting Research* (1976): 1–7.

18. Ibid., p. 5.

19. Ibid., pp. 1–7.

20. Robert Libby, "Discussion of Cognitive Changes Induced by Accounting Changes: Experimental Evidence on the Functional Fixation Hypothesis," supplement to *Journal of Accounting Research* (1976): 18–24.

21. Ibid., p. 23.

22. David B. Pearson, "Discussion of Cognitive Changes Induced by Accounting Changes: Experimental Evidence on the Functional Fixation Hypothesis," supplement to *Journal of Accounting Research* (1976): 25–28.

23. R. J. Swieringa, T. R. Dyckman, and R. E. Hoskin, "Empirical Evidence about the Effects of an Accounting Change on Information Processing," in T. J. Burns, ed., *Behavioral Experiments in Accounting II* (Columbus: Ohio State University Press, 1979), pp. 225–259.

24. T. R. Dyckman, R. E. Hoskin, and R. J. Swieringa, "An Accounting Change and Information Processing Changes," *Accounting, Organizations and Society* (February 1982): 1–11.

25. D. L. Chang and J. G. Birnberg, "Functional Fixity in Accounting Research: Perspective and New Data," *Journal of Accounting Research* (Autumn 1977): 300–312.

26. Ibid., p. 311.

27. R. A. Abdel-Khalik and T. F. Keller, "Earnings or Cash Flows: An Experiment on Functional Fixation and the Valuation of the Firm." *Studies in Accounting Research* 16 (Sarasota, Fla.: American Accounting Association, 1979).

28. Ibid., p. 17.

29. Robert Bloom, Pieter T. Elgers, and Dennis Murray, "Functional Fixation in Product Pricing: A Comparison of Individuals and Groups," *Accounting, Organizations and Society* 9, no. 1 (1984): 1–11.

30. Ibid., p. 8.

31. Neil Wilner and Jacob Birnberg, "Methodological Problems in Functional Fixation Research: Criticism and Suggestions," *Accounting, Organizations and Society* (February 1986): 74.

32. Robert W. McGee, "Software Accounting, Bank Lending Decisions, and Stock Prices," *Management Accounting* (July 1984): 20–23.

33. Ibid., p. 20.

34. Ahmed Belkaoui, "Accrual Accounting, Modified Cash Basis of Accounting and the Loan Decision: An Experiment in Functional Fixation" (Unpublished manuscript, University of Illinois at Chicago, 1988).

35. Robert E. Jensen, "An Experimental Design for the Study of Effects of Accounting Variations in Decision Making," *Journal of Accounting Research* (Autumn 1966): 224–238.

36. J. L. Livingstone, "A Behavioral Study of Tax Allocation in Electric Utility Regulation," *Accounting Review* (July 1967): 544–552.

37. Ibid., pp. 550–551.

38. Ibid., p. 552.

39. F. A. Mlynarczyk, Jr., "An Empirical Study of Accounting Methods and Stock Prices," supplement to *Journal of Accounting Research* (1969): 63–81.

40. W. H. Beaver, "The Behavior of Security Prices and Its Implications for Accounting Research Methods," supplement to *Accounting Review* (1972): 407–437.

41. Ibid., pp. 420–421.

42. K. E. Knight, "Effect of Effort on Behavioral Rigidity"; Barnes and Webb, "Management Information Changes and Functional Fixation."

43. Luchins and Luchins, "New Experimental Attempts."

44. J. A. Schumpeter, *Capitalism, Socialism and Democracy*, 3d ed. (New York: Harper and Row, 1950), pp. 123–124.

45. Robert R. Sterling, "On Theory Construction and Verification," *Accounting Review* (July 1970): 433.

46. L. Revsine, *Replacement Cost Accounting* (Englewood Cliffs, N.J.: Prentice-Hall, 1973), pp. 50–51.

47. D. Kahneman and A. Tversky, "Prospect Theory: An Analysis of Decision under Risk," *Econometrika* (March 1979): 263–291.

48. Ibid., p. 265.

49. Ibid., p. 268.

50. Ibid., p. 271.

51. R. S. Woodworth and H. Schosberg, *Experimental Psychology* (New York: Henry Holt and Co., 1954), p. 733.

52. Ibid.

53. G. E. Muller and F. Schumann, "Experimentelle Beitrage Zur Untersuchung des Gedachtnisses," *Zeitschrift für Psychologie* (1894): 81–190, 257–339.

54. A. C. Catania, *Learning* (Englewood Cliffs, N.J.: Prentice-Hall, 1979).

55. J. Kagan and E. Havemann, *Psychology: An Introduction,* 3d ed. (New York: Harcourt Brace Jovanovich, 1976), p. 149.

56. Susan Haka, Lauren Friedman, and Virginia Jones, "Functional Fixation and Interference Theory: A Theoretical and Empirical Investigation," *Accounting Review* (July 1986): 455–474.

57. Ibid., p. 460.

58. R. P. Barthol and Nari D. Ku, "Specific Regression under a Nonrelated Stress Situation," *American Psychologist* (February 1963): 482.

59. Ahmed Belkaoui, "Learning Order and the Acceptance of Accounting Techniques," *Accounting Review* (October 1975): 897–899.

60. Ibid., pp. 898–899.

61. C. Hovland, I. Jarvis, and H. Kelly, *Communication and Persuasion* (New Haven, Conn.: Yale University Press, 1953).

62. F. H. Lund, "The Psychology of Belief: IV. The Law of Primacy in Persuasion," *Journal of Abnormal and Social Psychology* (1925): 236–249; F. H. Kroner, "Experimental Studies of Changes in Attitudes: II. A Study of the Effect of Printed Arguments on Changes in Attitudes," *Social Psychology* (1936): 522–532.

63. R. Lana, "Controversy on the Topic and the Order of Presentation in Persuasive Communications," *Psychological Reports* (April 1963): 163–170.

64. C. A. Insko, "Primacy versus Recency in Persuasion as a Function of the Timing of Arguments and Measurement," *Journal of Abnormal and Social Psychology* (1964): 381–391.

65. Hovland, Jarvis, and Kelly, *Communication and Persuasion.*

66. David C. Morteson, *Communication: The Study of Human Interaction* (New York: McGraw-Hill, 1972).

67. Ahmed Belkaoui, "The Primacy-Recency Effect, Ego Involvement and the Acceptance of Accounting Techniques," *Accounting Review* (January 1977): 252–256.

68. Pearson, "Discussion of Cognitive Changes Induced by Accounting Changes."

69. Barnes and Webb, "Management Information Changes and Functional Fixation."

70. Luchins and Luchins, "New Experimental Attempts."

71. Barnes and Webb, "Management Information Changes and Functional Fixation."

72. Ibid., p. 12.

73. Flavell, Cooper, and Loisell, "Effect of the Number of Pre-utilization Functions."

74. Adamson and Taylor, "Functional Fixedness"; Flavell, Cooper, and Loisell, "Effect of the Number of Pre-utilization Functions."

75. N. A. Wilner and J. G. Birnberg, "A Comparison of the Accounting and Psychological Literature on Functional Fixation," (Unpublished working paper, 1984).

76. N. A. Wilner and J. G. Birnberg, "Methodological Problems in Functional Fixation Research: Criticisms and Suggestions," *Accounting, Organizations and Society* (February 1986): 75.

77. Ibid., pp. 75–78.

78. Ibid., pp. 78–79.

SELECT BIBLIOGRAPHY

Adamson, R. E. "Functional Fixation as Related to Problem Solving: A Repetition of Three Experiments." *Journal of Experimental Psychology* (October 1952): 288–291.

Adamson, R. E., and D. W. Taylor. "Functional Fixedness as Related to Elapsed Time and to Set." *Journal of Experimental Psychology* (February 1954): 122–126.

Ausubel, D., L. C. Robbins, and E. Blake. "Retroactive Inhibition and Facilitation in the Learning of School Materials." *Journal of Educational Psychology* (October 1957): 334–343.

Ausubel, D., M. Stager, and A. J. H. Gaite. "Retroactive Facilitation in Meaningful Verbal Learning." *Journal of Educational Psychology* (August 1968): 159–178.

Belkaoui, Ahmed. "Accrual Accounting, Modified Cash Basis of Accounting and the Loan Decision: An Experiment in Functional Fixation." Unpublished manuscript, University of Illinois at Chicago, 1988.

————. "Learning Order and the Acceptance of Accounting Techniques." *Accounting Review* (October 1975): 897–899.

————. "The Primacy-Recency Effect, Ego Involvement and the Acceptance of Accounting Techniques." *Accounting Review* (January 1977): 252–256.

Birch, H. G., and H. S. Rabinowitz. "The Negative Effect of Previous Experience on Productive Thinking." *Journal of Experimental Psychology* (February 1951): 121–125.

Catania, A. C. *Learning*. Englewood Cliffs, N.J.: Prentice-Hall, 1979.

Duncker, K. "On Problem Solving." *Psychological Monographs* 58, no. 5 (1945).

Dyckman, T. R., M. Gibbins, and R. J. Swieringa. "Experimental and Survey Research in Financial Accounting: A Review and Evaluation." In A. R. Abdel-Khalik and T. F. Keller, eds., *The Impact of Accounting Research on Practice and Disclosure*, pp. 48–105. Durham, N.C.: Duke University Press, 1978.

Flavell, J. H., A. Cooper, and R. H. Loisell. "Effect of the Number of Pre-utilization Functions on Functional Fixedness in Problem Solving." *Psychological Reports* (June 1958): 343–350.

Glucksberg, S., and J. H. Danks. "Functional Fixedness: Stimulus Equivalence Mediated by Semantic-Acoustic Similarity." *Journal of Experimental Psychology* (July 1967): 400–405.

Hoch, S. J. "Availability and Interference in Predictive Judgements." Working paper, Center for Decision Research, Graduate School of Business, University of Chicago, March 1984.

Hovland, C., I. Jarvis, and H. Kelly. *Communication and Persuasion*. New Haven, Conn.: Yale University Press, 1953.

Insko, C. A. "Primacy versus Recency in Persuasion as a Function of the Timing of Arguments and Measurement." *Journal of Abnormal and Social Psychology* (1964): 381–391.

Jensen, J. "On Functional Fixedness: Some Critical Remarks." *Scandinavian Journal of Psychology* (Winter 1960): 157–162.

Kagan, J., and E. Havemann. *Psychology: An Introduction*, 3d ed. New York: Harcourt Brace Jovanovich, 1976.

Kahneman, D., and A. Tversky. "Prospect Theory: An Analysis of Decision under Risk." *Econometrika* (March 1979): 263–291.

Knight, K. E. "Effect of Effort on Behavioral Rigidity in Luchins' Water Jar Task." *Journal of Abnormal and Social Psychology* (1960): 192–194.

Krowner, F. H. "Experimental Studies of Changes in Attitudes: II. A Study of the Effect of Printed Arguments on Changes in Attitudes." *Social Psychology* (1936): 522–532.

Lana, R. "Controversy on the Topic and the Order of Presentation in Persuasive Communications." *Psychological Reports* (April 1963): 163–170.

Larcker, D. F., and V. P. Lessig. "Perceived Usefulness of Information: A Psychometric Examination." *Decision Sciences* (January 1980): 121–134.

Luchins, A. S., and E. H. Luchins. "New Experimental Attempts at Presenting Mechanization in Problem Solving." In P. C. Watson and P. N. Johnson Laird, eds., *Thinking and Reasoning: Selected Readings*, pp. 42–44. Hammondsworth, Eng.: Penguin, 1968.

Lund, F. H. "The Psychology of Belief: IV. The Law of Primacy in Persuasion." *Journal of Abnormal and Social Psychology* (1925): 236–249.

Martin, E. "Verbal Learning Theory and Independent Retrieval Phenomena." *Psychological Review* (July 1971): 314–332.

Mehle, T., C. F. Gettys, C. Manning, S. Baca, and S. Fisher. "The Availability Explanation of Excessive Plausibility Assessment." *Acta Psychologica* (November 1981): 127–140.

Morteson, David C. *Communication: The Study of Human Interaction*. New York: McGraw-Hill, 1972.

Muller, G. E., and F. Schumann. "Experimentelle Bertrage Zur Untersuchung des Gedachtnisses." *Zeitschrift für Psychologie* (1894): 81–190, 257–339.

Roediger, H. L. "Recall as a Self-Limiting Process." *Memory and Cognition* (January 1978): 54–63.

Saugstad, P., and K. Raaheim. "Problem Solving, Past Experience and Availability of Functions." *British Journal of Psychology* (May 1960): 97–104.

Sherif, C. W., and M. Sherif. *Attitude, Ego Involvement, and Change*. New York: John Wiley and Sons, 1967.

Sherif, M., and C. I. Hovland. *Social Judgment: Assimilation and Contrast Effects and Attitude Change*. New Haven, Conn.: Yale University Press, 1961.

Sterling, Robert R. "Accounting Research, Education and Practice." *Journal of Accountancy* (September 1973): 44–52.

————. "A Case of Valuation and Learned Cognitive Dissonance." *Accounting Review* (April 1967): 376–378.

————. *Theory of Measurement of Enterprise Income*. Lawrence, Texas: Scholars Book Co., 1970.

Tversky, A. "Features of Similarity." *Psychological Review* (July 1977): 327–352.

Tversky, A., and D. Kahneman. "The Framing of Decisions and the Psychology of Choice." *Science* (January 1981): 453–458.

Wong, M. "Retroactive Inhibition in Meaningful Verbal Learning." *Journal of Educational Psychology* (October 1970): 410–415.

Woodworth, R. S., and H. Schosberg. *Experimental Psychology,* rev. ed. New York: Henry Holt and Co., 1954.

3

THE PRACTICE OF SLACK: A REVIEW

Cyert and March advanced the concept of organizational slack as a hypothetical construct to explain overall organizational phenomena.[1] Lewin and Wolf, on the other hand, have made the following warning: "Slack is a seductive concept; it 'explains' too much and 'predicts' too little."[2] Indeed, slack research needs to be categorized along more precise dimensions that better explain its nature and its impact. Accordingly, this chapter reviews the research on slack by differentiating between *organizational slack* and *budgetary slack*.

VIEWS ON SLACK

Slack arises from the tendency of organizations and individuals to refrain from using all the resources available to them. It describes a tendency to not operate at peak efficiency. In general, two types of slack have been identified in the literature, namely organizational slack and budgetary slack. Organizational slack basically refers to an unused capacity, in the sense that the demands put on the resources of the organization are less than the supply of these resources. Budgetary slack is found in the budgetary process and refers to the intentional distortion of information that results from an understatement of budgeted sales and an overstatement of budgeted costs.

The concepts of organizational slack and budgetary slack appear in other literature under different labels. Economists refer to an *X*-inefficiency in instances where resources are either not used to their full capacity or effectiveness or used in an extremely wasteful manner, as well as in instances where managers fail to make costless improvements. *X*-inefficiency is to be differentiated from allocative inefficiency, which refers to whether or not prices in a market are of the right kind, that is, whether they allocate input and output to those users who are willing to pay for them.[3] Categories of inefficiency of a nonallocative nature, or X-inefficiency, include inefficiency in (1) labor utilization, (2) capital utilization, (3) time sequence, (4) extent of employee cooperation, (5) information flow, (6) bargaining effectiveness, (7) credit availability utilization, and (8) heuristic procedures.[4]

Agency theory also refers to slack behavior. The problem addressed by the agency theory literature is how to design an incentive contract such that the total gains can be maximized, given (1) information asymmetry between principal and agent, (2) pursuit of self-interest by the agent, and (3) environmental uncertainty affecting the outcome of the agent's decisions.[5] Slack can occur when managers dwell in an ''excess consumption of perquisites'' or in a ''tendency to shrink.'' Basically, slack is the possible ''shrinking'' behavior of an agent.[6]

The literature in organizational behavior refers to slack in terms of defensive, tactical responses and deceptive behavior. By viewing organizations as political environments, the deceptive aspects of individual power-acquisition behavior become evident.[7] A variety of unobtrusive tactics in the operation of power,[8] covert intents and means of those exhibiting power-acquisition behaviors,[9] and a ''wolf in sheep's clothing'' phenomenon, whereby individuals profess a mission or goal strategy while practicing an individual-maximization strategy,[10] characterize these deceptive behaviors, which are designed to present an illusionary or false impression. Schein has provided the following examples of deceptive behaviors in communication, decision making, and presentation of self:

Communication. With regards to written or oral communications, there may be an illusion that these communications include all the information or that these communications are true, which masks the reality either of them consisting of only partial information or of their actually distorting the information.

Decision-Making. A manager may present the illusion that he is actually compromising or giving in with regard to a decision, whereas in reality he is purposely planning to lose this particular battle with the long-range objective of winning the war. Or a manager or a subunit may initiate a particular action and then work on plans and activities for implementing a program. This intensive planning and studying, however, may in reality be nothing more than a delaying tactic during which time the actual program will die or be forgotten. Underlying this illusion that one is selecting subordinates, members of boards of directors, or successors on the basis of their competency may be the reality that these individuals are selected for loyalty, compliancy, or conformity to the superior's image.

Presentation of Self. Many managers exude an apparent confidence, when in reality they are quite uncertain. Still other managers are skilled in organizing participatory group decision-making sessions, which in reality have been set up to produce a controlled outcome.[11]

Schein then hypothesized that the degree to which these behaviors are deceptive seems to be a function of both the nature of the organization and of the kinds of power exhibited (work-related or personal).[12] She relied on Cyert and March's dichotomization of organizations as either low- or high-slack systems.[13] Low-slack systems are characterized by a highly competitive environment that requires rapid and nonroutine decision making on the part of its members and a high level of productive energy and work outcomes to secure an effective performance. High-slack systems are characterized by a reasonably stable environment that requires routine decision making to secure an effective performance. Given these dichotomizations, Schein suggested that:

1. The predominant form of power acquisition behavior is personal in a high-slack organization and work-related in a low-slack organization.

2. The underlying basis of deception is an inherent covert nature of personal power acquisition behaviors in a high-slack organization and an organization illusion as to how work gets done in a low-slack organization.

3. The benefits of deception to members are the provisions of excitement and personal rewards in a high-slack organization and the facilitation of work accomplishment and organizational rewards in a low-slack organization.

4. The benefits of deception to organization are to foster illusion of a fast paced, competitive environment in a high-slack organization and to maintain an illusion of workability of the formal structure in a low-slack organization.[14]

ORGANIZATIONAL SLACK

Nature of Organizational Slack

There is no lack of definitions for organizational slack as can be seen from the definitions provided by Cyert and March,[15] Child,[16] Cohen, March, and Olsen,[17] March and Olsen,[18] Dimmick and Murray,[19] Litschert and Bonham,[20] and March,[21] and as shown in Exhibit 3.1.

What appears from these definitions is that organizational slack is a buffer created by management in its use of available resources to deal with internal as well as external events that may arise and threaten an established coalition. Slack, therefore, will be used by management as an agent of change in response to changes in both the internal and external environments.

Cyert and March's model explains slack in terms of cognitive and structural factors.[22] It provides the rationale for the unintended creation of slack. Individuals are assumed to "satisfice," in the sense that they set aspiration levels for performance rather than a maximization goal. These aspirations adjust upward or downward, depending on actual performance, and in a slower fashion than actual changes in performance. It is this lag in adjustment that allows excess resources from superior performance to accumulate in the form of organizational slack. This slack is then used as a stabilizing force to absorb excess resources in good

Exhibit 3.1
Definitions of Organizational Slack

Cyert & March [1963]

"[The] disparity between the resources available to the organization and the payments required to maintain the coalition" [p. 36].

E.g.: Excess dividends to stockholders

Prices lower than necessary to keep buyers

Wages greater than needed to keep labor

Perquisites to executives

Subunit growth beyond relative rate of contribution

"Supply of uncommitted resources" [p. 54].

"Resources funneled into the satisfaction of individual and sub-group [vs. organizational] objectives" [p. 98].

Child [1972]

"The margin or surplus [performance exceeding "satisficing" level] which permits an organization's dominant coalition to adopt structural arrangements which accord with their own preferences [vs. "goodness of fit" dictates of contingency theory], even at some extra administrative cost" [p. 11].

Cohen, March, & Olsen [1972]

"The difference between the resources of the organization and the combination of demands made on it" [p. 12].

March & Olsen [1976]

"The difference between existing resources and activated demands" [p. 87].

Dimmick & Murray [1978]

"Those resources which an organization has acquired which are not committed to a necessary expenditure. In essence, these are resources which can be used in a discretionary manner" [p. 616].

Operation = Avg. profit over 5 yrs., controlled for size ($ sales)

Litschert & Bonham [1978]

Using Cyert and March's [1963] definition, they gave the following suggested operation: Slack = the variation, from the average among comparable organizations on: ROE, ROTA, Net Sales, and Gross Profit as a percentage of Sales.

March [1979]

"Since organizations do not always optimize, they accumulate spare resources and unexploited opportunities which then become a buffer against bad times. Although the buffer is not necessarily intended, slack produces performance smoothing, reducing performance during good times and improving it during bad times" [quoted in *Stanford GSB*, p. 17].

Source: L. J. Bourgeois, "On the Measurement of Organizational Slack," *Academy of Management Review* 6, no. 1 (1981): 30. Reprinted with permission.

times without requiring a revision of aspirations and intentions regarding the use of these excess resources. "By absorbing excess resources it retards upward adjustment of aspirations during relatively good times . . . by providing a pool of emergency resources, it permits aspirations to be maintained during relatively bad times."[23]

Williamson has proposed a model of slack based on managerial incentives.[24] This model provides the rationale for managers' motivation and desire for slack resources. Under conditions where managers are able to pursue their own objectives, the model predicts that the excess resources available after target levels of profit have been reached are not allocated according to profit-maximization rules. Organizational slack becomes the means by which a manager achieves his or her personal goals, as characterized by four motives: income, job security, status, and discretionary control over resources. Williamson makes the assumption that the manager is motivated to maximize his or her personal goals subject to satisfying organizational objectives and that the manager achieves this by maximizing slack resources under his or her control. Williamson has suggested that there are four levels of profits: (1) a maximizing profit equal to the profit the firm would achieve when marginal revenue equals marginal cost, (2) actual profit equal to the true profit achieved by the firm, (3) reported profit equal to the accounting profit reported in the annual report, and (4) minimum profit equal to the profit needed to maintain the organizational coalition. If the market is non-competitive, various forms of slack emerge: (1) *slack absorbed as staff* equal to the difference between maximum profit and actual profit, (2) *slack in the form of cost* equal to the difference between reported and minimum profits, and (3) *discretionary spending for investment* equal to the difference between reported and minimum profits.

Income smoothing can be used to substantiate the efforts of management to neutralize environmental uncertainty and to create organizational slack by means of an accounting manipulation of the level of earnings. Kamin and Ronen have related organizational slack to income smoothing by reasoning that the decisions that affect the allocation of costs—such as budget negotiations, which often result in slack accumulation—are aimed at smoothing earnings.[25] They hypothesized that management-controlled firms were more likely to be engaged in smoothing as a manifestation of managerial discretion and slack. "Accounting" and "real" smoothing were tested by observing the behavior of discretionary expenses vis-à-vis the behavior of income numbers. Their results showed that (1) a majority of the firms behaved as if they were income smoothers, and (2) a particularly strong majority was found among management-controlled firms with high barriers to entry. This line of reasoning was pursued by Belkaoui and Picur.[26] Their study tested the effects of the dual economy on income-smoothing behavior. It was hypothesized that a higher degree of smoothing of income numbers would be exhibited by firms in the periphery sector than by firms in the core sector in reaction to different opportunity structures and experiences. Their results indicated that a majority of the firms may have been resorting to income smoothing. A higher number was found among firms in the periphery sector.

Lewin and Wolf proposed the following statements as a theoretical framework for understanding the concept of slack:

(1) Organizational slack depends on the availability of excess resources.

(2) Excess resources occur when an organization generates or has the potential to generate resources in excess of what is necessary to maintain the organizational coalition.

(3) Slack occurs unintentionally as a result of the imperfection of the resource allocation decision making process.

(4) Slack is created intentionally because managers are motivated to maximize slack resources under their control to insure achievement of personal goals subject to the achievement of organizational goals.

(5) The disposition of slack resources is a function of a manager's expense preference function.

(6) The distribution of slack resources is an outcome of the bargaining process setting organization and reflects the discretionary power of organization members in allocating resources.

(7) Slack can be present in a distributed or concentrated form.

(8) The aspiration of organizational participants for slack adjusts upward as resources become available. The downward adjustment of aspirations for slack resources, when resources become scarce, is resisted by organizational participants.

(9) Slack can stabilize short-term fluctuations in the firm's performance.

(10) Beyond the short-term, the reallocation of slack requires a change in organizational goals.

(11) Slack is directly related to organizational size, maturity and stability of the external environment.[27]

Functions of Organizational Slack

Because the definition of slack is often intertwined with a description of the functions that slack serves, Bourgeois discussed these functions as a means of making palpable the ways of measuring slack.[28] From a review of the administrative theory literature, he identified organizational slack as an independent variable that either "causes" or serves four primary functions: "(1) as an inducement for organizational actors to remain in the system, (2) as a resource for conflict resolution, (3) as a buffering mechanism in the work flow process, or (4) as a facilitator of certain types of strategic or creative behavior within the organization."[29] Exhibit 3.2 summarizes basic information on the first three of these functions.

Exhibit 3.2
Functions of Slack for Internal Maintenance

	Inducement (to maintain the coalition)	Conflict Resolution	Work flow Buffer
Authors and Concepts	I/C ratio [Barnard, 1937] I/C >1 [March & Simon, 1958] I > 1 = C [Cyert & March, 1963]	Goal incongruence [Pondy, 1967] Local rationality, goal conflict, local optimization [Cyert & March, 1963]	Technical core buffer (inventories, advertising) [Thompson, 1967] Systems model [Pondy, 1967] Reduced information-processing requirements [Galbraith, 1973]

Operation	I = Excess dividends
	    Low prices
	    High wages
	    Income and prestige
	    Executive "perks"
		Pursuit of pet projects
		Lowered ROI hurdle
		Increased/decreased financial authority
			Δ in inventory
			Δ in administrative intensity
			    * * *
			Reduced performance levels
			Longer delivery times
			Hire more labor
			Buy more equipment

Unit of Analysis	Individual (Σ for organization)	Subunit	Organization
Data Source	Questionnaire	Archival	Archival
Measure	$: static (one point in time)	$ or : relative (compared to previous period)	$: relative Time Labor intensity Static Excess capacity
Problems	Perceptual data Threatening Individual (vs. organizational) phenomenon	Sensitive data Subunit slack $\neq$ organizational slack	Slack consumption vs. slack creation

$ = Quantified in terms of monetary value

Δ = Change

Source: L. J. Bourgeois, "On the Measurement of Organizational Slack," *Academy of Management Review* 6, no. 1 (1981): 32. Reprinted with permission.

The concept of slack as an inducement to maintain the coalition was first introduced by Barnard in his treatment of the inducement/contribution ratio (I/C) as a way of attracting organizational participants and sustaining their membership.[30] March and Simon later described slack resources as the source of inducements through which the inducement/contribution ratio might exceed a value of one, which is equivalent to paying an employee more than would be required to retain his or her services.[31] This concept of slack was then explicitly introduced by Cyert and March as consisting of payments to members of the coalition in excess of what is required to maintain the organization.[32]

Slack as a resource for conflict resolution was introduced in Pondy's goal model.[33] In this model subunit goal conflicts are resolved partly by sequential attention to goals and partly by adopting a decentralized organizational structure. A decentralized structure is made possible by the presence of organizational slack.

A notion of slack as a technical buffer from the variances and discontinuities caused by environmental uncertainty was proposed by Thompson.[34] It was also acknowledged in Pondy's system model, which described conflict as a result of the lack of buffers between interdependent parts of an organization.[35] Galbraith saw buffering as an information processing problem: "Slack resources are an additional cost to the organization or the customer. . . . The creation of slack resources, through reduced performance levels, reduces the amount of information that must be processed during task execution and prevents the overloading of hierarchical channels."[36]

According to Bourgeois slack facilitates three types of strategic or creative behavior within the organization: (1) providing resources for innovative behavior, (2) providing opportunities for a satisficing behavior, and (3) affecting political behavior.[37] Exhibit 3.3 summarizes the fundamental characteristics of these types of behavior and their strategic implications for the organization.

First, as a facilitator of innovative behavior, slack tends to create conditions that allow the organization to experiment with new strategies[38] and introduce innovation.[39] Second, as a facilitator of suboptimal behavior, slack defines the threshold of acceptability of a choice, or "bounded search,"[40] by people whose bounded rationality leads them to satisfice.[41] Third, the notion that slack affects political activity was advanced by Cyert and March, who argued that slack reduces both political activity and the need for bargaining and coalition-forming activity.[42] Furthermore, Astley has argued that slack created by success results in self-aggrandizing behavior by managers, who engage in political behavior to capture more than their fair share of the surplus.[43]

Measurement of Organizational Slack

One problem in investigating empirically the presence of organizational slack relates to the difficulty of securing an adequate measurement of the phenomenon. As Exhibits 3.2 and 3.3 show, various methods have been suggested. In addition to these methods, eight variables that appear in public data, whether they are created by managerial actions or made available by the environment, may explain a change in slack.[44] The model, suggested by Bourgeois, is as follows:

Slack = f (RE, DP, GαA, WC/S, D/E, CR, I/P, P/E)

where

RE   = Retained earnings
DP   = Dividend payout

Exhibit 3.3
Slack as a Facilitator of Strategic Behavior

	Innovation	Satisficing	Politics
Authors and Concepts	Experimentation with new strategies [Hambrick & Snow, 1977] Funds for innovation [Cyert & March, 1963]	Bounded search [Simon, 1957; March & Simon, 1958]	Bargaining activity [Cyert & March, 1963] Self-aggrandizement; conflict and coalition [Astley, 1978]
Opera-tions	New products New markets New processes R&D and market research	Search time Search team Number of alterna-tives generated or considered	New resource infu-sion and subsequent distribution Policy conflicts between managers, coalition formation
Unit of Analysis	Organization	Organization or top management team	Organization or top management team
Data Source	Archival Interview	Interview	Archival Interview Organization

Measure	Products
	Clients, longitu-
	  region dinal
	$: static
		Time
		$ longitudinal
		Process
			$
			      longitu-
			Behavior dinal

$ = quantified in terms of monetary value.

Source: L. J. Bourgeois, "On the Measurement of Organizational Slack," *Academy of Management Review* 6, no. 1 (1981): 35. Reprinted with permission.

$G\alpha A$ = General and administrative expense

WC/S = Working capital as a percentage of sales

D/E = Debt as a percentage of equity

CR = Credit rating

I/P = Short-term loan interest compared to prime rate

P/E = Price/earnings ratio

RE, $G\alpha A$, WC/S, and CR are assumed to have a positive effect on changes in slack, whereas DP, D/E, P/E, and I/P are assumed to have a negative effect on changes in slack.

Some of these measures have also been suggested by other researchers. For example, Rosner used profit and excess capacity as slack measures,[45] and Lewin and Wolf used selling, general, and administrative expenses as surrogates for slack.[46] Bourgeois and Singh refined these measures by suggesting that slack could be differentiated on an ''ease-of-recovery'' dimension.[47] Basically, they considered excess liquidity to be *available slack*, not yet earmarked for particular uses. Overhead costs were termed *recoverable slack*, in the sense that they are absorbed by various organizational functions but can be recovered when needed elsewhere. In addition, the ability of a firm to generate resources from the environment, such as the ability to raise additional debt or equity capital, was considered *potential slack*. All of these measures were divided by sales to control for company size.

Building on Bourgeois and Singh's suggestions, Lant opted for the four following measures:

1. Administrative Slack = (General and Administrative Expenses)/Cost of Goods Sold
2. Available Liquidity = (Cash + Marketable Securities − Current Liabilities)/Sales
3. Recoverable Liquidity = (Accounts Receivable + Inventory)/Sales
4. Retained Earnings = (Net Profit − Dividends)/Sales[48]

Lant used these measures to show empirically that (*a*) available liquidity and general and administrative expenses have significantly higher variance than profit across firms and across time, and (*b*) the mean change in slack is significantly greater than the mean change in profit. She concluded as follows:

These results are logically consistent with the theory that slack absorbs variance in actual profit. They also suggest that the measures used are reasonable measures for slack. Thus, it supports prior work which has used these measures, and implies that further large sample models using slack as a variable is feasible since financial information is readily available for a large number of firms. Before these results can be generalized, however, the tests conducted here should be replicated using different samples of firms from a variety of industries.[49]

BUDGETARY SLACK

Nature of Budgetary Slack

The literature on organizational slack shows that managers have the motives necessary to desire to operate in a slack environment. The literature on budgetary slack considers the budget as the embodiment of that environment and, therefore, assumes that managers will use the budgeting process to bargain for slack budgets. As stated by Schiff and Lewin, ''managers will create slack in budgets through a process of *understating revenues and overstating costs*.''[50] The general definition of budgetary slack, then, is the understatement of revenues and the overstatement of costs in the budgeting process. A detailed description of the creation of budgetary slack by managers was reported by Schiff and Lewin in their study of the budget process of three divisions of multidivision companies.[51] They found evidence of budgetary slack through underestimation of gross revenue, inclusion of discretionary increases in personnel requirements, establishment of marketing and sales budgets with internal limits on funds to be spent, use of manufacturing costs based on standard costs that do not reflect process improvements operationally available at the plant, and inclusion of discretionary "special projects."

Evidence of budgetary slack has also been reported by others. Lowe and Shaw found a downward bias, introduced through sales forecasts by line managers, which assumed good performance where rewards were related to forecasts.[52] Dalton reported various examples of department managers allocating resources to what they considered justifiable purposes even though such purposes were not authorized in their budgets.[53] Shillinglaw noted the extreme vulnerability of budgets used to measure divisional performance given the great control exercised by divisional management in budget preparation and the reporting of results.[54]

Slack creation is a generalized organizational phenomenon. Many different organizational factors have been used to explain slack creation, in particular organizational structure, goal congruence, control system, and managerial behavior. Slack creation is assumed to occur in cases where a Tayloristic organizational structure exists,[55] although it is also assumed to occur in a participative organizational structure.[56] It may be due to conflicts that arise between the individual and organizational goals, leading managers intentionally to create slack. It may also be due to the attitudes of management toward the budget and to workers' views of the budgets as a device used by management to manipulate them.[57] Finally, the creation of slack may occur whether or not the organization is based on a centralized or decentralized structure.[58] With regard to this last issue, Schiff and Lewin have reported that the divisional controller appears to have undertaken the tasks of creating and managing divisional slack and is most influential in the internal allocation of slack.

Budgeting and the Propensity to Create Budgetary Slack

The budgeting system has been assumed to affect a manager's propensity to create budgetary slack, in the sense that this propensity can be increased or decreased by the way in which the budgeting system is designed or complemented. Onsi was the first to investigate empirically the connections between the type of budgeting system and the propensity to create budgetary slack.[59] From a review of the literature, he stated the following four assumptions:

(1) Managers influence the budget process through bargaining for slack by understating revenues and overstating costs. . . .

(2) Managers build up slack in "good years" and reconvert slack into profit in "bad years." . . .

(3) Top management is at a "disadvantage" in determining the magnitude of slack. . . .

(4) The divisional controller in decentralized organizations participates in the task of creating and managing divisional slack.[60]

Personal interviews of 32 managers of five large, national and international companies and statistical analysis of a questionnaire were used to identify the important behavioral variables that influence slack buildup and utilization. The questionnaire's variables were grouped into the following eight dimensions:

1. *Slack attitude* described by the variables indicating a manager's attitude to slack.

2. *Slack manipulation* described by the variables indicating how a manager builds-up and uses slack.

3. *Slack institutionalization* described by the variables that make a manager less inclined to reduce his slack.

4. *Slack detection* described by the variables indicating the superior's ability to detect slack based on the amount of information he receives.

5. *Attitude towards the top management control system* described by the variables indicating an authoritarian philosophy towards budgeting being attributed to top management by divisional managers.

6. *Attitudes towards the divisional control system* described by variables on attitudes toward subordinates, sources of pressure, budget autonomy, budget participation, and supervisory uses of budgets.

7. *Attitudes towards the budget described* by variables on attitude towards the level of standards, attitude towards the relevancy of budget attainment to valuation of performance, and the manager's attitude (positive or negative) towards the budgetary system in general, as a managerial tool.

8. *Budget relevancy* described by variables indicating a manager's attitudes towards the relevancy of standards for his department's operation.[61]

Factor analysis reduced these dimensions to seven factors and showed a relationship between budgetary slack and what Onsi called "an authoritarian top management budgetary control system." Thus, he stated:

Budgetary slack is created as a result of pressure and the use of budgeted profit attainment as a basic criterion in evaluating performance. Positive participation could encourage less need for building-up slack. However, the middle managers' perception of pressure was an overriding concern. The positive correlation between managers' attitudes and attainable level of standards is a reflection of this pressure.[62]

Cammann explored the moderating effects of subordinates' participation in decision making and the difficulty of subordinates' jobs on their responses to different uses of control systems by their superiors.[63] His results showed that the use of control systems for contingent reward allocation produced defensive responses by subordinates under all conditions, which included the creation of budgetary slack. Basically, when superiors used budgeting information as a basis for allocating organizational rewards, their subordinates' responses were defensive. Allowing participation in the budget processes reduced this defensiveness.

Finally, Merchant conducted a field study designed to investigate how managers' propensities to create budgetary slack are affected by the budgeting system and the technical context.[64] He hypothesized that the propensity to create budgetary slack is positively related to the importance placed on meeting budget targets and negatively related to the extent of participation allowed in budgeting processes, the degree of predictability in the production process, and the superiors' abilities to create slack. Unlike earlier studies that had drawn across functional areas, 170 manufacturing managers responded to a questionnaire measuring the propensity to create slack, the importance of meeting the budget, budget participation, the nature of technology in terms of work-flow integration and product standardization, and the ability of superiors to detect slack. The results suggested that managers' propensities to create slack (1) do vary with the setting and with how the budgeting system is implemented; (2) are lower where managers actively participate in budgeting, particularly when technologies are relatively predictable; and (3) are higher when a tight budget requires frequent tactical responses to avoid overruns.

Budgetary Slack Information Distortion and Truth-Inducing Incentive Schemes

Budgetary slack involves a deliberate distortion of input information. Distortion of input information in a budget setting arises, in particular, from the need of managers to accommodate their expectations about the kinds of payoffs associated with different possible outcomes. Several experiments have provided evidence of such distortion of input information. Cyert, March, and Starbuck showed in a laboratory experiment that subjects adjusted the information they transmitted in a complex decision-making system to control their payoffs.[65] Similarly, Lowe and Shaw have shown that in cases where rewards were linked to forecasts, sales managers tended to distort the input information and to induce biases in their sales forecast.[66] Dalton also provided some rich situational descriptions of information distortion in which lower-level managers distorted the budget information and allocated resources to what were perceived to be justifiable objectives.[67] Finally, given the existence of a payoff structure that can induce a forecaster to bias intentionally his or her forecast, Barefield provided a model of forecast behavior that showed a "rough" formulation of a possible link between a forecaster's biasing and the quality of the forecaster as a source of data for an accounting system.[68]

Taken together, these studies suggest that budgetary slack, through systematic distortion of input information, can be used to accommodate the subjects' expectations about the payoffs associated with various possible outcomes. They fail, however, to provide a convincing rationalization of the link between distortion of input information and the subjects' accommodation of their expectations. Agency theory and issues related to risk aversion may provide such a link. Hence, given the existence of divergent incentives and information asymmetry between the controller (or employer) and the controllee (or employee) and the high cost of observing employee skill or effort, a budget-based employment contract (that is, where employee compensation is contingent on meeting the performance standard) can be Pareto-superior to fixed pay or linear sharing rules (where the employer and employee split the output).[69] However, these budget-based schemes impose a risk on the employee, as job performance can be affected by a host of uncontrollable factors. Consequently, risk-averse individuals may resort to slack budgeting through systematic distortion of input information. In practice, moreover, any enhanced (increased) risk aversion would lead the employee to resort to budgetary slack. One might hypothesize that, without proper incentives for truthful communication, the slack budgeting behavior could be reduced. One suggested avenue is the use of truth-inducing, budget-based schemes.[70] These schemes, assuming risk neutrality, motivate a worker to reveal truthfully private information about future performance and to maximize performance regardless of the budget.

Accordingly, Young conducted an experiment to test the effects of risk aversion and asymmetric information on slack budgeting.[71] Five hypotheses related to budgetary slack were developed and tested using a laboratory experiment. The hypotheses were as follows:

Hypothesis 1: A subordinate who participates in the budgeting process will build slack into the budget. . . .

Hypothesis 2: A risk-averse subordinate will build in more budget slack than a non-risk-averse subordinate. . . .

Hypothesis 3: Social pressure not to misrepresent productive capability will be greater for a subordinate whose information is known by management than for a subordinate having private information. . . .

Hypothesis 4: As social pressure increases for the subordinate, there is a lower degree of budgetary slack. . . .

Hypothesis 5: A subordinate who has private information builds more slack into the budget than a subordinate whose information is known by management.[72]

The results of the experiment confirmed the hypotheses that a subordinate who participates builds in budgetary slack and that slack is, in part, attributable to a subordinate's risk preferences. Given state uncertainty and a worker-manager information asymmetry about performance capability, the subjects in the experiment created slack even in the presence of a truth-inducing scheme. In addition, risk-averse workers created more slack than non-risk-averse workers did. Similarly, Chow, Cooper, and Waller provided evidence that, given a worker-manager information asymmetry about performance capability, slack is lower under a truth-inducing scheme than under a budget-based scheme with an incentive to create slack.[73]

Both Young's and Chow, Cooper, and Waller's studies were found to have limitations.[74] With regard to Young's study, Waller found three limitations:

First, unlike the schemes examined in the analytical research, the one used in his study penalized outperforming the budget, which limits its general usefulness. Second, there was no manipulation of incentives, so variation in slack due to incentives was not examined. Third, risk preferences were measured using the conventional lottery technique of which the validity and reliability are suspect.[75]

With regard to Chow, Cooper, and Waller's study, Waller found to be limitations the assumption of state certainty and the failure to take risk preference into account. Accordingly, Waller conducted an experiment under which subjects participatively set budgets under either a scheme with an incentive for creating slack or a truth-incentive scheme like those examined in the analytical research. In addition, risk neutrality was induced for one-half of the subjects and constant, absolute risk aversion for the rest, using a technique discussed by Berg, Daley, Dickhaut, and O'Brien that allows the experimenter to induce (derived) utility functions with any shape.[76] The results of the experiment show that when a conventional truth-inducing scheme is introduced, slack decreases for risk-neutral subjects but not for risk-averse subjects. Added to the evidence provided by the other studies, this study indicates that risk preference is an important determinant of slack, especially in the presence of a truth-inducing scheme.

Budgetary Slack and Self-Esteem

The enhancement of risk aversion and the resulting distortion of input information can be more pronounced when self-esteem is threatened. It was found that persons who have low opinions of themselves are more likely to cheat than persons with higher self-esteem.[77] A situation of dissonance was created in an experimental group by giving out positive feedback about a personality test to some participants and negative feedback to others. All the participants were then asked to take part in a competitive game of cards. The participants who received a blow to their self-esteem cheated more often than those who had received positive feedback about themselves. Could it also be concluded that budgetary slack through information distortion may be a form of dishonest behavior, arising from the enhancement of risk aversion caused by a negative feedback on self-esteem? A person's expectations can be an important determinant of his or her behavior. A negative impact on self-esteem can lead an individual to develop an expectation of poor performance. At the same time, the individual who is given negative feedback about his or her self-esteem would be more risk averse than others and would be ready to resort to any behavior to cover the situation. Consequently, the person may attempt to distort the input information in order to have an attainable budget. Belkaoui accordingly tested the hypothesis that individuals given negative feedback about their self-esteem would introduce more bias into estimates than individuals given positive or neutral feedback about their self-esteem.[78] One week after taking a self-esteem test, subjects were provided with false feedback (either positive or negative) and neutral feedback about their self-esteem score. They were then asked to make two budgeting decisions, first one cost estimate and then one sales estimate for a fictional budgeting decision. The results showed that, in general, the individuals who were provided with information that temporarily caused them to lower their self-esteem were more apt to distort input information than those who were made to raise their self-esteem. It was concluded that, whereas slack budgeting may be consistent with generally low self-esteem feedback, it is inconsistent with generally high or neutral self-esteem feedback.

Toward a Theoretical Framework for Budgeting

A theoretical framework aimed at structuring knowledge about biasing behavior was proposed by Lukka.[79] It contains an explanatory model for budgetary biasing and a model for budgetary biasing at the organizational level.

The explanatory model of budgetary biasing at the individual level is presented in Exhibit 3.4. It draws from the management accounting and organizational behavior literature and related behavioral research to suggest a set of intentions and determinants of budgetary biasing. Budgetary biasing is at the center of many interrelated and sometimes contradictory factors with the actor's intentions as the synthetic core of his or her behavior.

The model for budgetary biasing at the organizational level is presented in Exhibit 3.5. It shows that the "bias contained in the final budget is not the result of one actor's intentional behavior, but rather the result of the dialectics of the negotiations.[80] While budgetary biases 1 and 2 are the original biases created in the budget by the controlling unit and the controlled unit, biases 3 and 4 are the final biases to end up in the budget after the budgetary negotiations, which are

Exhibit 3.4
Intentions and Determinants of Budgetary Biasing

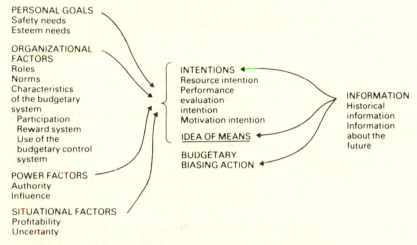

Source: Kari Lukka, ''Budgetary Biasing in Organizations: Theoretical Framework and Empirical Evidence,'' *Accounting, Organizations and Society* (February 1988): 291. Reprinted with permission.

Exhibit 3.5
Budgetary Process from the Biasing Viewpoint

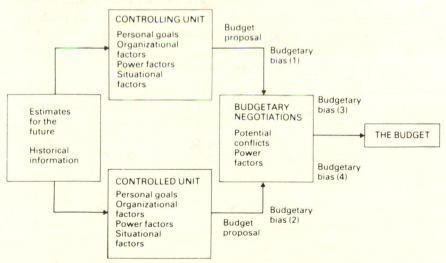

Source: Kari Lukka, ''Budgetary Biasing in Organizations: Theoretical Framework and Empirical Evidence,'' *Accounting, Organizations and Society* (February 1988): 292. Reprinted with permission.

characterized by potential conflicts and power factors. The results of semi-structured interviews at different levels of management of a large decentralized company verified the theoretical framework. The usefulness of this theoretical framework rests on further refinements and empirical testing.

Positive versus Negative Slack

Although the previous sections have focused on budgetary, or positive, slack, budgetary bias is in fact composed of both budgetary slack and an upward bias, or a negative slack. While budgetary slack refers to bias in which the budget is designed intentionally so as to make it easier to achieve the forecast, upward bias refers to overstatement of expected performance in the budget. Otley has described the difference as follows: "Managers are therefore likely to be conservative in making forecasts when future benefits are sought (positive slack) but optimistic when their need for obtaining current approval dominates (negative slack)."[81]

Evidence for negative slack was first provided by Read, who showed that managers distort information to prove to their superiors that all is well.[82] He cited several empirical studies of budgetary control that indicated that managers put a lot of effort and ingenuity into assuring that messages conveyed by budgetary information serve their own interests.[83] Following earlier research by Barefield, Otley argued that forecasts may be the mode, rather than the means, of people's intuitive probability distributions.[84] Given that the distribution of cost and revenue is negatively skewed, there will be a tendency for budget forecasts to become unintentionally biased in the form of negative slack. Data collected from two organizations verified the presence of negative slack.

Reducing Budgetary Slack: A Bonus-Based Technique

In general, firms use budgeting and bonus techniques to overcome slack budgeting. One such approach consists of paying higher rewards when budgets are set high and achieved, and lower rewards when budgets are either set high but not met or set low and achieved. Mann presented a bonus system that gave incentives for managers to set budget estimates as close to achievable levels as possible.[85] The following two formulas were proposed:

Formula 1 applies for bonus if actual performance is equal to or greater than budget.

$$(\text{Multiplier no. 2} \times \text{budget goal}) + (\text{multiplier no. 1} \times [\text{actual level achieved - budget goal}])$$

Formula 2 applies for bonus if actual performance is less than budget.

$$(\text{Multiplier no. 2} \times \text{budget goal}) + (\text{multiplier no. 3} \times [\text{actual level achieved - budget goal}])$$

Exhibit 3.6
Reducing Slack through a Bonus System

(1)	(2)	(3)	(4) Bonus I	(5) Bonus II
Budget Sales	Actual Sales	State of Nature	Multiple No. 1 = $.05 Multiple No. 2 = $.10 Multiple No. 3 = $.15	Multiple no. 1 = .01 Multiple no. 2 = .10 Multiple No. 3 = .30
200,000	180,000	Over estimation	$17,000	$14,000
200,000	200,000	Actual = Budget	20,000	20,000
200,000	220,000	Under estimation	21,000	22,000

The three multipliers set by management served as factors in calculating different components of bonuses. They were defined as follows:

Multiplier no. 1 (which must be less than multiplier no. 2, and which in turn must be less than multiplier no. 3) is used when actual performance is greater than budget. It provides a smaller bonus per unit for the part of actual performance that exceeds the budgeted amount. . . .

Multiplier no. 2 is the rate per unit used to determine the basic bonus component. It is based on the budgeted level of activity which equals multiplier no. 2 times the budgeted level.

Multiplier no. 3 is the rate used to reduce the bonus when the achieved level is less than the budget (multiplier no. 3 times work of units by which actual performance fell short of budget).[86]

Exhibit 3.6 shows an illustration of the application of the method and the effect of variations in multipliers or bonuses. As the exhibit shows, the manager will be rewarded for accurate estimation of the level of rates. In addition, the multipliers can be set with greater flexibility for controlling the manager's estimates.

CONCLUSION

Organizational slack and budgetary slack are two hypothetical constructs to explain organizational phenomena that are prevalent in all forms of organizations. Evidence linking both constructs to organizational, individual, and contextual factors is growing and in the future may contribute to an emerging theoretical framework for an understanding of slack. Further investigation into the potential determinants of organizational and budgetary slack remains to be done. This effort is an important one, as the behavior of slack is highly relevant to the achievement of internal economic efficiency in organizations.

NOTES

1. Richard M. Cyert and James G. March, eds., *A Behavioral Theory of the Firm* (Englewood Cliffs, N.J.: Prentice-Hall, 1963).

2. Arie Y. Lewin and Carl Wolf, "The Theory of Organizational Slack: A Critical Review," *Proceedings: Twentieth International Meeting of TIMS* (1976): 648–654.

3. Harvey Leibenstein, "Allocative Efficiency vs. 'X-Efficiency,'" *American Economic Review* (June 1966): 392–415.

4. Harvey Leibenstein, "X-Efficiency: From Concept to Theory," *Challenge* (September–October 1979): 13–22.

5. Nandan Choudhury, "Incentives for the Divisional Manager," *Accounting and Business Research* (Winter 1985): 11–21.

6. S. Baiman, "Agency Research in Managerial Accounting: A Survey," *Journal of Accounting Literature* (Spring 1982): 154–213.

7. D. Packard, *The Pyramid Climber* (New York: McGraw-Hill, 1962); E. A. Buttler, "Corporate Politics—Monster or Friend?" *Generation* 3 (1971): 54–58, 74; A. N. Schoomaker, *Executive Career Strategies* (New York: American Management Association, 1971).

8. J. Pfeffer, "Power and Resource Allocation in Organizations," in B. M. Shaw and G. R. Salancik, eds., *New Directions in Organizational Behavior* (Chicago: St. Clair Press, 1977).

9. V. E. Schein, "Individual Power and Political Behaviors in Organizations: An Inadequately Explored Reality," *Academy of Management Review* (January 1977): 64–72.

10. B. Bozeman and W. Malpive, "Goals and Bureaucratic Decision-Making: An Experiment," *Human Relations* (June 1977): 417–429.

11. V. E. Schein, "Examining an Illusion: The Role of Deceptive Behaviors in Organizations," *Human Relations* (October 1979): 288–289.

12. Ibid., p. 290.

13. Cyert and March, *A Behavioral Theory of the Firm.*

14. Schein, "Examining an Illusion," p. 293.

15. Cyert and March, *A Behavioral Theory of the Firm.*

16. John Child, "Organizational Structure, Environment, and Performance: The Role of Strategic Choice," *Sociology* 6, no. 1 (1972): 2–22.

17. M. D. Cohen, J. G. March and J. P. Olsen, "A Garbage Can Model of Organizational Choice," *Administrative Science Quarterly* 17, no. 1 (1972): 1–25.

18. J. G. March and J. P. Olsen, *Ambiguity and Choice* (Bergen: Universitetsforlagt, 1976).

19. D. E. Dimmick and V. V. Murray, "Correlates of Substantive Policy Decisions in Organizations: The Case of Human Resource Management," *Academy of Management Journal* 21, no. 4 (1978): 611–623.

20. R. J. Litschert and T. W. Bonham, "A Conceptual Model of Strategy Formation," *Academy of Management Review* 3, no. 2 (1978): 211–219.

21. James G. March, interview by Stanford Business School Alumni Association, *Stanford GSB* 47, no. 3 (1978–79): 16–19.

22. Cyert and March, *A Behavioral Theory of the Firm.*

23. Ibid., p. 38.

24. Oliver E. Williamson, "A Model of Rational Managerial Behavior," in Richard M. Cyert and James G. March, eds., *A Behavioral Theory of the Firm* (Englewood Cliffs, N.J.: Prentice-Hall, 1963); idem, *The Economics of Discretionary Behavior: Managerial Objectives in a Theory of the Firm* (Englewood Cliffs, N.J.: Prentice-Hall, 1964).

25. J. Y. Kamin and J. Ronen, "The Smoothing of Income Numbers: Some Empirical Evidence on Systematic Differences among Management-Controlled and Owner-Controlled Firms," *Accounting, Organizations and Society* (October 1978): 141–157.

26. Ahmed Belkaoui and R. D. Picur, "The Smoothing of Income Numbers: Some Empirical Evidence on Systematic Differences between Core and Periphery Industrial Sectors," *Journal of Business Finance and Accounting* (Winter 1984): 527–545.

27. Lewin and Wolf, "The Theory of Organizational Slack," p. 653.

28. L. J. Bourgeois, "On the Measurement of Organizational Slack," *Academy of Management Review* 6, no. 1 (1981): 29–39.

29. Ibid., p. 31.

30. C. I. Barnard, *Functions of the Executive* (Cambridge, Mass.: Harvard University Press, 1938).

31. James G. March and H. A. Simon, *Organizations* (New York: John Wiley and Sons, 1958).

32. Cyert and March, *A Behavioral Theory of the Firm*, p. 36.

33. L. R. Pondy, "Organizational Conflict: Concepts and Models," *Administrative Science Quarterly* 12, no. 2 (1967): 296–320.

34. J. D. Thompson, *Organizations in Action* (New York: McGraw-Hill, 1967).

35. Pondy, "Organizational Conflict."

36. Jay Galbraith, *Designing Complex Organizations* (Reading, Mass.: Addison-Wesley, 1973), p. 15.

37. Bourgeois, "On the Measurement of Organizational Slack," p. 34.

38. D. C. Hambrick and C. C. Snow, "A Contextual Model of Strategic Decision Making in Organizations," in R. L. Taylor, J. J. O'Connell, R. A. Zawaki and D. D. Warrick, eds., *Academy of Management Proceedings* (1977): 109–112.

39. Cyert and March, *A Behavioral Theory of the Firm.*

40. March and Simon, *Organizations.*

41. H. A. Simon, *Administrative Behavior* (New York: Free Press, 1957).

42. Cyert and March, *A Behavioral Theory of the Firm.*

43. W. G. Astley, "Sources of Power in Organizational Life" (Ph.D. diss., University of Washington, 1978).

44. Bourgeois, "On the Measurement of Organizational Slack," p. 38.

45. Martin M. Rosner, "Economic Determinant of Organizational Innovation," *Administrative Science Quarterly* 12 (1968): 614–625.

46. Arie Y. Lewin and Carl Wolf, "Organizational Slack: A Test of the General Theory," *Journal of Management Studies* (Forthcoming).

47. L. J. Bourgeois and Jitendra V. Singh, "Organizational Slack and Political Behavior within Top Management Teams," (Working paper, Graduate School of Business, Stanford University, 1983).

48. Theresa K. Lant, "Modeling Organizational Slack: An Empirical Investigation," Stanford University Research Paper, no. 856 (July 1986).

49. Ibid., p. 14.

50. Michael Schiff and Arie Y. Lewin, "The Impact of People on Budgets," *Accounting Review* (April 1970): 259–268.

51. Michael Schiff and Arie Y. Lewin, "Where Traditional Budgeting Fails," *Financial Executive* (May 1968): 51–62.

52. A. E. Lowe and R. W. Shaw, "An Analysis of Managerial Biasing: Evidence from a Company's Budgeting Process," *Journal of Management Studies* (October 1968): 304–315.

53. M. Dalton, *Men Who Manage* (New York: John Wiley and Sons, 1961), pp. 36–38.

54. G. Shillinglaw, "Divisional Performance Review: An Extension of Budgetary Control," in C. P. Bonini, R. K. Jaedicke, and H. M. Wagner, eds., *Management Controls: New Directors in Basic Research* (New York: McGraw-Hill, 1964), pp. 149–163.

55. C. Argyris, *The Impact of Budgets on People* (New York: Controllership Foundation, 1952), p. 25.

56. E. H. Caplan, *Management Accounting and Behavioral Sciences* (Reading, Mass.: Addison-Wesley, 1971).

57. Argyris, *The Impact of Budgets on People*.

58. Schiff and Lewin, "Where Traditional Budgeting Fails," pp. 51–62.

59. Mohamed Onsi, "Factor Analysis of Behavioral Variables Affecting Budgetary Slack," *Accounting Review* (July 1973): 535–548.

60. Ibid., p. 536.

61. Ibid., p. 539.

62. Ibid., p. 546.

63. Cortlandt Cammann, "Effects of the Use of Control Systems," *Accounting, Organizations and Society* (January 1976): 301–313.

64. Kenneth A. Merchant, "Budgeting and the Propensity to Create Budgetary Slack," *Accounting, Organizations and Society* (May 1985): 201–210.

65. Richard M. Cyert, J. G. March, and W. H. Starbuck, "Two Experiments on Bias and Conflict in Organizational Estimation," *Management Science* (April 1961): 254–264.

66. Lowe and Shaw, "An Analysis of Managerial Biasing."

67. Dalton, *Men Who Manage*.

68. R. M. Barefield, "A Model of Forecast Biasing Behavior," *Accounting Review* (July 1970): 490–501.

69. J. S. Demski and G. A. Feltham, "Economic Incentives in Budgetary Control Systems," *Accounting Review* (April 1978): 336–359.

70. Y. Ijiri, J. Kinard, and F. Putney, "An Integrated Evaluation System for Budget Forecasting and Operating Performance with a Classified Budgeting Bibliography," *Journal of Accounting Research* (Spring 1968): 1–28; M. Loeb and W. Magat, "Soviet Success Indicators and the Evaluation of Divisional Performance," *Journal of Accounting Research* (Spring 1978): 103–121; P. Jennergren, "On the Design of Incentives in Business Firms—A Survey of Some Research," *Management Science* (February 1980): 180–201; M. Weitzman, "The New Soviet Incentive Model," *Bell Journal of Economics* (Spring 1976): 251–257.

71. Mark S. Young, "Participative Budgeting: The Effects of Risk Aversion and Asymmetric Information on Budgetary Slack," *Journal of Accounting Research* (Autumn 1985): 829–842.

72. Ibid., pp. 831–832.

73. C. Chow, J. Cooper, and W. Waller, "Participative Budgeting: Effects of a Truth-Inducing Pay Scheme and Information Asymmetry on Slack and Performance" (Working paper, 1986).

74. William S. Waller, "Slack in Participative Budgeting: The Joint Effect of a Truth-Inducing Pay Scheme and Risk Preferences," *Accounting, Organizations and Society* (December 1987): 87–98.

75. Ibid., p. 88.

76. J. Berg, L. Daley, J. Dickhaut, and J. O'Brien, "Controlling Preferences for Lotteries on Units of Experimental Exchange," *Quarterly Journal of Economics* (May 1986): 281–306.

77. E. Aronson and D. R. Mettee, "Dishonest Behavior as a Function of Differential Levels of Induced Self-Esteem," *Journal of Personality and Social Psychology* (January 1968): 121–127.

78. Ahmed Belkaoui, "Slack Budgeting, Information Distortion and Self-Esteem," *Contemporary Accounting Research* (Fall 1985): 111–123.

79. Kari Lukka, "Budgetary Biasing in Organizations: Theoretical Framework and Empirical Evidence," *Accounting, Organizations and Society* (February 1988): 281–301.

80. Ibid., p. 292.

81. David T. Otley, "The Accuracy of Budgetary Estimates: Some Statistical Evidence," *Journal of Business Finance and Accounting* (Fall 1985): 416.

82. W. H. Read, "Upward Communication in Industrial Hierarchies," *Human Relations* (1962): 3–16.

83. G. H. Hofstede, *The Game of Budget Control* (London: Tavistock, 1968); A. G. Hopwood, "An Empirical Study of the Role of Accounting Data in Performance Evaluation," supplement to *Journal of Accounting Research* (1972): 156–182; David T. Otley, "Budget Use and Managerial Performance," *Journal of Accounting Research* (Spring 1978): 122–149.

84. R. M. Barefield, "Comments on a Measure of Forecasting Performance," *Journal of Accounting Research* (Autumn 1969): 324–327; Otley, "The Accuracy of Budgetary Estimates."

85. G. S. Mann, "Reducing Budget Slack," *Journal of Accountancy* (August 1988): 118–122.

86. Ibid., p. 119.

SELECT BIBLIOGRAPHY

Antle, R., and G. Eppen. "Capital Rationing and Organizational Slack in Capital Budgeting." *Management Science* (February 1985): 163–174.

Argyris, C. *The Impact of Budgets on People*. New York: Controllership Foundation, 1952.

Aronson, E., and D. R. Mettee. "Dishonest Behavior as a Function of Differential Levels of Induced Self-Esteem.'' *Journal of Personality and Social Psychology* (January 1968): 121–127.

Astley, W. G. ''Sources of Power in Organizational Life.'' Ph.D. diss., University of Washington, 1978.

Barefield, R. M. ''A Model of Forecast Biasing Behavior.'' *Accounting Review* (July 1970): 490–501.

Barnard, C. I. *Functions of the Executive.* Cambridge, Mass.: Harvard University Press, 1937.

Barnea, A., J. Ronen, and S. Sadan. ''Classifactory Smoothing of Income with Extraordinary Items.'' *Accounting Review* (January 1976): 110–122.

Belkaoui, Ahmed. *Conceptual Foundations of Management Accounting.* Reading, Mass.: Addison-Wesley, 1980.

———. *Cost Accounting: A Multidimensional Emphasis.* Hinsdale, Ill.: Dryden Press, 1983.

———. ''The Relationships between Self-Disclosure Style and Attitudes to Responsibility Accounting.'' *Accounting, Organizations and Society* (December 1981): 281–289.

———. ''Slack Budgeting, Information Distortion and Self-Esteem.'' *Contemporary Accounting Research* (Fall 1985): 111–123.

Belkaoui, Ahmed, and R. D. Picur. ''The Smoothing of Income Numbers: Some Empirical Evidence on Systematic Differences Between Core and Periphery Industrial Sectors.'' *Journal of Business Finance and Accounting* (Winter 1984): 527–545.

Berg, J., L. Daley, J. Dickhaut, and J. O'Brien. ''Controlling Preferences for Lotteries on Units of Experimental Exchange.'' *Quarterly Journal of Economics* (May 1986): 281–306.

Bonin, J. P. ''On the Decision of Managerial Incentive Structures in a Decentralized Planning Environment.'' *American Economic Review* (September 1976): 682–687.

Bonin, J. P., and A. Marcus. ''Information, Motivation, and Control in Decentralized Planning: The Case of Discretionary Managerial Behavior.'' *Journal of Comparative Economics* (September 1979): 235–253.

Bourgeois, L. J. ''On the Measurement of Organizational Slack.'' *Academy of Management Review* 6, no. 1 (1981): 29–39.

Bourgeois, L. J., and W. G. Astley. ''A Strategic Model of Organizational Conduct and Performance.'' *International Studies of Management and Organization* 9, no. 3 (1979): 40–66.

Bourgeois, L. J., and Jitendra V. Singh. ''Organizational Slack and Political Behavior within Top Management Teams.'' Working paper, Graduate School of Business, Stanford University, 1983.

Brownell, P. ''Participation in the Budgeting Process—When It Works and When It Doesn't.'' *Journal of Accounting Literature* (Spring 1982): 124–153.

Caplan, E. H. *Management Accounting and Behavioral Sciences.* Reading, Mass.: Addison-Wesley, 1971.

Carter, E. ''The Behavioral Theory of the Firm and Top-Level Corporate Decisions.'' *Administrative Science Quarterly* 16, no. 4 (1971): 413–428.

Child, John. "Organizational Structure, Environment, and Performance: The Role of Strategic Choice." *Sociology* 6, no. 1 (1972): 2–22.

Chow, C. "The Effects of Job Standard Tightness and Compensation Scheme on Performance: An Exploration of Linkages." *Accounting Review* (October 1983): 667–685.

Chow, C., J. Cooper, and W. Waller. "Participative Budgeting: Effects of a Truth-Inducing Pay Scheme and Information Asymmetry on Slack and Performance." Working paper, 1986.

Christensen, J. "The Determination of Performance Standards and Participation." *Journal of Accounting Research* (Autumn 1982): 589–603.

Cohen, M. D., J. G. March, and J. P. Olsen. "A Garbage Can Model of Organizational Choice." *Administrative Science Quarterly* 17, no. 1 (1972): 1–25.

Collins, F. "Managerial Accounting Systems and Organizational Control: A Role Perspective." *Accounting, Organizations and Society* (May 1982): 107–122.

Conn, D. "A Comparison of Alternative Incentive Structures for Centrally Planned Economic Systems." *Journal of Comparative Economics* (September 1979): 261–278.

Cyert, Richard M., and James G. March. "Organizational Factors in the Theory of Oligopoly." *Quarterly Journal of Economics* (April 1956): 44–66.

———, eds. *A Behavioral Theory of the Firm.* Englewood Cliffs, N.J.: Prentice-Hall, 1963.

Cyert, Richard M., J. G. March, and W. H. Starbuck. "Two Experiments on Bias and Conflict in Organizational Estimation." *Management Science* (April 1961): 254–264.

Dalton, M. *Men Who Manage.* New York: John Wiley and Sons, 1961.

Demski, J. S., and G. A. Feltham. "Economic Incentives in Budgetary Control Systems." *Accounting Review* (April 1978): 336–359.

Dimmick, D. E., and V. V. Murray. "Correlates of Substantive Policy Decisions in Organizations: The Case of Human Resource Management." *Academy of Management Journal* 21, no. 4 (1978): 611–623.

Fitts, W. F. *Interpersonal Competence: The Wheel Model.* Nashville, Tenn.: Counselor Recording and Tests, 1970.

———. *Manual for the Tennessee Self-Concept Scale.* Nashville, Tenn.: Counselor Recording and Tests, 1965.

———. *The Self-Concept and Behavior: Overview and Supplement.* Nashville, Tenn.: Counselor Recordings and Tests, 1972.

———. *The Self-Concept and Performance.* Nashville, Tenn.: Counselor Recording and Tests, 1972.

———. *The Self-Concept and Psychopathology.* Nashville, Tenn.: Counselor Recording and Tests, 1972.

Fitts, W. F., and W. T. Hammer. *The Self-Concept and Delinquency.* Nashville, Tenn.: Counselor Recording and Tests, 1969.

Fitts, W. F., J. L. Adams, G. Radford, W. C. Richard, B. K. Thomas, M. M. Thomas, and W. Thompson. *The Self-Concept and Self-Actualization.* Nashville, Tenn.: Counselor Recording and Tests, 1971.

Galbraith, Jay. *Designing Complex Organizations*. Reading, Mass.: Addison-Wesley, 1973.

Gonik, J. "Tie Salesmen's Bonuses to Their Forecasts." *Harvard Business Review* (May–June 1978): 116–123.

Gordon, M. J., B. N. Horwitz, and P. T. Myers. "Accounting Measurements and Normal Growth of the Firm." In R. K. Jaedicke, Y. Ijiri, and O. Nieslen, eds., *Research in Accounting Measurement*. Sarasota, Fla.: American Accounting Association, 1966.

Hambrick, D. C., and C. C. Snow. "A Contextual Model of Strategic Decision Making in Organizations." In R. L. Taylor, J. J. O'Connell, R. A. Zawacki, and D. D. Warrick, eds., *Academy of Management Proceedings* (1977): 109–112.

Hershey, J., H. Kunreuther, and P. Schoemaker. "Bias in Assessment Procedures for Utility Functions." *Management Science* (August 1982): 936–954.

Hopwood, A. G. "An Empirical Study of the Role of Accounting Data in Performance Evaluation." Supplement to *Journal of Accounting Research* (1972): 156–182.

Ijiri, Y., J. Kinard, and F. Putney. "An Integrated Evaluation System for Budget Forecasting and Operating Performance with a Classified Budgeting Bibliography." *Journal of Accounting Research* (Spring 1968): 1–28.

Itami, H. "Evaluation Measures and Goal Congruence under Uncertainty." *Journal of Accounting Research* (Spring 1975): 163–180.

Jennergren, P. "On the Design of Incentives in Business Firms—A Survey of Some Research." *Management Science* (February 1980): 180–201.

Kamin, J. Y., and J. Ronen. "The Smoothing of Income Numbers: Some Empirical Evidence on Systematic Differences among Management-Controlled and Owner-Controlled Firms." *Accounting, Organizations and Society* (October 1978): 141–157.

Kerr, S., and W. Slocum, Jr. "Controlling the Performances of People in Organizations." In W. Starbuck and P. Nystrom, eds., *Handbook of Organizational Design* 2:116–134. New York: Oxford University Press, 1981.

Lecky, P. *Self-Consistency*. New York: Island Press, 1945.

Leibenstein, Harvey. "Allocative Efficiency vs. 'X-Efficiency.' " *American Economic Review* (June 1966): 392–415.

––––––. "X-Efficiency: From Concept to Theory." *Challenge* (September–October 1979): 13–22.

Levinthal, D., and J. G. March. "A Model of Adaptive Organizational Search." *Journal of Economic Behavior and Organization* (May 1981): 307–333.

Lewin, Arie Y., and Carl Wolf. "Organizational Slack: A Test of the General Theory." *Journal of Management Studies* (Forthcoming).

––––––. "The Theory of Organizational Slack: A Critical Review." *Proceedings: Twentieth International Meeting of TIMS* (1976): 648–654.

Litschert, R. J., and T. W. Bonham. "A Conceptual Model of Strategy Formation." *Academy of Management Review* 3, no. 2 (1978): 211–219.

Locke, E., and D. Schweiger. "Participation in Decision Making: One More Look." In B. Staw, ed., *Research in Organizational Behavior*, pp. 265–339. Greenwich, Conn.: JAI Press, 1979.

Loeb, M., and W. Magat. "Soviet Success Indicators and the Evaluation of Divisional Performance." *Journal of Accounting Research* (Spring 1978): 103–121.

Lowe, A. E., and R. W. Shaw. "An Analysis of Managerial Biasing: Evidence from a Company's Budgeting Process." *Journal of Management Studies* (October 1968): 304–315.

March, James G. "Decisions in Organizations and Theories of Choice." In Andrew H. Van de Ven and William F. Joyce, eds., *Perspectives on Organizational Design and Behavior*. New York: John Wiley and Sons, 1981.

————. Interview by Stanford Business School Alumni Association, *Stanford GSB* 47, no. 3 (1978–79): 16–19.

March, James G., and H. A. Simon. *Organizations*. New York: John Wiley and Sons, 1958.

Merchant, Kenneth A. "The Design of the Corporate Budgeting System: Influences on Managerial Behavior and Performance." *Accounting Review* (October 1981): 813–829.

Mezias, Stephen J. "Some Analytics of Organizational Slack." Working paper, Graduate School of Business, Stanford University, November 1985.

Miller, J., and J. Thornton. "Effort, Uncertainty, and the New Soviet Incentive System." *Southern Economic Journal* (October 1978): 432–446.

Mitroff, I. I., and J. R. Emshoff. "On Strategic Assumption-Making: A Dialectical Approach to Policy and Planning." *Academy of Management Review* 4, no. 1 (1979): 1–12.

Moch, M. K., and L. R. Pondy. "The Structure of Chaos: Organized Anarchy as a Response to Ambiguity." *Administrative Science Quarterly* 22, no. 2 (1977): 351–362.

Onsi, Mohamed. "Factor Analysis of Behavioral Variables Affecting Budgetary Slack." *Accounting Review* (July 1973): 535–548.

Parker, L. D. "Goal Congruence: A Misguided Accounting Concept." *ABACUS* (June 1976): 3–13.

Pondy, L. R. "Organizational Conflict: Concepts and Models." *Administrative Science Quarterly* 12, no. 2 (1967): 296–320.

Radner, R. "A Behavioral Model of Cost Reduction." *Bell Journal of Economics* (Fall 1975): 196–215.

Rogers, C. R. *Client Centered Therapy*. Boston: Houghton Mifflin, 1951.

Rosner, Martin M. "Economic Determinant of Organizational Innovation." *Administrative Science Quarterly* 12 (1968): 614–625.

Schein, V. E. "Examining an Illusion: The Role of Deceptive Behaviors in Organizations." *Human Relations* (October 1979): 287–295.

Schiff, Michael. "Accounting Tactics and the Theory of the Firm." *Journal of Accounting Research* (Spring 1966): 62–67.

Schiff, Michael, and Arie Y. Lewin. *Behavioral Aspects of Accounting*. Englewood Cliffs, N.J.: Prentice-Hall, 1974.

————. "The Impact of People on Budgets." *Accounting Review* (April 1970): 259–268.

————. "Where Traditional Budgeting Fails." *Financial Executive* (May 1968): 51–62.

Simon, H. A. *Administrative Behavior*. New York: Free Press, 1957.

Singh, Jitendra V. "Performance, Slack, and Risk Taking in Organizational Decision Making." *Academy of Management Journal* (September 1986): 562–585.

———. "Performance, Slack, and Risk Taking in Strategic Decisions: Test of a Structural Equation Model. Ph.D. diss., Stanford Graduate School of Business, 1983.

Snowberger, V. "The New Soviet Incentive Model: Comment." *Bell Journal of Economics* (Autumn 1977): 591–600.

Snygg, D., and A. W. Combs. *Individual Behavior*. New York: Harper and Row, 1949.

Staw, B. M. "Rationality and Justification in Organizational Life." In B. M. Staw and L. L. Cummings, eds., *Research in Organizational Behavior* 2. Greenwich, Conn.: JAI Press, 1980.

Swieringa, R. J., and R. H. Moncur. "The Relationship between Managers' Budget Oriented Behavior and Selected Attitudes, Position, Size and Performance Measures." Supplement to *Journal of Accounting Research* (1972): 19.

Thompson, J. D. *Organizations in Action*. New York: McGraw-Hill, 1967.

Thompson, W. *Correlates of the Self-Concept*. Nashville, Tenn.: Counselor Recording and Tests, 1972.

Waller, William S. "Slack in Participative Budgeting: The Joint Effect of a Truth-Inducing Pay Scheme and Risk Preferences." *Accounting, Organizations and Society* (December 1987): 87–98.

Waller, William S., and C. Chow. "The Self-Selection and Effort of Standard-Based Employment Contracts: A Framework and Some Empirical Evidence." *Accounting Review* (July 1985): 458–476.

Weitzman, M. "The New Soviet Incentive Model." *Bell Journal of Economics* (Spring 1976): 251–257.

Williamson, Oliver E. *The Economics of Discretionary Behavior: Managerial Objectives in a Theory of the Firm*. Englewood Cliffs, N.J.: Prentice-Hall, 1964.

———. "A Model of Rational Managerial Behavior." In Richard M. Cyert and James G. March, eds., *A Behavioral Theory of the Firm*. Englewood Cliffs, N.J.: Prentice-Hall, 1963.

Winter, Sidney G. "Satisficing, Selection, and the Innovating Remnant." *Quarterly Journal of Economics* 85 (1971): 237–257.

Woot, P. D., H. Heyvaert, and F. Martou. "Strategic Management: An Empirical Study of 168 Belgian Firms." *International Studies of Management and Organization* 7 (1977): 60–73.

Wylie, R. C. *The Self-Concept: A Critical Survey of Pertinent Research Literature*. Lincoln: University of Nebraska Press, 1961.

Young, Mark S. "Participative Budgeting: The Effects of Risk Aversion and Asymmetric Information on Budgetary Slack." *Journal of Accounting Research* (Autumn 1985): 829–842.

4

ACCOUNTING AND LANGUAGE

The idea that accounting can be viewed as a language has generated numerous empirical attempts to evaluate the denotations and connotations of accounting constructs. Research in accounting has employed many of the theories and methods used in the study of language, in particular the Sapir-Whorf hypothesis of linguistic relativism, sociolinguistics, and psycholinguistics. This chapter, therefore, will discuss the attempts so far in the literature to analyze accounting as a language and to use the theories and methods prevalent in the study of language.

THE STUDY OF LANGUAGE

The ability to acquire language and use it for communication constitutes the most significant difference between humans and animals. Humans use language as an elaborate symbolic system with which to organize their cognitive experience, as well as a system of social conventions that specify relationships between sets of symbols and sets of ideas. Language is the keystone of human culture. It gives people of a given culture a history, a representation of collective experiences, by assigning meanings to their world.

The study of language as a communication form or as a cultural form is important for the understanding of human behavior. In general, the study of language has focused primarily on four areas: *structural linguistics, developmental psycholinguistics, linguistic relativity,* and *sociolinguistics.*

Structural linguistics devotes itself to the process of language acquisition and the identification of formal structural properties. Developmental psycholinguistics considers language acquisition and use as special instances of more general cognitive functioning.[1]

Another objective of language study is to acquire a better understanding of the human thinking process through the examination of grammatical organization and transformation. Linguistic relativity examines the role of language in our conception of the world. In brief, as speakers of a language, our worldview, or weltanschauung, forces us to interpret the world through the unique grammatical forms and categories that the language supplies.[2]

Sociolinguistics, or the sociology of language, concerns itself with the existence of different linguistic repertories in a single language, which are associated with different social strata and correspond to different social behaviors.[3] Sociolinguistics studies the characteristics of language varieties, their functions, and their speakers, as well as how these characteristics constantly interact and change one another within a speech community.[4]

ACCOUNTING AS A LANGUAGE

It is customary to call accounting a language or, more precisely, the language of business, because it is an important means of communicating information about business. Accounting textbooks often emphasize the notion that accounting is a language. Following this general perception of accounting, Ijiri contended:

As the language of business, accounting has many things in common with other languages. The various business activities of a firm are reported in accounting statements using accounting language, just as news events are reported in newspapers in the English language. To express an event in accounting or in English, we must follow certain rules. Without following certain rules diligently, not only does one run the risk of being misunderstood, but one also risks a penalty for misrepresentation, lying, or perjury. Comparability of statements is essential to the effective functioning of a language whether it is in English or in accounting. At the same time, language has to be flexible enough to adapt to a changing environment.[5]

The linguistic nature of accounting is clearly evident in the profession's continuous efforts to publish accounting terminology bulletins. It is also visible in the emerging empirical literature on accounting and language.

The question arises, What makes accounting a language? Hawes defined a language as follows:

Man's symbols are not randomly arranged signs which lead to the conceptualization of isolated and discrete referents. Rather, man's symbols are arranged in a systematic or patterned fashion with certain rules governing their usage. This arrangement of symbols is called a language and the rules which influence the patterning and usage of symbols constitute the grammar of the language.[6]

This definition identifies two components of language, namely symbols and grammatical rules. Therefore, the perception of accounting as a language rests on the identification of accounting symbols and rules. The following argument can be made:

1. The symbols or lexical characteristics of a language are the "meaningful" units or words identifiable in any language. These symbols are linguistic objects used to identify particular concepts. These symbolic representations do exist in accounting. Numerals and words, and debits and credits can be viewed as symbols that are generally accepted and unique to the accounting discipline.[7]

2. The grammatical rules of a language refer to the syntactical arrangements existing in any given language. Such rules also exist in accounting. They constitute the general set of procedures used for the creation and dissemination of accounting data. This parallel between grammatical and accounting rules was established in the following manner:

> The CPA (the expert in accounting) certifies the correctness of the application of accounting rules as does an accomplished speaker of a language for the grammatical correctness of the sentence. Accounting rules formalize the structure of accounting in the same way as grammar formalizes the inherent structure of a natural language.[8]

Given the existence of both symbols and rules as major components, accounting can be defined a priori as a language. As for the study of language, accounting can be researched using theories and methods of structural linguistics, developmental psycholinguistics, linguistic relativity, and sociolinguistics.

LINGUISTIC RELATIVITY IN ACCOUNTING

The Sapir-Whorf Hypothesis of Linguistic Relativity

Anthropologists have always emphasized the study of language in their studies of culture. Sapir would refer to the "linguistic symbolism" of a given culture.[9] He perceived language to be an instrument of thought for the communication of thought. In other words, a given language predisposed its users to a distinct belief. All of these premises led to the formulation of the main principle of linguistic relativity: that language is an active determinant of thought. Similarly, Whorf maintained that ways of speaking indicate the metaphysics of a culture. These metaphysics consist of unstated premises that shape the perception and thought of those who participate in a culture and predispose them to a certain method of perception:

> Formulation of ideas is not an independent process, strictly rational in the old sense, but it is part of a particular grammar, and differs, from slightly to greatly, between different grammars. . . . We are thus introduced to a new principle of relativity, which holds that all observers are not led by the same physical evidence to the same picture of the universe, unless their linguistic backgrounds are similar or in some way may be calibrated.[10]

At its most extreme, the linguistic relativity hypothesis claims that linguistic structure directly constrains cognitive organization. Fishman explained this claim as follows:

Some languages recognize far more tenses than do others. Some languages recognize a gender of nouns (and, therefore, also require markers of gender in the verb and adjective systems), whereas others do not. Some languages build into the verb system recognition of certainty or uncertainty of past, present, or future action. Other languages build into the verb system a recognition of the size, shape, and color of nouns referred to.[11]

The linguistic relativity hypothesis usually is contrasted with either a *neutral view of language,* a *cultural relativity hypothesis,* or a *linguistic reflection hypothesis.*

According to the *neutral view,* language provides a verbalized inventory of real items in the world. This inventory is always the same. Words are only referents that differ from one language to another. They are expressions of a common world of experiences shared by all people independently of language. In this school of thought, the Sapir-Whorf view maintains that the inventory does not exist independent of language; it is *determined* by any given language. Consequently, the structure of a person's language is a kind of mode that fixes his or her cognitive function. Reality is not present in the same forms for all people. Human beings may be restricted because they can only think what their language allows them to think.

The *cultural relativity hypothesis* holds that cultural patterns determine behavior. The Sapir-Whorf hypothesis differs from cultural relativity by prescribing the major determining role to linguistic patterns. Cultural patterns affect to some degree the way one perceives the world. Conversely, linguistic categories affect cultural experience. For example, Whorf held: "Our linguistically determined thought world not only collaborates with our cultural idols and ideals but engages even our unconscious personal reactions in its patterns and gives them a certain character—characteristics."[12]

In the *linguistic reflection view,* language primarily reflects rather than creates specific behavior and orientations. It was developed to replace the rather strong claims of the linguistic relativity hypothesis as a constraint of sociocultural organizations. The differences between the linguistic relativity hypothesis and the linguistic reflection view have been eloquently expressed as follows: "One (the 'Linguistic Relativity Hypothesis') posits that language structure and language usage are fundamental and 'given' and that all behavior is influenced thereby. The other claims that social organization and behavior are prior and language merely reflects them."[13] Both positions are important. Whether language is a mere reflection of the sociocultural structure or a constraint that causes particular behavior rests on how one interprets the results of the empirical studies on the Sapir-Whorf hypothesis.

Exhibit 4.1
A Systematic Version of the Sapir-Whorf Hypothesis

	Data of speaker's behavior	
Data about language characteristics	Linguistic data	Nonlinguistic data
Lexical characteristics	1	2
Grammatical characteristics	3	4

Systematization of the Sapir-Whorf Hypothesis

Fishman provided some order and systematization to the Sapir-Whorf hypothesis by using a four-fold analytic scheme (see Exhibit 4.1).[14] He distinguished between two levels of language, lexical and grammatical, and two types of behavior, linguistic and nonlinguistic. They can be described as follows:

1.   The lexical level consists of all words that compose a language. Languages differ in the number of terms used to describe a phenomenon. For example, the two words "financial leverage" in English are denoted by six words in French: "Effet financier du coup de levier."

2.   The grammatical level of language primarily refers to the manner in which the structural units are organized. It is a syntactical arrangement procedure. "Double-entry bookkeeping" is denoted in French as "Compatibilité à partie double," since noun and adjective are arranged differently in the two languages.

3.   Linguistic behavior refers to choices among *words,* whereas nonlinguistic behavior refers to choices among *objects.* This distinction will become clearer after the explanation of each of the cells identified in Exhibit 4.1.

Cell 1 implies a relationship between the lexical properties of a language and the speaker's linguistic behavior. Phenomena are codified differently in each language. What requires a highly differentiated codification in one language is minimally codified in another language. Therefore, the linguistic behavior or choice of words to express a particular phenomenon will differ from one language to another. For example, there are several terms for horses among speakers of Arabic and various terms for snow among speakers of Eskimo.

Cell 2 implies a relationship between the lexical properties of a language and the nonlinguistic behavior of its users. It assumes that speakers of a language who make certain lexical distinctions will be able to perform particular nonlinguistic tasks better and more rapidly than the speakers of languages who do not. Brown and Lenneberg, Lenneberg, Lantz and Steffre, and others showed that the availability of labels for certain colors enabled subjects to recognize them more readily than colors for which no labels were available.[15] They also demonstrated that the most highly codified colors in a given language are recognized and recalled more often by subjects. A highly codified color is described by a fewer number of words.

Cell 3 implies a relationship between grammatical characteristics and linguistic behavior. Whorf primarily concerned himself with the relationship between language and worldview.[16] The level of the hypothesis assumes that the speakers of one language who use specific grammatical rules are predisposed to a different worldview from that of the speakers of other languages. Whorf based his conclusions on an analysis of Hopi that compared the language with Standard Average European (SAE) languages, including English. Hoijer argued the same position in an analysis of Navaho.[17] The work of Ervin-Tripp on bilingualism also can be used to support this level of the Sapir-Whorf hypothesis.[18] She used as subjects bilingual Japanese women who were married to U.S. servicemen. When asked to converse in Japanese, the context of their conversation was more typical of women in Japan. Similarly, when asked to converse in English, the context was more typical of women in the United States.

Cell 4 implies a relationship between grammatical characteristics and nonlinguistic behavior. Carroll and Casagrande found some support for this level of the hypothesis.[19] They attempted to evaluate whether the speakers of a language that codes for color, shape, and size by using the same verb, such as the Navaho language, classify objects differently from the speakers of a language that only codes for tense, person, and number with its verbs, as does English. They found that Navaho-dominant Navahos chose objects as predicted by the grammatical verb more often than did the English-dominant Navahos.

From this discussion emerges the main paradigm of linguistic relativity: that cognitive organization can be directly influenced by linguistic structure. Accounting, as a language, also mediates users' behavior.

Systematization of Linguistic Relativism in Accounting

Evidence in support of the Sapir-Whorf hypothesis exists at each of the levels identified by Fishman.[20] In order to assert that accounting affects the user's cognitive behavior like a language does, a similar systematization is necessary to guide future accounting research on the subject. The propositions derived from such a systematization can be used to justify conceptually some of the research findings on the impact of accounting information on decision making. Because the number of articles dealing with the impact of information content on decision making is quite large, only a few research findings will be used here to illustrate linguistic relativism in accounting.

Exhibit 4.2
Propositions of Linguistic Relativism in Accounting

Data about accounting characteristics	Data of user's behavior	
	Linguistic behavior	Nonlinguistic behavior
Symbolic representation	1	2
Manipulation rules	3	4

To accomplish the systematization, characteristics of accounting language and data of cognitive behavior are differentiated. The characteristics of accounting language already have been defined as symbolic representations and manipulation rules. The data of cognitive behavior in accounting refers to the user's behavior, which may be either linguistic or nonlinguistic. For instance, a portfolio decision is an example of nonlinguistic behavior, whereas a similarity judgment between two stocks shows linguistic behavior. This systematization leads to a four-fold analytical scheme, which is portrayed in Exhibit 4.2.

Cell 1 involves the relationship between the symbolic representations of accounting and the linguistic behavior of the user. For example, an accountant will find a business phenomenon easier to describe than a nonaccountant. It may be said that the codification structure of accounting is more differentiated than that of ordinary English, leading to a different linguistic behavior of users. The first level of the Sapir-Whorf hypothesis in accounting can be described in the following manner: Users who make certain lexical distinctions in accounting are able to talk and/or solve problems that cannot easily be solved by users who do not.

It can be used as a conceptual justification for most studies that evaluate the semantic meaning of accounting concepts or content.[21] Oliver used the semantic differential technique to measure the semantic meaning of eight important accounting concepts for seven professional groups involved in the production and use of accounting data. The results indicated that accounting educators' perceptions of the meanings of these concepts do not conform to the perceptions of the other six professional groups. In other words, following the first hypothesis, these results show that the accounting concepts first had an impact on the linguistic behavior of different professional users and, second, were understood differently by the users.

Cell 2 involves the relationship between the symbolic representations of accounting and the nonlinguistic behavior of the user. Following Brown and

Lenneberg's study, it can be conjectured that phenomena or concepts that are highly codified in accounting will be recalled and responded to more often than less highly codified concepts.[22] This second level of the Sapir-Whorf hypothesis in accounting may be expressed as follows: Users who make certain lexical distinctions in accounting are able to perform (nonlinguistic) tasks more rapidly or more completely than those users who do not.

This proposition can be used as a theoretical net for those studies that evaluate the impact of accounting content (extent of codification) on the user's decision making.[23] Abdel-Khalik reported on an empirical study concerning the assumption that detailed financial information is more useful for lending decision making.[24] Although his results support imputing a higher utility for detailed data under only certain conditions, they are conceptually justifiable by the second Sapir-Whorf hypothesis in the sense that the extent of aggregation (or codification) of data implies a different utility and a different nonlinguistic behavior.

Cell 3 involves the relationship between the accounting manipulation rules and linguistic behavior. For example, a description of the financial position of a given firm will differ, depending on whether the firm has adopted LIFO or FIFO. The third level of the Sapir-Whorf hypothesis in accounting can be expressed as follows: Users who process accounting (grammatical) rules are more predisposed to particular managerial styles or emphases than those who do not.

Such a position can accommodate any findings on differences in common stock perception and preferences that may arise from the use of alternative accounting techniques. More specifically, if subjects in a laboratory experiment are presented with different combinations of accounting information on various stocks and if an individual's stock perception can be assumed to be fully represented by his or her similarity judgments on all possible pairs of stocks, one can find axes in the multidimensional space of perceptual judgments.[25] Green and Maheshwari adopted such a procedure and concluded that the axes or dimensions could be interpreted as the mean or variance of return advocated in the normative models of portfolio theory. They used two groups of subjects. Group A represented the "high-information" group, in that all subjects received a supplementary information sheet for each stock. Group B, representing the "low-information" group, received only the industry classification of each company. The two groups' perceptual maps, obtained by the use of the Torgeson and Young multidimensional scaling program, were different. Following our second hypothesis, the results show that the accounting manipulation rules and results had an impact on the linguistic behavior of the subjects in Group A and Group B.

Finally, Cell 4 involves the relationship between accounting manipulation rules and nonlinguistic behavior. The adoption of LIFO or FIFO, for example, may affect the investment decision of a user. The fourth level of the Sapir-Whorf hypothesis in accounting can be expressed as follows: Accounting techniques tend either to facilitate or to render more difficult (nonlinguistic) managerial behaviors on the part of users.

Some behavioral accounting findings on the impact of alternative accounting methods on the user's decision making can be reconciled with this fourth accounting proposition of the Sapir-Whorf hypothesis.[26] Elias attempted to determine whether an investment decision would be made differently with the addition of information provided by a human resource accounting system. His participants came from several groups with different levels of sophistication in and orientations toward accounting.[27] They were asked to select one company as the best investment on the basis of financial statements prepared in the conventional manner and financial statements that included "human assets" treatment. One of the results of his study was that the selected company was associated with the experimental accounting treatment. Although exploratory, these results are in line with our fourth hypothesis and show the impact of accounting manipulation rules on the nonlinguistic behavior of users, specifically the selection of a portfolio.

ACCOUNTING RESEARCH IN LINGUISTIC RELATIVITY

According to the Sapir-Whorf hypothesis, accounting has lexical characteristics and grammatical rules that affect the linguistic and nonlinguistic behavior of users. Thus, four propositions were introduced to integrate conceptually research findings on the impact of accounting information on user's behavior.[28] They are as follows:

1. Users who make certain lexical distinctions in accounting are able to talk and/or solve problems that cannot easily be solved by users who do not.
2. Users who make certain lexical distinctions in accounting are able to perform (nonlinguistic) tasks more rapidly or more completely than those users who do not.
3. Users who process accounting (grammatical) rules are more predisposed to particular managerial styles or emphases than those who do not.
4. Accounting techniques tend either to facilitate or to render more difficult (nonlinguistic) managerial behaviors on the part of users.

Most empirical research, however, has investigated the role of accounting as a language and as a vehicle of communication without explicit reference to the linguistic relativity hypothesis and without focusing on the connotative meanings of accounting constructs. The notion that all types of accounting constructs can have connotative as well as denotative meanings led to various investigations of the connotative meanings of accounting constructs. The denotative meaning of a construct communicates an objective description of the construct. A connotative meaning describes a subjective attitude or emotion about the construct. There are, therefore, positive and negative connotations of accounting constructs.

Haried first investigated the semantic dimensions of financial statements using the *semantic differential technique,* which had been developed by Osgood, Suci, and Tannenbaum to measure connotative meanings.[29] In a second study he reported on an adaptation of a second technique, the *antecedent-consequent method,* which was developed by Triandis and Kilty to measure denotative meanings.[30] The purpose of the second study was to test the hypothesis that the semantic differential, the antecedent-consequent method, or both, could adapt to the systematic gathering and analyzing of evidence relevant to semantic problems in external accounting communication. The results, based on the answers of five different groups of users, favored the use of the antecedent-consequent method. Haried concluded:

The antecedent-consequent method was shown to be adaptable to financial report terminology and useful in systematically gathering and analyzing empirical evidence relevant to hypotheses about semantic problems in external accounting communications. The technique meets the general criteria of a measurement instrument and generates analytical results that are relatively easy to interpret and apply to the problems at hand. Moreover, it measures those aspects of meaning that appear to be most important in identifying differences between the meaning intended and that actually conveyed by the use of a word in financial reports. The semantic differential is also adaptable as a sensitive, reliable, and valid instrument for measuring connotative meanings conveyed by terms used in financial reports. My research, however, shows that it is less capable of providing evidence which is necessarily relevant to hypotheses regarding the semantic problems in external accounting communication.[31]

Other studies, however, relied on the semantic differential. Oliver used it to measure the semantic meaning of eight accounting concepts using seven professional groups involved in the production and use of accounting data to obtain information about relative communication among groups.[32] His findings showed a highly significant difference in meaning for six of the eight concepts among the professional groups as well as a major role for academicians in causing the lack of communication. He advised that "if accounting educators sincerely desire an influential role in the continuing development and utilization of accounting information, it appears they should structure their future attempts to interject their positions within a communication network in phase with the nonacademics.[33]

Flamholtz and Cook used the area of human resource accounting as a vehicle to study the role of connotative meaning in the process of change in accounting.[34] They relied on the semantic differential technique to identify the dimensions of selected traditional and human resource accounting constructs and to position these constructs in a semantic space. The results showed the presence of two clusters of constructs: traditional and nontraditional. It was then argued that a "semantic halo effect" differentiates the connotative meanings of traditional and nontraditional accounting constructs. This could explain resistance to accounting innovations such as human resource accounting or socioeconomic accounting. The use of the term "halo effect" was explained as follows:

As used in psychology, the term "halo effect" refers to a tendency to generalize an overall impression of a person to specific traits or characteristics. As used in this article, the semantic halo effect refers to a tendency to generalize to specific characteristics of a construct based upon whether the construct is perceived as traditional or nontraditional.[35]

Most recently, Houghton used the semantic differential technique to examine the connotative meaning (and the cognitive structure within which that meaning is held) of "true and fair view" from the point of view of accountants and private (noninstitutional) shareholders.[36] Significant differences were found in the responses given by accountants and private shareholders. In addition, the factor or cognitive structure of the "expert" accountant groups was seen to be more complex than that of the private shareholders.

Two studies have relied on a psycholinguistic technique, the *cloze procedure*. As defined by its creator, cloze is a "method of intercepting a message from a transmitter (writer or speaker), mutilating its language patterns by deleting parts, and so administering it to receivers (readers or listeners) that their attempts to make patterns whole again potentially yield a considerable number of cloze units.[37]

In the first study, Adelberg used the cloze readability procedure to measure the understandability of various accounting communications.[38] His empirical evidence showed that differential understandability exists across some, but not all, of the following: financial report preparers, financial report messages, and financial report users. It also showed that (1) users do not well understand accounting policies, footnotes, and management analyses of operations, and (2) narrative disclosures are not well understood by commercial bank loan officer trainees.

Adelberg then used the cloze readability procedure to evaluate empirically the communication of authoritative pronouncements in accounting.[39] The evidence showed that communication problems do not exist for either authoritative bodies or classes of accountants but do exist for two of the fifteen authoritative pronouncements tested. The cloze readability procedure is most suitable to the analysis of narration. In particular, Adelberg suggested, it could be used to test the comprehensibility of authoritative pronouncements:

Authoritative bodies use the cloze procedure to provide feedback via field trials of the comprehensibility of early drafts of their authoritative pronouncements to see if the understandability is appropriate to the intended audience. If the scores compared unfavorably with the 57% criterion level, revisions could be initiated until the scores of a subsequent cloze test would compare favorably with the 57% criterion level.[40]

RELEVANCE OF SOCIOLINGUISTICS TO ACCOUNTING

The Sapir-Whorf hypothesis emphasizes the role of language as a mediator and shaper of the environment. Mediation can differ, as it does when a speaker belongs to several organizations and communities and tends to develop his or her own verbal repertoires. Language then becomes one of the ways of distinguishing these communities and ceases to be merely a means of interpersonal communication and influence. Fishman has suggested:

It [language] is not merely a *carrier* of content, whether latent or manifest. Language itself is constant, a referent for loyalties and animosities, an indicator of social statuses and personal relationships, a marker of situations and topics as well as of the societal goals and the large-scale value-laden arenas of interaction that typify every speech community.[41]

This expansive role of language, in defining communities and social relationships, is the realm of sociolinguistics.

Sociolinguistics assumes that language largely determines the socialization of individual consciousness and the social molding of personality.[42] The discipline deals with the interaction of two aspects of human behavior—the use of language and the social organization of behavior. Our focus has been on the generally accepted social organization of language use within speech communities. This focus, known as the descriptive sociology of language, seeks to discover who speaks or writes what linguistic codes to whom, when, and why. A second focus concerns itself with the discovery of the determinants that explain changes in the social organization of language use and behavior. It is known as the dynamic sociology of language. Both focuses imply the existence in any speech community of several varieties of languages or "verbal repertoires." Thus the sociology of language attempts to explain the underlying causes of the verbal repertories of a given speech community. This implies that within each language there are linguistic codes that play an important role as a mediator of the perceptual cognitive processes employed in defining the social environment.[43]

In relating this to accounting, Belkaoui assumed that professional affiliations in accounting create linguistic repertoires or codes for intragroup and/or intergroup communications, which lead to different understandings of accounting and social relationships.[44] Specifically, a selected set of accounting concepts was subjected to analysis using multidimensional scaling techniques to evaluate the intergroup perceptual differences between three groups of users. A sociolinguistic construct was used to justify the possible lack of consensus on the meaning of accounting concepts. The dimensions of the common perceptual space were identified as conjunctive, relational, and disjunctive by analogy to the process of concept formation. The sociolinguistic thesis was verified for both the conjunctive and the disjunctive concepts. Other issues for future research have also been identified: (1) the presence and the nature of the "institutional language" within accounting professional groups; (2) the presence of a profession-linked linguistic code in accounting composed of a "formal language" and a "public language"; and (3) testing whether the public language is understood by users of public data (for example, financial analysts) and whether the formal language is understood by users of formal data (such as students).[45]

Libby used multidimensional scaling techniques to investigate bankers' and auditors' perceptions of the message communicated by the audit report.[46] This study falls into the area of sociolinguistics and accounting because members of different occupational groups were compared as to their perception of an accounting construct, namely the audit report. However, the study argued that the research question could be structured within Hammond's cognitive conflict paradigm, which is based on the lens model. Libby stated: "In the paradigm, differential perceptions concerning the message intended by the reports would be indicated by the differential weighing of cues and dimensions on which the reports vary. Besides providing a method of conceptualizing perceptual disagreements, Hammond's work provides a suggested method for reducing disagreements, if this is desired."[47]

Surprisingly, no disagreements were found. The study reported that three tests of auditors' and bankers' perceptions revealed no significant differences. This is the only study to have reported no differences in the perceptions of connotative meanings of accounting constructs between members of different occupational groups.

RELEVANCE OF BILINGUALISM TO ACCOUNTING

Although accounting is itself a language, its lexical and grammatical characteristics are expressed in many different languages. Therefore, communication problems inevitably arise between unilingual accountants from different countries. Following the Sapir-Whorf hypothesis, linguistic behavior, or the choice of words for a particular phenomenon, will differ from one language to another. A second problem can affect bilingual speakers. Namely, two language systems available to bilingual speakers can bring about linguistic and perceptual confusion instead of cognitive enrichment. Another problem facing bilinguals concerns whether switching from one language to another leads to better perception. In effect, language switching has been found to be related to high levels of creativity, cognitive feasibility,[48] concept formation,[49] verbal intelligence[50] and psycholinguistic abilities.[51]

The three problems that have been identified affect the perception of accounting concepts by bilingual and unilingual speakers. Monti-Belkaoui and Belkaoui conducted an experiment to evaluate the extent of these problems.[52] A selected set of accounting concepts were subjected to analysis through multidimensional scaling techniques. The purpose was to evaluate the intergroup perceptual differences of four experimental groups made up of unilingual French, unilingual English, and bilingual students. The findings supported the contention that unilingual speakers of separate languages differ from each other and from bilingual speakers in their perception of accounting concepts. Some of the findings provided support for the contention that language switching may enhance understanding.

Language differences result not only in general communication problems across national boundaries but also in specific perceptual differences in understanding concepts used in the accounting discipline. Monti-Belkaoui and Belkaoui offered the following advice:

The increasing volume of international trade during recent years and the decline in the competitive position previously enjoyed by U.S. firms in the international market is seen in part as a function of the linguistic barrier faced by typically unilingual American corporate executives and professionals in dealing with overseas customers and colleagues. . . .

. . . The evidence suggests that fluency in two languages aids in the uniform acquisition and comprehension of professional concepts. The need for (and efficacy of) the bilingual professional is an area that requires further attention from social sciences, economic planners, and the standard-setters of professional organizations.[53]

CONCLUSION

The examination of connotative and denotative meanings of accounting constructs and the investigation of differences in the perception of these constructs by users and preparers are new facets of behavioral accounting. Attempts so far have generally been characterized by successful use of the various methodologies used in the study of language, namely the semantic differential, antecedent-consequent methods, the cloze procedure, and multidimensional scaling techniques. Some of these attempts have gone beyond the mere use of these techniques to support research questions with theoretical models from linguistics, in particular the Sapir-Whorf hypothesis of linguistic relativism, sociolinguistics, and bilingualism. Much remains to be done, as (1) accounting innovations have different connotative meanings to professional groups and special interest groups; (2) various "institutional" accounting language repertoires arise out of the particular needs and interests of members of linguistic communities; and (3) the increase in international trade and the efforts to harmonize international accounting create communication problems of perception and expectation among speakers of different languages and holders of different cultures. Both the profession and academia need to be attuned to these developing problems, because they can affect the harmonious growth of the discipline internationally and within any country.

NOTES

1. Noam Chomsky, *American Power and the New Mandarins* (New York: Pantheon Books, 1969); idem, *Aspects of the Theory of Syntax* (Cambridge, Mass.: MIT Press,

1965); J. A. Fodor, "How to Learn to Talk: Some Simple Ways," in F. Smith and G. Miller, eds., *The Genesis of Language: A Psycholinguistic Approach* (Cambridge, Mass.: MIT Press, 1966).

2. E. Sapir, *Culture, Language and Personality: Selected Essays,* ed. D. G. Mandelbaum (Berkeley and Los Angeles: University of California Press, 1956); B. L. Whorf, *Language, Thought and Reality: Selected Writings,* ed. J. B. Caroll (Cambridge, Mass.: MIT Press, 1956).

3. B. Bernstein, "Some Sociological Determinants of Perception: An Enquiry in Subcultural Differences," *British Journal of Sociology* (1958): 159–174.

4. Joshua A. Fishman, *Sociolinguistics: A Brief Introduction* (New York: Newbury House Publishers, 1972).

5. Yuji Ijiri, *Theory of Accounting Measurement,* Studies in Accounting Research no. 10 (Sarasota, Fla.: American Accounting Association, 1975).

6. Leonard C. Hawes, *Pragmatics of Analoguing* (Reading, Mass.: Addison-Wesley, 1975).

7. Daniel McDonald, *Comparative Accounting Theory* (Reading, Mass.: Addison-Wesley, 1972).

8. Tribhowan N. Jain, "Alternative Methods of Accounting and Decision Making: A Psycholinguistic Analysis," *Accounting Review* (January 1973): 95–104.

9. Sapir, *Culture, Language and Personality.*

10. Whorf, *Language, Thought and Reality,* pp. 212, 214.

11. Fishman, *Sociolinguistics,* p. 156.

12. B. L. Whorf, "The Relation of Habitual Thought and Behavior to Language," in L. Spier, ed., *Language, Culture and Personality* (Salt Lake City: University of Utah Press, 1941), pp. 75–93.

13. Fishman, *Sociolinguistics,* p. 156.

14. Joshua A. Fishman, "A Systematization of the Whorfian Hypothesis," *Behavioral Science* (1960): 323–339.

15. R. W. Brown and E. H. Lenneberg, "A Study in Language and Cognition," *Journal of Abnormal and Social Psychology* (1954): 454–462; Eric H. Lenneberg, "Cognition in Ethnolinguistics," *Language* (1973): 463–471; De Lee Lantz and Volney Steffre, "Language and Cognition Revisited," *Journal of Abnormal and Social Psychology* (1953): 454–462.

16. Whorf, *Language, Thought and Reality.*

17. H. Hoijer, "Cultural Implications of the Navaho Linguistic Categories," *Language* (1951): 111–120.

18. Susan Ervin-Tripp, "Sociolinguistics," in L. Berkowitz, ed., *Advances in Experimental Social Psychology* (New York: Academic Press, 1960): 91–165.

19. J. B. Carroll and J. B. Casagrande, "The Functions of Language Classification in Behavior," in E. E. Maccoby, T. M. Newcomb, and E. L. Hartley, eds., *Readings in Social Psychology,* 3d ed. (New York: Holt, Rinehart and Winston, 1958).

20. Fishman, "A Systematization of the Whorfian Hypothesis.

21. Bruce L. Oliver, "The Semantic Differential: A Device for Measuring the Interprofessional Communication of Selected Accounting Concepts," *Journal of Accounting Research* (Autumn 1974): 299–316; Andrew A. Haried, "Measurement of Meaning in Financial Reports," *Journal of Accounting Research* (Spring 1973): 117–145; Ahmed

Belkaoui and Alain Cousineau, "Accounting Information, Nonaccounting Information, and Common Stock Perception: An Application of Multidimensional Scaling Techniques," *Journal of Business* (July 1977): 334–343.

22. Brown and Lenneberg, "A Study in Language and Cognition."

23. Edward J. Lusk, "Cognitive Aspects of Annual Reports: Field Independence/Dependence," *Empirical Research in Accounting: Selected Studies* (1973): 191–202.

24. Rashad A. Abdel-Khalik, "The Effect of Aggregating Accounting Reports on the Quality of the Lending Decision: An Empirical Investigation," *Empirical Research in Accounting: Selected Studies* (1973): 104–138.

25. P. E. Green and A. Maheshwari, "Common Stock Perception and Preference: An Application of Multidimensional Scaling," *Journal of Business* (October 1969): 439–457.

26. Thomas R. Dyckman, "The Effects of Alternative Accounting Techniques on Certain Management Decisions," *Journal of Accounting Research* (Spring 1964): 91–107; Robert E. Jensen, "An Experimental Design for the Study of Effects of Accounting Variations in Decision Making," *Journal of Accounting Research* (Autumn 1966): 224–238; J. Dickhaut, "Alternative Information Structures and Probability Revisions," *Accounting Review* (January 1973).

27. Nabil Elias, "The Effects of Human Asset Statements on the Investment Decision: An Experiment," *Empirical Research in Accounting: Selected Studies* (1972): 215–240.

28. Ahmed Belkaoui, "Linguistic Relativity in Accounting," *Accounting Organizations and Society* (October 1978): 97–104.

29. Andrew A. Haried, "The Semantic Dimensions of Financial Statements," *Journal of Accounting Research* (Autumn 1972): 376–391; Charles E. Osgood, George J. Suci, and Percy H. Tannenbaum, *The Measurement of Meaning* (Urbana: University of Illinois Press, 1957).

30. Haried, "Measurement of Meaning in Financial Reports"; Harry C. Triandis and Keith M. Kilty, *Cultural Influences upon the Perception of Implicative Relationships among Concepts and the Analysis of Values,* Group Effectiveness Research Laboratory Technical Report no. 56 (Urbana, Ill.: Group Effectiveness Research Laboratory, 1968), p. 4.

31. Haried, "Measurement of Meaning in Financial Reports," p. 143.

32. Oliver, "The Semantic Differential."

33. Ibid., p. 312.

34. Eric Flamholtz and Ellen Cook, "Connotative Meaning and Its Role in Accounting Change: A Field Study," *Accounting, Organizations and Society* (October 1978): 115–140.

35. Ibid., pp. 134–135.

36. K. A. Houghton, "True and Fair View: An Empirical Study of Connotative Meaning," *Accounting, Organizations and Society* (March 1987): 143–152.

37. W. Taylor, "Cloze Procedure: A New Tool for Measuring Readability," *Journalism Quarterly* (Fall 1953): 415–433.

38. Arthur Harris Adelberg, "A Methodology for Measuring the Understandability of Financial Report Messages," *Journal of Accounting Research* (Autumn 1979): 565–592.

39. Arthur Harris Adelberg, "An Empirical Evaluation of the Communication of Authoritative Pronouncements in Accounting," *Accounting and Finance* (November 1982): 73–94.

40. Ibid., p. 89.

41. Fishman, *Sociolinguistics*, p. 1.

42. Ibid., p. 4.

43. Bernstein, "Some Sociological Determinants of Perception"; L. Schatzman and A. Strauss, "Social Class and Modes of Communication," *American Journal of Sociology* (1955): 329–338; Ervin-Tripp, "Sociolinguistics"; M. Whiteman and M. Deutsch, "Social Disadvantage as Related to Intellect and Language Development," in M. Deutsch, I. Katz, and A. R. Jensen, eds., *Social Class, Race and Psychological Development* (New York: Holt, Rinehart and Winston, 1968).

44. Ahmed Belkaoui, "The Interprofessional Linguistic Communication of Accounting Concepts: An Experiment in Sociolinguistics," *Journal of Accounting Research* (Autumn 1980): 362–374.

45. Robert Libby, "Message Communicated by the Audit Report," *Journal of Accounting Research* (Spring 1979): 99–122.

46. Ibid., p. 101.

47. Ibid., p. 101.

48. E. Peal and W. Lambert, "The Relationship of Bilingualism to Intelligence," *Psychological Monographs* (1962): 76.

49. W. W. Liedke and L. D. Nelson, "Concept Formation and Bilingualism," *Alberta Journal of Education Research* (1968): 4.

50. W. E. Lambert and G. R. Tucker, "The Benefits of Bilingualism," *Psychology Today* (September 1973).

51. M. C. Casserly and A. P. Edwards, "Detrimental Effects of Grade One Bilingualism Programs: An Exploratory Study" (Paper presented to the annual conference of the Canadian Psychological Association, 1973).

52. J. Monti-Belkaoui and Ahmed Belkaoui, "Bilingualism and the Perception of Professional Concepts," *Journal of Psycholinguistic Research* 12, no. 2 (1983): 111–127.

53. Ibid., p. 124.

SELECT BIBLIOGRAPHY

Abdel-Khalik, Rashad A. "The Effect of Aggregating Accounting Reports on the Quality of the Lending Decision: An Empirical Investigation." *Empirical Research in Accounting: Selected Studies* (1973): 104–138.

Adelberg, Arthur Harris. "An Empirical Evaluation of the Communication of Authoritative Pronouncements in Accounting." *Accounting and Finance* (November 1982): 73–94.

———. "A Methodology for Measuring the Understandability of Financial Report Messages." *Journal of Accounting Research* (Autumn 1979): 565–592.

Balkan, L. *Les Effets du Bilinguisme Francais-Anglais sur les Aptitudes Intellectuelles*. Bruxelles: Aimav, 1970.

Belkaoui, Ahmed. "The Impact of Socio-economic Accounting Statements on the Investment Decision: An Empirical Study." *Accounting, Organizations and Society* (September 1980): 263–283.

———. "The Interprofessional Linguistic Communication of Accounting Concepts: An

Experiment in Sociolinguistics." *Journal of Accounting Research* (Autumn 1980): 362–374.

―――. "Linguistic Relativity in Accounting." *Accounting, Organizations and Society* (October 1978): 97–104.

―――. "A Test of the Linguistic Relativity in Accounting." *Canadian Journal of Administrative Sciences* (December 1984): 238–255.

Belkaoui, Ahmed, and Alain Cousineau. "Accounting Information, Nonaccounting Information, and Common Stock Perception: An Application of Multidimensional Scaling Techniques." *Journal of Business* (July 1977): 334–343.

Bernstein, B. "Some Sociological Determinants of Perception: An Enquiry in Subcultural Differences." *British Journal of Sociology* (1958): 159–174.

Brown, R. W., and E. H. Lenneberg. "A Study in Language and Cognition." *Journal of Abnormal and Social Psychology* (1954): 454–462.

Caroll, J. B., and J. B. Casagrande. "The Functions of Language Classification in Behavior." In E. E. Maccoby, T. M. Newcomb, and E. L. Hartley, eds., *Readings in Social Psychology*, 3d ed. New York: Holt, Rinehart and Winston, 1958.

Casserly, M. C., and A. P. Edwards. "Detrimental Effects of Grade One Bilingualism Programs: An Exploratory Study." Paper presented to the annual conference of the Canadian Psychological Association (1973).

Chomsky, Noam. *American Power and the New Mandarins.* New York: Pantheon Books, 1969.

―――. *Aspects of the Theory of Syntax.* Cambridge, Mass.: MIT Press, 1965.

Dickhaut, J. "Alternative Information Structures and Probability Revisions." *Accounting Review* (January 1973).

Dyckman, Thomas R. "The Effects of Alternative Accounting Techniques on Certain Management Decisions." *Journal of Accounting Research* (Spring 1964): 91–107.

Elias, Nabil. "The Effects of Human Asset Statements on the Investment Decision: An Experiment." *Empirical Research in Accounting: Selected Studies* (1972): 215–240.

Ervin-Tripp, Susan. "Sociolinguistics." In L. Berkowitz, ed., *Advances in Experimental Social Psychology*, pp. 91–165. New York: Academic Press, 1960.

Fishman, Joshua A. *Sociolinguistics: A Brief Introduction.* New York: Newbury House Publishers, 1972.

―――. "A Systematization of the Whorfian Hypothesis." *Behavioral Science* (1960): 323–339.

Flamholtz, Eric, and Ellen Cook. "Connotative Meaning and Its Role in Accounting Change: A Field Study." *Accounting, Organizations and Society* (October 1978): 115–140.

Fodor, J. A. "How to Learn to Talk: Some Simple Ways." In F. Smith and G. Miller, eds., *The Genesis of Language: A Psycholinguistic Approach.* Cambridge, Mass.: MIT Press, 1966.

Green, P. E., and A. Maheshwari. "Common Stock Perception and Preference: An Application of Multidimensional Scaling." *Journal of Business* (October 1969): 439–457.

Haried, Andrew A. "Measurement of Meaning in Financial Reports." *Journal of Accounting Research* (Spring 1973): 117–145.

———. "The Semantic Dimensions of Financial Statements." *Journal of Accounting Research* (Autumn 1972): 376–391.

Harris, A. J. *Effective Teaching of Reading*. New York: D. McKay Co., 1962.

Hawes, Leonard C. *Pragmatics of Analoguing*. Reading, Mass.: Addison-Wesley, 1975.

Heitzman, A., and R. H. Bloomer. "The Effect of Non-overt Reinforced Cloze Procedure upon Reading Comprehension." *Journal of Reading* (December 1967): 213–223.

Hoijer, H. "Cultural Implications of the Navaho Linguistic Categories." *Language* (1951): 111–120.

Houghton, K. A. "True and Fair View: An Empirical Study of Connotative Meaning." *Accounting, Organizations and Society* (March 1987): 143–152.

Hunt, D. E., and C. I. Hovland. "Order of Consideration of Different Types of Concepts." *Journal of Experimental Psychology* (1960): 220–225.

Jain, Tribhowan N. "Alternative Methods of Accounting and Decision Making: A Psycholinguistic Analysis." *Accounting Review* (January 1973): 95–104.

Jensen, Robert E. "An Experimental Design for the Study of Effects of Accounting Variations in Decision Making." *Journal of Accounting Research* (Autumn 1966): 224–238.

Kittell, J. E. "Intelligence Test Performance of Children from Bilingual Environments." *Elementary School Journal* (1963): 64.

Lambert, W. E., and G. R. Tucker. "The Benefits of Bilingualism." *Psychology Today* (September 1973).

Landry, R. G. "A Comparison of Second Language Learners and Monolinguals on Diverging Thinking Tasks at the Elementary School Level." *Modern Language Journal* (1974): 58.

Lantz, D. L. "Language and Cognition Revisited." *Journal of Abnormal and Social Psychology* (1953): 454–462.

Lenneberg, Eric H. "Cognition in Ethnolinguistics." *Language* (1973): 463–471.

Libby, Robert. "Bankers' and Auditors' Perceptions of the Message Communicated by the Audit Report." *Journal of Accounting Research* (Spring 1979): 99–122.

Liedke, W. W., and L. D. Nelson. "Concept Formation and Bilingualism." *Alberta Journal of Education Research* (1968): 4.

Lusk, Edward J. "Cognitive Aspects of Annual Reports: Field Independence/Dependence." *Empirical Research in Accounting: Selected Studies* (1973): 191–202.

McDavid, J. W., and H. Harari. *Psychology and Social Behavior*. New York: Harper and Row, 1974.

McDonald, Daniel. *Comparative Accounting Theory*. Reading, Mass.: Addison-Wesley, 1972.

Monti-Belkaoui, J., and Ahmed Belkaoui. "Bilingualism and the Perception of Professional Concepts." *Journal of Psycholinguistic Research* 12, no. 2 (1983): 111–127.

Moriarity, Shane. "Communicating Financial Information through Multidimensional Graphics." *Journal of Accounting Research* (Spring 1979): 205–224.

Oliver, Bruce L. "The Semantic Differential: A Device for Measuring the Interprofessional Communication of Selected Accounting Concepts." *Journal of Accounting Research* (Autumn 1974): 299–316.

Osgood, Charles E., George J. Suci, and Percy H. Tannenbaum. *The Measurement of Meaning.* Urbana: University of Illinois Press, 1957.

Pashalian, S., and J. E. Crissy. "How Readable Are Corporate Annual Reports." *Journal of Applied Psychology* (August 1950): 244–248.

Peal, E., and W. Lambert. "The Relationship of Bilingualism to Intelligence." *Psychological Monographs* (1962): 76.

Peterson, J., E. Paradis, and N. Peters. "Revalidation of the Cloze Procedure as a Measure of Instructional Level for High School Students." In *Investigations Relating to Mature Reading,* pp. 144–149. Milwaukee: National Reading Conference, 1973.

————. "Validation of the Cloze Procedure as a Measure of Readability with High School, Trade School, and College Populations." In *Investigations Relating to Mature Readings.* Milwaukee: National Reading Conference, 1972.

Rankin, E. "The Cloze Procedure—Its Validity and Utility." In *Starting and Improving College Reading Programs,* pp. 131–144. Milwaukee: National Reading Conference, 1959.

————. "An Evaluation of the Cloze Procedure as a Technique for Measuring Reading Comprehension." Ph.D. diss., University of Michigan, 1957.

————. "Grade Level Interpretation of Cloze Readability Scores." In *Reading: The Right to Participate,* pp. 30–37. Milwaukee: National Reading Conference, 1971.

Rankin, E., and J. Culhane. "Comparable Cloze and Multiple-Choice Comprehension Tests." *Journal of Reading* (December 1969): 193–198.

Sapir, E. *Culture, Language and Personality: Selected Essays.* Edited by D. G. Mandelbaum. Berkeley and Los Angeles: University of California Press, 1956.

Schmidt, W. H. *Child Development: The Human, Cultural and Educational Context.* New York: Harper and Row, 1973.

Schramm, W. "How Communication Works." In W. Schramm, ed., *The Process and Effects of Mass Communication.* Urbana: University of Illinois Press, 1954.

Smith, J. E., and N. P. Smith. "Readability: A Measure of the Performance of the Communication Function of Financial Reporting." *Accounting Review* (July 1971): 352–361.

Soper, F. J., and R. Dolphin, Jr. "Readability and Corporate Annual Reports." *Accounting Review* (April 1964): 358–362.

Taylor, W. "Application of 'Cloze' and Entropy Measures to the Study of Contextual Constraint in Samples of Continuous Prose." Ph.D. diss., University of Illinois, 1954.

————. "Cloze Procedure: A New Tool for Measuring Readability." *Journalism Quarterly* (Fall 1953): 415–433.

————. "Cloze Readability Scores as Indices of Individual Differences in Comprehension and Aptitude." *Journal of Applied Psychology* (February 1957): 19–26.

————. "New Developments in the Use of Cloze Procedure." *Journalism Quarterly* (Winter 1956): 42–48, 99.

Triandis, Harry C., and Keith M. Kilty. *Cultural Influences upon the Perception of Implicative Relationships among Concepts and the Analysis of Values.* Group

Effectiveness Research Laboratory Technical Report no. 56. Urbana, Ill.: Group
Effectiveness Research Laboratory, 1968.

Weaver, W., and A. Kingston. "A Factor Analysis of the Cloze Procedure and Other
Measures of Reading and Language Ability." *Journal of Communication* (December 1963): 252–261.

Whorf, B. L. *Language, Thought and Reality: Selected Writings*. Edited by J. B. Caroll.
Cambridge, Mass.: MIT Press, 1956.

————. "The Relation of Habitual Thought and Behavior to Language." In L. Spier,
ed., *Language, Culture and Personality*, pp. 75–93. Salt Lake City: University of
Utah Press, 1941.

Zaltman, Gerald, C. R. A. Pison, and Reinhard Angelman. *Metatheory and Consumer
Research*. New York: Holt, Rinehart and Winston, 1973.

5

GOAL SETTING,
PARTICIPATIVE BUDGETING,
AND PERFORMANCE

Both the psychological and the behavioral accounting literature have focused on the effects of goal setting, or standard setting, on performance. In addition, while the conventional accounting literature has assumed participation in goal setting to be a means for affecting performance, behavior, and task performance, the behavioral accounting literature has examined the effects of participative budgeting on attitudes and performance. This chapter will elaborate on the results of research into the effects of goal setting in general and participative budgeting in particular on task and/or attitude outcomes.

GOAL SETTING AND TASK PERFORMANCE

Evidence in Psychology

A goal can be defined as "what an individual is trying to accomplish . . . the object or aim of an action."[1] Its equivalent in accounting is the performance standard. Goal setting, or standard setting, is assumed to affect motivation, behavior, and task performance.

Among the attributes of goals are (1) *goal specifity,* which refers to the extent to which the performance level to be accomplished is explicit as to its content and clarity;[2] and (2) *goal difficulty,* which is the probability of accomplishment. A survey of empirical studies has shown that most studies support the hypothesis that specific, hard goals produce better performance than medium, easy, do-your-best, or no goals.[3]

Mechanisms, psychological processes, and cognitive activities that influence the effects of goal-setting include: (1) *direction,* which refers to the fact that goals indicate what needs to be done in the work setting; (2) *effort* mobilized to accomplish the goal; (3) *persistence* of the individual at the task; and (4) *strategy development,* which refers to the development of strategies, or action plans, for attaining goals. In addition, feedback on progress toward a goal, rewards given for goal attainment, and participation in the setting of goals have been found to mediate the positive effects of goal setting on performance. Of the individual differences, only need for achievement and self-esteem appear promising as moderating variables of the relationship between goal setting and task performance.

Evidence in Accounting

Several studies have examined the effects of setting budget goals on performance.[4] Rockness tested the effect of goal-setting difficulty, alternative reward structures, and performance feedback on both performance measures and satisfaction.[5] The results of the experiment verified parts of a budgetary model that predicted that (1) subjects in the high-budget condition differed from those in the medium-budget condition, (2) absolute performance increased with more direct reward structure, and (3) differences in planned performance existed between subjects receiving formal feedback and those receiving nonformal feedback.

A second study by Chow explored the linkages between job-standard tightness, type of compensation scheme, and performance.[6] In addition to conducting the conventional investigation of the relation between goal setting (in this case job-standard tightness) and performance, Chow built on the agency research and adverse selection studies to suggest that goal setting and type of compensation scheme affect not only workers' effort but also their self-selection among employment contracts and, through these, job performance.[7] The results of the experiment indicated that (1) for subjects with assigned treatments, job-standard tightness and type of compensation scheme had significant independent but insignificant interactive effects on performance; (2) when permitted a choice of compensation schemes (given an assigned job standard), subjects self-selected among them by skill; and (3) the selection of one's own compensation scheme enhanced performance.

Toward a Theoretical Framework: The Role of Task Uncertainty

As these results suggest, accounting studies concur with the psychological literature in the finding that setting specific difficult budget goals leads to higher task performance than setting either specific moderate goals, specific easy goals, or general goals. Naylor and Ilgen have suggested, however, that research should expand to search for the moderating variables that mediate the relationship between goal setting and performance.[8] Hirst gave the following two reasons to make such a search:

First, it has the potential to delineate situations in which goal setting does *not* have a positive effect on performance. This is significant because it suggests a need to control for moderator variables in future studies that empirically investigate both the direct effects of goal setting on performance, and the way goal setting combines with other factors (e.g., participation) to affect performance. Second, knowledge about moderator variables can have practical implications. In particular, the designers of goal setting programs can use such knowledge to anticipate the effects of their programs, and to introduce goal setting interventions in one of those situations where they are expected to have a positive effect on performance.[9]

In fact, Hirst proposed a theoretical framework that traced the effect of a potential moderating variable, task uncertainty, on the relationship between goal setting and performance.[10] As shown in Exhibit 5.1, the relationship between goal setting and performance is linked by a hypothesized sequence of activities in line with models of task performance provided by Locke et al. and Porter, Lawler, and Hackman.[11] The model includes four conditional mechanisms along the path linking goal setting to task outcomes. These are (1) goal setting, in terms of difficulty and specificity; (2) a set of cognitive activities—interpretation, strategy search, and selection of valid strategies; (3) intentions, in terms of direction, level, and duration of effort; and (4) action, in terms of the task performance. Hirst argued that difficulties can arise in performing the cognitive activities where task uncertainty is high. The complete argument is shown in Exhibit 5.2. It postulates the negative effects of task uncertainty on the completeness of task knowledge and the positive effects of goal setting based on complete task knowledge. As a result, Hirst proposed a hypothesis of task uncertainty as a moderating variable:

H_1: There is an interaction between goal setting and task uncertainty affecting task performance.[12]

While the focus has been on task uncertainty, future theoretical and empirical attempts will focus on identifying other moderating variables and integrating the findings to provide a sound basis for the design of budgetary control systems.

PARTICIPATIVE BUDGETING AND PERFORMANCE

Participation in budgeting entails the involvement of subordinates in the setting of standards that affect their operations and rewards. The implied benefit of participative budgeting is that it will improve attitudes, productivity, and/or performance. The results, however, have been mixed. Some studies have supported the argument that budgetary participation leads to higher job satisfaction,[13] higher motivation to achieve the budget,[14] and higher performance.[15] Other studies, however, found either a weak association between participation and performance,[16] or a negative association between the two variables.[17]

Exhibit 5.1
The Effects of Task Uncertainty on the Relation between Goal Setting and Task Performance

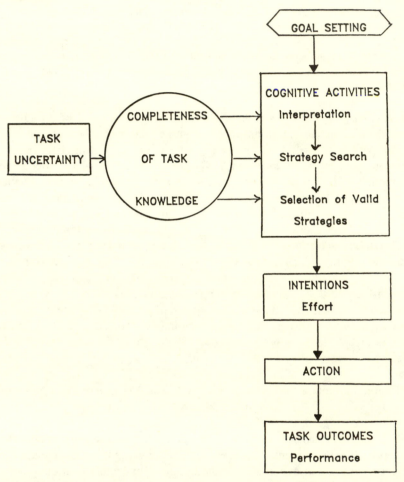

Source: Mark K. Hirst, "The Effects of Setting Budget Goals and Task Uncertainty on Performance: A Theoretical Analysis," *Accounting Review* (October 1987): 776. Reprinted with permission.

While findings on the relationship between participative budgeting and performance have been mixed, participation in decision making has been broadly defined as the "organizational process whereby individuals are involved in, and have influence on, decisions that have direct effects on those individuals."[18] Brownell reviewed participation in decision making and found evidence of

Exhibit 5.2
The Relation between Goal Setting and Task Performance

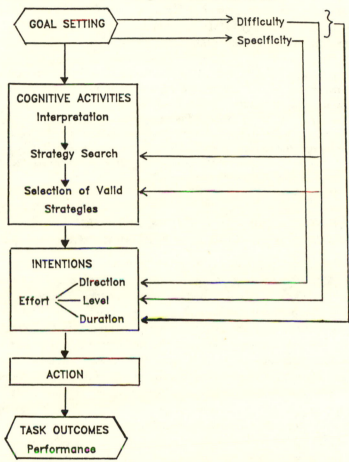

Source: Mark K. Hirst, "The Effects of Setting Budget Goals and Task Uncertainty on Performance: A Theoretical Analysis," *Accounting Review* (October 1987): 778. Reprinted with permission.

positive effects of *antecedent moderators* on participation and positive effects of participation on outcomes conditioned by *consequence moderators*. The anteced-ent moderators included (1) the cultural variables of nationality,[19] legislative systems,[20] race,[21] and religion; and (2) the organizational variables of environ-mental stability,[22] technology,[23] task uncertainty,[24] and organizational struc-ture.[25] The consequence moderators included: (1) the interpersonal variables of task stress,[26] group size,[27] intrinsic satisfaction of task,[28] and congruence between task and individual;[29] and (2) the individual level variables of locus of control,[30] authoritarianism,[31] external reference points,[32] and perceived emphasis placed on accounting information.[33] A comprehensive review of participation in decision making (hereafter PDM) was attempted by Locke and Schweiger.[34] They reached the following interesting conclusions:

(1) The use of PDM is a practical rather than a moral issue; (2) the concept of participation refers to shared or joint decision making, and therefore excludes delegation; (3) there are numerous mechanisms both cognitive and motivational through which PDM may produce high morale and performance; (4) research findings yield equivocal support for the thesis that PDM necessarily leads to increased satisfaction and productivity, although the evidence for the former outcome is stronger than the evidence for the latter; (5) the evidence indicates that the effectiveness of PDM depends upon numerous contextual factors; and (6) PDM is the only way to motivate employees.[35]

MODERATING FACTORS IN THE LINK BETWEEN PARTICIPATIVE BUDGETING AND PERFORMANCE

The view that the relationship between participation and performance holds under all conditions is known as the universalistic perspective. As we have seen, support for this view is mixed. Another view, that the relationship between participation and performance is moderated by organizational, task-related, structural, attitudinal, and personality variables, is known as the contingency perspective. This perspective accounts for the moderating effects of motivation, leadership style, task uncertainty, role ambiguity, reward structure, cognitive dissonance, authoritarianism, locus of control, and the Pelz effect. Findings on the impact of these moderating variables demonstrate the superiority of the contingency perspective in the analysis of the relationship between participative budgeting and performance. Before reviewing these findings, it is appropriate to note that the literature on participation in decision making has also identified more intervening mechanisms that mediate the effects of participation in decision making. These proposed effects and mechanisms are portrayed in Exhibit 5.3.

MOTIVATION, PARTICIPATIVE BUDGETING, AND PERFORMANCE

Participative budgeting has long been assumed to enhance managerial performance by positively affecting motivation.[36] Cost-accounting textbooks have made such claims in advocating the use of participative budgeting.[37] The accuracy of this assertion rests on establishing positive connections between participation and performance, participation and motivation, and motivation and performance, as well as an intervening linkage between participation and performance through motivation.

Exhibit 5.3
Proposed Effects and Mechanisms of Participation in Decision Making (PDM)

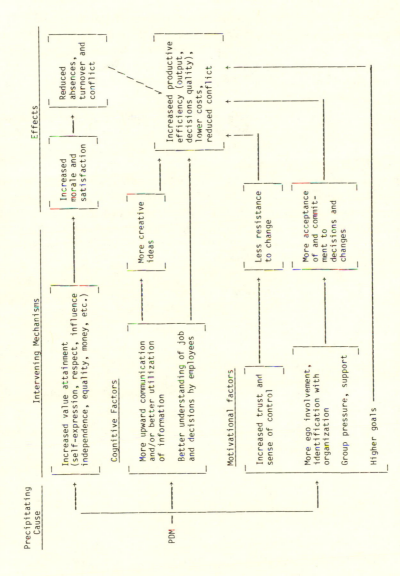

Source: Edwin A. Locke and David M. Schweiger, ''Participation in Decision-Making: One More Look.'' in Barry M. Staw, ed., *Research in Organizational Behavior* (Greenwich, Conn.: JAI Press, 1979), 1:279. Reprinted with permission.

First, as was seen earlier in this chapter, the relationship between participation and performance is unsure at best, suggesting the need to examine the impact of moderating variables.

Second, with regard to the connection between participative budgeting and motivation, the evidence has been supportive.[38] To measure motivation, these studies relied upon: (1) Vroom's expectancy model; (2) subordinates' ratings of their superiors' budget-related behaviors to assess the superiors' motivation; and (3) the three-item instruments developed by either Hackman and Lawler or Hackman and Porter.[39]

Third, with regard to the relationship between motivation and performance, both the accounting and the organizational behavior literature give strong evidence of a positive relationship.[40]

Fourth, Brownell and McInnes provided results that failed to confirm the hypothesis that motivation mediates the effect of participation on performance, although participation and performance were found to be positively related.[41] Basically, the path between participation and performance through motivation was not evident. The expectancy model developed by House and introduced in the accounting literature by Ronen and Livingstone was used to measure motivation.[42] The model is as follows:

$$M = IV_b + P_1 \left[IV_a + \sum_{i=1}^{n} (P_{2i}EV_i) \right],$$

$$i = 1, \ldots, n$$

where

M = motivation,

IV_a = intrinsic valence associated with work-goal accomplishment,

IV_b = intrinsic valence associated with goal-directed behavior,

EV_i = extrinsic valence associated with the ith extrinsic reward contingent on work-goal accomplishment,

P_1 = the expectancy that goal-directed behavior will lead to work-goal accomplishment, and

P_{2i} = the expectancy that work-goal accomplishment will lead to the ith extrinsic reward.

In the Brownell and McInnes study, the expectancies were positively related to participative budgeting, while the intrinsic values were negatively related to participative budgeting. The following interpretation was proposed: "Hence, a possible interpretation of the study's findings is that managers negotiate slack budgets in response to participation's reinforcements of the expectation of formal rewards being based on attaining budget, in essence trading off expectations of intrinsic for extrinsic rewards."[43]

LEADERSHIP STYLE, ORGANIZATIONAL PERFORMANCE, AND PARTICIPATIVE BUDGETING

Studies of the relationship between managerial leadership styles and measures of organizational effectiveness, such as performance of subordinates, have produced various results. Early findings were that the effectiveness of budgetary systems is associated with supervisory leadership style.[44] Then Hopwood investigated the impact of three styles of evaluation that make distinctly different uses of data: budget-constrained style, profit-conscious style, and nonaccounting style. He suggested that one significant dimension of budget use is the relative importance attached to the budget in evaluating managerial performance.[45] The leadership style characterized by a heavy emphasis on budget-related performance was found to be significantly associated with job-related tension. Noting Hopwood's primary emphasis on the effect of budget use on managers' beliefs and feelings, Otley extended the hypotheses to include the overall effectiveness of operation.[46] He stated the hypotheses as follows:

When a manager perceives that he is evaluated primarily on his ability to meet his budget (rather than on the basis of a more flexible use of budgetary information), he is more likely to (a) experience job-related and budget-related tension; (b) distrust his superior; (c) be clear about how his performance is evaluated; (d) consider his evaluation to be unfair. His response to such feelings will be such that he is more likely to (e) bias his budget estimates by building in "slack" so that the budget becomes easier to attain; (f) have a short-term view of his job in that his performance measure is short-term; (g) perform poorly, particularly on those aspects of performance which yield only long-term benefits.[47]

Otley's results suggested that superior performance levels are associated with a budget-focus leadership, the reverse of Hopwood's finding. To reconcile the conflicting results, Brownell confirmed the hypothesis that directly observable associations between leadership evaluative style and performance should not be expected, because the relationship will be moderated by budgetary participation.[48] The foundations for the hypotheses were based on the operant-conditioning[49] and balance[50] theoretical paradigms.

TASK UNCERTAINTY AND PARTICIPATIVE BUDGETING

Galbraith and later Tushman and Nadler have argued that the effectiveness of participation in decision making depends on task uncertainty.[51] As the task environment of a subunit becomes more uncertain, the need for information and greater information-processing capacity at the subunit level increases. As uncertainty increases, the organization develops strategies to deal with the need to process information. One strategy, of a decentralizing nature, consists of creating lateral relations, which is equivalent to moving the level of decision making down to where the information exists instead of bringing the information upward in the hierarchy. Lawrence and Lorsch provided some empirical evidence in their finding that, faced with higher environmental uncertainty, successful firms resort to a design of organizational structure that facilitates the flow of information both horizontally and vertically, allowing for higher participation in decision making.[52] While Lawrence and Lorsch focused on the relationship between uncertainty and participation in decision making, Govindarajan extended the analysis to participative budgeting, arguing that the greater the environmental uncertainty the greater the positive impact of participation on managerial performance or attitudes.[53] Data from responsibility-center managers verified the assertion. Task uncertainty was also used to explain the dysfunctional behavior of subordinates associated with different uses of accounting information. Hirst developed the hypothesis that a medium to high (medium to low) reliance on such measures minimizes the incidence of dysfunctional behavior in situations of low (high) task uncertainty.[54] Furthermore, the results of a field study by Brownell and Hirst supported the hypothesis that compatible combinations of participation and budget emphasis (high/high and low/low) are more effective in reducing job-related tension in low, as opposed to high, task uncertainty activities.[55]

ROLE AMBIGUITY AND PARTICIPATIVE BUDGETING

Role ambiguity has been viewed as the extent to which clear information is missing with regard to expectations associated with a role, methods for fulfilling role expectations, and/or the consequences of role performance.[56] Role ambiguity was found to be negatively related to job satisfaction,[57] performance,[58] effort,[59] and productivity.[60] It has also been found to be negatively related to participative budgeting.[61] Given these findings on role ambiguity, Chenhall and Brownell proposed that an understanding of participative budgeting's effects on job satisfaction and performance could best be reached by considering the intervening effect that role ambiguity has in these relationships.[62] They hypothesized that the relationship between participative budgeting and job satisfaction or subordinated performance could be explained by an *indirect* effect, in which participation reduces role ambiguity and thereby enhances job satisfaction and subordinate performance. Empirical results based on a survey of 36 middle-level managers and a path analysis confirmed the hypothesis that participative budgeting is most helpful in decreasing managers' role ambiguity, which in turn improves job satisfaction and performance.

REWARD STRUCTURE AND PARTICIPATIVE BUDGETING

Cherrington and Cherrington argued that it is not budgets per se that affect people, but rather the positive and negative reinforcing consequences and the reward contingencies associated with budgets.[63] They contended that the principles of operant conditioning, as introduced by Skinner, can be applied to the budgeting process to predict or control attitudes and behavior.[64] Cherrington and Cherrington predicted that (1) task performance is a function of the reward contingencies—high performance is expected in conditions where appropriate reinforcements are made contingent upon high performance; and (2) there is a direct relationship between the occurrence of appropriate reinforcement and measures of satisfaction. Their findings provided significant evidence of the strong intervening effect of reward on the relationship between participative budgeting and performance.

COGNITIVE DISSONANCE AND PARTICIPATIVE BUDGETING

Cognitive dissonance has been defined as

a negative drive state which occurs whenever an individual simultaneously holds two cognitions (ideas, beliefs, opinions) which are psychologically inconsistent. Stated differently, two cognitions are dominant if, considering these two cognitions alone, the opposite of one follows from the other. Since the occurrence of dissonance is presumed to be unpleasant, individuals strive to reduce it.[65]

Individuals choose among alternatives but find that they themselves experience dissonance as a result of the choice. They try to reduce the dissonance by seeking information or adopting attitudes that emphasize the positive aspects of the choice and deemphasize the negative aspects. Similarly, when asked to participate in the setting of performance standards, individuals need to reduce the dissonance that results from their choice by connecting themselves to the chosen standard. Foran and DeCoster advanced the theory that feedback about the acceptability of a choice allows dissonance reduction to begin through the commitment to the chosen alternative.[66] They tested the validity of this model by investigating the effect on the dependent variables of cognitive dissonance and postdecisional modes of dissonance reduction of the following independent variables: (1) channeled and nonchanneled communication networks, (2) the personality of authoritarianism, and (3) feedback about performance standards. The findings of their study show that favorable feedback results in significantly more commitment to standards than does unfavorable feedback. They concluded as follows:

This finding allows speculation about the policy implications for accountants. Participation in the process of establishing standards is not adequate to insure workers' commitment to performance standards. The workers must participate and then be given feedback about their selections. Thus, based on this study, accountants must consider the development of performance standards as a multistep process including participation, involvement, free choice, and feedback (favorable if possible) about the results of planning. Only then will there be commitment to the performance standards.[67]

Tiller tested a dissonance model of participative budgeting that specified three conditions under which participative budgeting would lead to increased commitment to budget achievement and increased performance on the part of the subjects: conditions of low pay (insufficient justification), a high budget (aversive consequence), and participation (perceived decision freedom).[68] The experiment demonstrated that when the budgeting context allows individuals to perceive themselves as having exercised freedom of decision in the setting of difficult-to-achieve budgets, participative budgeting yields both increased commitment toward budget achievement and increased performance, even in the absence of a performance-contingent reward structure.

PERSONALITY FACTORS AND PARTICIPATIVE BUDGETING

The search for moderating variables in the relationship between participative budgeting and measures of managerial performance has included several personality variables.

Authoritarianism

Authoritarianism has been examined as one moderating variable of the effectiveness of participation in budgeting. It has been known to have a potential for affecting individuals' work attitudes.[69] As a moderating variable of the impact of participation, its effect has been mixed, with some evidence showing participation to be most effective among low authoritarians[70] and other evidence finding it to be of no effect.[71] These studies, however, only examined the authoritarianism of one individual, usually the subordinate, which could explain their mixed results. Accordingly, Chenhall hypothesized and confirmed that the effects of participative budgeting on subordinates' satisfaction with their jobs and budgets are moderated by the configuration of authoritarianism between the subordinate and superior.[72] More specifically, participative budgeting results in strong positive attitudes in homogeneous dyads, that is, in pairings of superiors and subordinates who have the same level of authoritarianism, be it high or low. Similar findings in psychology have related homogeneous dyads to cooperative personal exchanges[73] and low-authoritarian dyads to trusting behavior.[74]

Locus of Control

Another personality variable, locus of control, has been examined as a moderating variable, or "conditional factor," in the relationship between budgetary participation and performance. As a construct, locus of control denotes the distribution of individuals according to the degree to which they accept personal responsibility for what happens to them.[75] As a general principle:

Internal control refers to the perception of positive and/or negative events as being a consequence of one's own actions and thereby under personal control; external control refers to the perception of positive and/or negative events as being unrelated to one's own behaviors in certain situations and therefore beyond personal control.[76]

Following the basic psychological tenet that task performance is a function of personality/situation congruence, Brownell suggested the potential for significant interaction between budgetary participation and locus of control that would affect performance.[77] Basically, he stated:

Characterizing high budgetary participation as an internally controlled situation, this will be congruent only for individuals who are internals on the locus of control dimension and they are hypothesized to perform better in this situation. Conversely, low participation will be congruent only for externals, and they are hypothesized to perform better under low than under high participation conditions.[78]

The result of a laboratory experiment showed a statistical significant interaction between participation and locus of control that affected performance. A field study by the same author confirmed the moderating effect of locus of control.[79]

The Pelz Effect

Researchers of superior-subordinate communication have studied the effect of leadership style and a superior's upward influence on his or her relationship with subordinates. The evidence, known as the Pelz effect, shows a positive association between a superior's upward hierarchical influence and the subordinate's satisfaction with the performance of the superior, provided the superior also exhibits a "supportive" leadership style in interactions with the employee. As Pelz noted: "If the superior has *little* power or influence, then neither his helpful behavior nor his restraining behavior will have much concrete effect on the employees."[80] Several studies have supported the Pelz effect.[81]

In accordance with the findings on the Pelz effect, it could be argued that dyadic configurations of leadership style and a superior's upward influence create situations where budget participation affects subordinate satisfaction with work and budget. As Exhibit 5.4 shows, there are four possible combinations of dyads defined in terms of leadership style and superior's upward influence. Two are homogeneous in the sense that both variables are high or both variables are low. Two are heterogeneous in the sense that one variable is high while the other is low.

Exhibit 5.4
Dyadic Configuration Resulting from Dimensions of Superior's Leadership Style and Upward Influence

		Supervisor's Leadership Support Style	
		High	Low
Supervisor's Upward Influence	High	+ (1)	− (2)
	Low	− (2)	+ (1)

(1) Homogeneous group implying a positive relationship between budget participation and subordinate satisfaction.
(2) Heterogeneous group implying a negative relationship between budget participation and subordinate satisfaction.

It is hypothesized that in the homogeneous dyads, participative budgeting will have a positive effect on attitudes toward the job and the budget. In the case where both leadership support style and upward influence are high, the superior's reliance on support and high status in the firm create a predisposition toward budget participation and subordinate satisfaction. In the case where both leadership support style and upward influence are low, it is hypothesized that subordinate satisfaction with budget and job will still exist. Subordinate attitudes will be at their most negative in this instance where superiors are perceived to be low in upward influence as well as nonsupportive.

It is also hypothesized that in the heterogeneous dyads, mixed subordinate attitudes toward the job and the budget will be associated with participative budgeting. If the leader is supportive but has an organizationally marginal status, studies supporting the Pelz effect suggest there will be an impact on budget participation. People will be less inclined to participate under those conditions. Similarly, if the leader is nonsupportive but has an organizationally high status, the Pelz effect will also lead to low budget participation and low satisfaction with the budget.

Therefore, Belkaoui has proposed the following hypothesis: "For subordinates who perceive their superiors as supportive and their level of hierarchical influence high, budget participation affects positively subordinate job satisfaction and their satisfaction with the budget."[82] A field study presented evidence that a superior's leadership style and upward influence in work-related decisions mediate the effect of participation in job and budget satisfaction.

CONCLUSION

What appears from the literature covered in this chapter is the need for an investigation of additional moderating variables that can mediate the link between goal setting in general, participative budgeting in particular, and task performance. Development of a theoretical framework that incorporates moderating variables as a link between goal setting and participative budgeting on the one hand and performance on the other should be a first step before empirical investigation. The practical results of investigating the moderating variables will be the help they provide to designers of goal-setting programs not only to anticipate the impact of their programs, but also to give a role to moderating variables in those situations where they are expected to have an impact.

NOTES

1. E. A. Locke, K. N. Shaw, L. M. Saari, and G. P. Latham, "Goal Setting and Task Performance: 1969–1980," *Psychological Bulletin* (1981): 126.

2. Ibid., p. 131.

3. Ibid.

4. A. Stedry and E. Kay, "The Effects of Goal Difficulty on Performance: A Field Experiment," *Behavioral Science* (November 1966): 459–470; G. H. Hofstede, *The Game of Budget Control* (London: Tavistock, 1968); H. O. Rockness, "Expectancy Theory in a Budgetary Setting: An Empirical Examination," *Accounting Review* (October 1977): 893–903; C. W. Chow, "The Effects of Job Standard Tightness and Compensation Scheme on Performance: An Exploration of Linkages," *Accounting Review* (October 1983): 667–685.

5. H. O. Rockness, "Expectancy Theory in a Budgetary Setting."

6. Chow, "The Effects of Job Standard Tightness and Compensation Scheme on Performance."

7. J. S. Demski and G. A. Feltham, "Economic Incentives in Budgetary Control Systems," *Accounting Review* (April 1978): 336–359.

8. J. C. Naylor and D. R. Ilgen, "Goal Setting: A Theoretical Analysis of a Motivational Technology," in B. M. Staw and L. L. Cummings, eds., *Research in Organizational Behavior* (Greenwich, Conn.: JAI Press, 1984), 6:95–140.

9. Mark K. Hirst, "The Effects of Setting Budget Goals and Task Uncertainty on Performance: A Theoretical Analysis," *Accounting Review* (October 1987): 774–784.

10. Ibid., p. 775.

11. Locke et al., "Goal Setting and Task Performance"; L. W. Porter, E. E. Lawler III, and J. R. Hackman, *Behavior in Organizations* (New York: McGraw-Hill, 1975).

12. Hirst, "The Effects of Setting Budget Goals and Task Uncertainty on Performance," p. 780.

13. R. J. Swieringa and R. H. Moncur, *Some Effects of Participative Budgeting on Managerial Behavior* (New York: National Association of Accountants, 1974).

14. Hofstede, *The Game of Budget Control;* D. Searfoss and R. Monczka, "Perceived Participation in the Budget Process and Motivation to Achieve the Budget." *Academy of Management Journal* (December 1973): 541–554.

15. I. Kenis, "Effects of Budgetary Goal Characteristics on Managerial Attitudes and Performance," *Accounting Review* (October 1979): 707–721.

16. K. W. Milani, "The Relationship of Participation in Budget-Setting to Industrial Supervisor Performance and Attitudes: A Field Study," *Accounting Review* (April 1975): 274–285.

17. A. C. Stedry, *Budget Control and Cost Behavior* (Englewood Cliffs, N.J.: Prentice-Hall, 1960); J. F. Bryan and E. A. Locke, "Goal Setting as a Means of Increasing Motivation," *Journal of Applied Psychology* (1967): 274–277.

18. P. Brownell, "Participation in the Budgeting Process: When It Works and When It Doesn't," *Journal of Accounting Literature* (Spring 1982): 124–153.

19. Industrial Democracy in Europe International Research Group, "Participation: Formal Rules, Influence and Involvement," *Industrial Relations* (Fall 1979): 273–294; L. Coch and J. R. P. French, Jr., "Overcoming Resistance to Change," *Human Relations* (August 1948): 512–532; J. R. P. French, Jr., J. Israel, and D. Ho, "An Experiment on Participation in a Norwegian Factory: Interpersonal Discussions of Decision-Making," *Human Relations* (February 1960): 3–19.

20. C. D. King and M. van de Vall, *Models of Industrial Democracy* (New York: Mouton, 1978).

21. S. Melman, "Managerial vs. Cooperation Decision in Israel," *Studies in Comparative International Development* 6 (1970–1971).

22. P. R. Lawrence and J. W. Lorsch, *Organization and Environment,* (Cambridge, Mass.: Harvard University Graduate School of Business Administration, 1967).

23. J. D. Thompson, *Organizations in Action* (New York: McGraw-Hill, 1967).

24. Jay Galbraith, *Designing Complex Organizations* (Reading, Mass.: Addison-Wesley, 1973).

25. W. J. Burns, Jr., and J. H. Waterhouse, "Budgetary Control and Organizational Structure," *Journal of Accounting Research* (Autumn 1975): 177–203.

26. A. W. Halpin, "The Leadership Behavior and Combat Performance of Airplane Commanders," *Journal of Abnormal and Social Psychology* (1954): 19–22.

27. H. H. Meyer, "The Effective Superior: Some Surprising Findings," in A. J. Marrow, ed., *The Failure of Success* (New York: Amacom, 1972).

28. R. J. House, A. C. Filley, and S. Kerr, "Relation of Leader Consideration and Initiating Structure to R. D. Subordinates' Satisfaction," *Administrative Science Quarterly* (March 1971): 19–30.

29. R. W. Griffin, "Relationships among Individual, Taste Design, and Leader Behavior Variables," *Academy of Management Journal* (December 1980): 665–683.

30. P. Brownell, "Participation in Budgeting, Locus of Control and Organizational Effectiveness," *Accounting Review* (October 1981): 844–860.

31. V. H. Vroom, *Some Personality Determinants of the Effects of Participation* (Englewood Cliffs, N.J.: Prentice-Hall, 1960).

32. Hofstede, *The Game of Budget Control.*

33. P. Brownell, "The Role of Accounting Data in Performance Evaluation, Budgetary Participation and Organizational Effectiveness," *Journal of Accounting Research* (Spring 1982): 12–27.

34. E. A. Locke and D. M. Schweiger, "Participation in Decision-Making: One More Look," in B. M. Staw, ed., *Research in Organizational Behavior* (Greenwich, Conn.: JAI Press, 1979), 1:325.

35. Ibid.

36. C. Argyris, *The Impact of Budgets on People* (New York: Controllership Foundation, 1952); S. W. Becker and D. Green, "Budgeting and Employee Behavior," *Journal of Business* (October 1962): 352–402.

37. Ahmed Belkaoui, *Cost Accounting: A Multidimensional Emphasis* (Hinsdale, Ill.: Dryden Press, 1983); idem, *Conceptual Foundations of Management Accounting* (Reading, Mass.: Addison-Wesley, 1980); idem, *Handbook of Management Control Systems* (New Haven, Conn.: Greenwood Press, 1986).

38. Hofstede, *The Game of Budget Control;* D. G. Searfoss, "Some Behavioral Aspects of Budgeting for Control: An Empirical Study," *Accounting, Organizations and Society* (November 1976): 375–385; Kenis, "Effects of Budgetary Goal Characteristics on Managerial Attitudes and Performance"; Searfoss and Monczka, "Perceived Participation in the Budget Process and Motivation to Achieve the Budget"; Kenneth A. Merchant, "The Design of the Corporate Budgeting System: Influences on Managerial Behavior and Performance," *Accounting Review* (October 1981): 813–829.

39. V. H. Vroom, *Work and Motivation* (New York: John Wiley and Sons, 1964); J. R. Hackman and E. E. Lawler, "Employee Reactions to Job Characteristics," *Journal of Applied Psychology* (June 1971): 259–286; J. R. Hackman and L. W. Porter, "Expectancy Theory Predictions of Work Effectiveness," *Organizational Behavior and Human Performance* (November 1968): 417–426.

40. K. R. Ferris, "A Test of the Expectancy Theory of Motivation in an Accounting Environment," *Accounting Review* (July 1977): 605–615; Rockness, "Expectancy Theory in a Budgetary Setting"; Milani, "The Relationship of Participation in Budget-Setting to Industrial Supervisor Performance and Attitudes"; T. R. Mitchell, "Expectancy Models of Job Satisfaction, Occupational Preference, and Effort: A Theoretical, Methodological, and Empirical Appraisal," *Psychological Bulletin* (December 1974): 1053–1077; M. A. Wahba and R. J. House, "Expectancy Theory in Work and Motivation—Some Logical and Methodological Issues," *Human Relations* (February 1974): 121–147; T. Connolly, "Some Conceptual and Methodological Issues in Expectancy Models of Work Performance Motivation," *Academy of Management Review* (October 1976): 37–47; J. P. Campbell and R. D. Pritchard, "Motivation Theory in Industrial and Organizational Psychology," in M. D. Dunnette, ed., *Handbook of Industrial and Organizational Psychology* (Chicago: Rand McNally, 1976), pp. 63–130; T. R. Mitchell, "Organizational Behavior," *Annual Review of Psychology* (1979): 243–281.

41. P. Brownell and M. McInnes, "Budgetary Participation, Motivation and Managerial Performance," *Accounting Review* (October 1986): 587–603.

42. R. J. House, "A Path-Goal Theory of Leader Effectiveness," *Administrative Science Quarterly* (September 1971): 321–338; J. Ronen and J. L. Livingstone, "An Expectancy Theory Approach to the Motivational Impacts of Budgets," *Accounting Review* (October 1975): 671–685.

43. Brownell and McInnes, "Budgetary Participation, Motivation and Managerial Performance," p. 597.

44. Argyris, *The Impact of Budgets on People;* D. T. DeCoster and J. P. Fertakis, "Budget-Induced Pressure and Its Relationship to Supervisory Behavior," *Journal of Accounting Research* (Autumn 1968): 237–246.

45. A. G. Hopwood, "An Empirical Study of the Role of Accounting Data in Performance Evaluation," supplement to *Journal of Accounting Research* (1972): 156–182.

46. David T. Otley, "Budget Use and Managerial Performance," *Journal of Accounting Research* (Spring 1978): 122–179.

47. Ibid., p. 176.

48. Brownell, "The Role of Accounting Data in Performance Evaluation, Budgetary Participation, and Organizational Effectiveness."

49. B. F. Skinner, *The Behavior of Organisms* (New York: Appleton-Century-Crofts, 1938).

50. F. Heider, "Attitudes and Cognitive Organization," *Journal of Psychology* (January 1946): 107–112.

51. Galbraith, *Designing Complex Organizations;* M. L. Tushman and D. A. Nadler, "Information Processing as an Integrating Concept in Organizational Design," *Academy of Management Review* (1978): 613–624.

52. Lawrence and Lorsch, *Organization and Environment.*

53. V. Govindarajan, "Impact of Participation in the Budgetary Process on Managerial Attitudes and Performance: Universalistic and Contingency Perspectives," *Decision Sciences* (February 1986): 496–516.

54. Hirst, "Accounting Information and the Evaluation of Subordinate Performance."

55. P. Brownell and M. K. Hirst, "Reliance on Accounting Information, Budgetary Participation, and Task Uncertainty: Tests of a Three-Way Interaction," *Journal of Accounting Research* (Autumn 1986): 841–849.

56. G. Graen, "Role-Making Processes within Complex Organizations," in M. D. Dunnette, ed., *Handbook of Industrial Psychology* (Chicago: Rand McNally, 1976).

57. T. A. Beehr, J. T. Walsh, and T. D. Taber, "Relationship of Stress to Individually and Organizationally Valued States: Higher Order Needs as a Moderator," *Journal of Applied Psychology* (1976): 41–47; R. D. Caplan, S. Cobba, J. R. P. French, R. Van Harrison, and S. R. Pinneas, *Job Demands and Worker Health: Main Effects and Occupational Differences* (Washington, D.C.: Government Printing Office, 1975); C. N. Greene, "Relationships among Role Accuracy, Compliance, Performance Evaluation and Satisfaction within Managerial Dyads," *Academy of Management Journal* (1972): 205–215; W. C. Hamner and H. W. Tosi, "Relationships of Role Conflict and Role Ambiguity to Job Involvement Measures," *Journal of Applied Psychology* (1974): 497–499; T. W. Johnson and J. E. Stinton, "Role Ambiguity, Role Conflict, and Satisfaction: Moderating Effects of Individual Influences," *Journal of Applied Psychology* (1975): 329–333; R. J. Paul, "Role Clarity as a Correlate of Satisfaction, Job-Related Strain, and Propensity to Leave—Male vs. Female," *Journal of Applied Psychology* (1974): 233–245; J. R. Rizzo, R. J. House, and S. I. Lirtzman, "Role Conflict and Ambiguity in Complex Organizations," *Administrative Service Quarterly* (June 1970): 150–163.

58. Hamner and Tosi, "Relationships of Role Conflict and Role Ambiguity to Job Involvement Measures"; A. D. Brief and R. J. Alday, "Correlates of Role Indices," *Journal of Applied Psychology* (1976): 468–472.

59. Beehr, Walsh, and Taber, "Relationship of Stress to Individually and Organizationally Valued States."

60. A. R. Cohen, "Situational Structure, Self-Esteem, and Threat Oriented Reactions to Power," in D. Cartwright., ed., *Studies in Social Power* (Ann Arbor: University of Michigan Press, 1959).

61. H. Tosi and D. Tosi, "Some Correlates of Role Conflict and Ambiguity among

Public School Teachers,'' *Journal of Human Relations* (1970): 1068–1075; R. S. Schuler, ''A Role and Expectancy Perception Model of Participation in Decision Making,'' *Academy of Management Journal* (June 1980): 331–340.

62. R. H. Chenhall and P. Brownell, ''The Effects of Participative Budgeting on Job Satisfaction and Performance: Role Ambiguity as an Intervening Variable,'' *Accounting, Organizations and Society* 13, no. 3 (1988): 225–233.

63. D. J. Cherrington and J. O. Cherrington, ''Appropriate Reinforcement Contingencies in the Budgeting Process,'' supplement to *Journal of Accounting Research* (1973): 225–253.

64. B. F. Skinner, *Contingencies of Reinforcement* (New York: Appleton-Century-Crofts, 1969).

65. E. Aronson, ''Dissonance Theory: Progress and Problems,'' in R. P. Abelson, E. Aronson, W. J. McGuire, T. M. Newcomb, M. J. Rosenberg, and P. H. Tannenbaum, eds., *Theories of Cognitive Consistency: A Sourcebook* (Chicago: Rand McNally, 1968), pp. 5–6.

66. Michael F. Foran and Don T. DeCoster, ''An Experimental Study of the Effects of Participation, Authoritarianism, and Feedback on Cognitive Dissonance in a Standard Setting Situation,'' *Accounting Review* (October 1974): 751–763.

67. Ibid., p. 762.

68. M. G. Tiller, ''The Dissonance Model of Participative Budgeting: An Empirical Exploration,'' *Journal of Accounting Research* (Autumn 1983): 581–595.

69. B. D. Slack and J. O. Cook, ''Authoritarian Behavior in a Conflict Situation,'' *Journal of Personality and Social Psychology* (January 1973): 130–136.

70. Vroom, *Some Personality Determinants of the Effects of Participation;* Hofstede, *The Game of Budget Control;* R. E. Seiler and R. W. Bartlett, ''Personality Variables as Predictors of Budget Systems Characteristics,'' *Accounting, Organizations and Society* (December 1982): 381–403.

71. Foran and DeCoster, ''An Experimental Study of the Effects of Participation, Authoritarianism, and Feedback on Cognitive Dissonance in a Standard Setting Situation''; A. A. Abdel-Halim and K. M. Rowland, ''Some Personality Determinants of the Effects of Participation: A Further Investigation,'' *Personnel Psychology* (Spring 1976); Frank Collins, ''The Interaction of Budget Characteristics and Personality Variables with Budgetary Response Attitudes,'' *Accounting Review* (April 1978): 324–335.

72. Robert H. Chenhall, ''Authoritarianism and Participative Budgeting: A Dyadic Analysis,'' *Accounting Review* (April 1986): 263–272.

73. Slack and Cook, ''Authoritarian Behavior in a Conflict Situation''; W. Haythorn, A. Conch, D. Haefner, P. Langham, and L. Carter, ''The Behavior of Authoritarian and Equalitarian Personalities in Small Groups,'' *Human Relations* (February 1956): 57–74.

74. M. Deutsch, ''Trust, Trustworthiness and the F-Scale,'' *Journal of Abnormal and Social Psychology* (July 1960): 138–140.

75. J. B. Rolter, M. Seeman, and S. Liverant, ''Internal versus External Control of Reinforcement: A Major Variable in Behavioral Theory'' in N. F. Washburne, ed., *Decisions, Values and Groups* (New York: Pergamon Press, 1962), pp. 473–516.

76. H. M. Lefcourt, ''Internal versus External Control of Reinforcement: A Review,'' *Psychological Bulletin* (April 1966): 206–220.

77. Brownell, "Participation in Budgeting, Locus of Control and Organizational Effectiveness."

78. Ibid., p. 847.

79. P. Brownell, "A Field Study Examination of Budgetary Participation and Locus of Control," *Accounting Review* (October 1982): 766–777.

80. D. Pelz, "Influence: A Key to Effective Leadership in the First Line Supervisor," *Personnel* (1952): 209–271.

81. K. H. Roberts and C. A. O'Reilly, "Failures in Upward Communication: Three Possible Culprits," *Academy of Management Journal* (1974): 205–215; A. P. Jones, L. R. James, and J. R. Bruni, "Perceived Leadership Behavior and Employee Confidence in the Leader as Moderated by Job Involvement," *Journal of Applied Psychology* (1978): 146–149; C. A. O'Reilly and K. H. Roberts, "Supervisor Influence and Subordinate Mobility Aspirations as Moderators of Consideration and Initiating Structure," *Journal of Applied Psychology* (1978): 96–102; F. M. Jablin, "Superior's Upward Influence, Satisfaction and Openness in Superior-Subordinate Communication: A Reexamination of the 'Pelz Effect,'" *Human Communication Research* (1980): 210–220.

82. Ahmed Belkaoui, "Leadership Style, Dimensions of Superior's Upward Influence and Participative Budgeting" (Working paper, University of Illinois at Chicago, June 1988).

SELECT BIBLIOGRAPHY

Becker, S. W., and D. Green. "Budgeting and Employee Behavior." *Journal of Business* (October 1962): 352–402.

Belkaoui, Ahmed. "Leadership Style, Dimensions of Superior's Upward Influence and Participative Budgeting." Working paper, University of Illinois at Chicago, June 1988.

Brownell, P. "A Field Study Examination of Budgetary Participation and Locus of Control." *Accounting Review* (October 1982): 766–777.

_____. "Participation in Budgeting, Locus of Control and Organizational Effectiveness." *Accounting Review* (October 1981): 844–860.

_____. "Participation in the Budgeting Process: When It Works and When It Doesn't." *Journal of Accounting Literature* (Spring 1982): 124–153.

_____. "The Role of Accounting Data in Performance Evaluation, Budgetary Participation, and Organizational Effectiveness." *Journal of Accounting Research* (Spring 1982): 12–27.

Brownell, P., and M. K. Hirst. "Reliance on Accounting Information, Budgetary Participation, and Task Uncertainty: Tests of a Three-Way Interaction." *Journal of Accounting Research* (Autumn 1986): 841–849.

Brownell, P., and M. McInnes. "Budgetary Participation, Motivation and Managerial Performance." *Accounting Review* (October 1986): 587–603.

Bryan, J. F., and E. A. Locke. "Goal Setting as a Means of Increasing Motivation." *Journal of Applied Psychology* (1967): 274–277.

Burns, W. J., Jr., and J. H. Waterhouse. "Budgetary Control and Organizational Structure." *Journal of Accounting Research* (Autumn 1975): 177–203.

Campbell, J. P., and R. D. Pritchard. "Motivation Theory in Industrial and Organizational Psychology." In M. D. Dunnette, ed., *Handbook of Industrial and Organizational Psychology*, pp. 63–130. Chicago: Rand McNally, 1976.

Chenhall, Robert H. "Authoritarianism and Participative Budgeting: A Dyadic Analysis." *Accounting Review* (April 1986): 263–272.

Chenhall, Robert H., and P. Brownell. "The Effects of Participative Budgeting on Job Satisfaction and Performance: Role Ambiguity as an Intervening Variable." *Accounting, Organizations and Society* 13, no. 3 (1988): 225–233.

Cherrington, D. J., and J. O. Cherrington. "Appropriate Reinforcement Contingencies in the Budgeting Process," Supplement to *Journal of Accounting Research* (1973): 225–253.

Chow, C. W. "The Effects of Job Standard Tightness and Compensation Scheme on Performance: An Exploration of Linkages." *Accounting Review* (October 1983): 667–685.

Coch, L., and J. R. P. French, Jr. "Overcoming Resistance to Change." *Human Relations* (August 1948): 512–532.

Collins, Frank. "The Interaction of Budget Characteristics and Personality Variables with Budgetary Response Attitudes." *Accounting Review* (April 1978): 324–335.

Connolly, T. "Some Conceptual and Methodological Issues in Expectancy Models of Work Performance Motivation." *Academy of Management Review* (October 1976): 37–47.

DeCoster, D. T., and J. P. Fertakis. "Budget-Induced Pressure and Its Relationship to Supervisory Behavior." *Journal of Accounting Research* (Autumn 1968): 237–246.

Demski, J. S., and G. A. Feltham. "Economic Incentives in Budgetary Control Systems." *Accounting Review* (April 1978): 336–359.

Ferris, K. R. "A Test of the Expectancy Theory of Motivation in an Accounting Environment." *Accounting Review* (July 1977): 605–615.

Foran, Michael F., and Don T. DeCoster. "An Experimental Study of the Effects of Participation, Authoritarianism, and Feedback on Cognitive Dissonance in a Standard Setting Situation." *Accounting Review* (October 1974): 751–763.

French, J. R. P., Jr., J. Israel, and D. Ho. "An Experiment on Participation in a Norwegian Factory: Interpersonal Discussions of Decision-Making." *Human Relations* (February 1960): 3–19.

Govindarajan, V. "Impact of Participation in the Budgetary Process on Managerial Attitudes and Performance: Universalistic and Contingency Perspectives." *Decision Sciences* (February 1986): 496–516.

Griffin, R. W. "Relationships among Individual, Task Design, and Leader Behavior Variables." *Academy of Management Journal* (December 1980): 665–683.

Hackman, J. R., and E. E. Lawler. "Employee Reactions to Job Characteristics." *Journal of Applied Psychology* (June 1971): 259–286.

Hackman, J. R., and L. W. Porter. "Expectancy Theory Predictions of Work Effectiveness." *Organizational Behavior and Human Performance* (November 1968): 417–426.

Halpin, A. W. "The Leadership Behavior and Combat Performance of Airplane Commanders." *Journal of Abnormal and Social Psychology* (1954): 19–22.

Haythorn, W., A. Conch, D. Haefner, P. Langham, and L. Carter. "The Behavior of

Authoritarian and Equalitarian Personalities in Small Groups." *Human Relations* (February 1956): 57–74.

Hirst, Mark K. "Accounting Information and the Evaluation of Subordinate Performance: A Situational Approach." *Accounting Review* (October 1981): 771–784.

———. "The Effects of Setting Budget Goals and Task Uncertainty on Performance: A Theoretical Analysis." *Accounting Review* (October 1987): 774–784.

Hofstede, G. H. *The Game of Budget Control*. London: Tavistock, 1968.

Hopwood, A. G. "An Empirical Study of the Role of Accounting Data in Performance Evaluation." Supplement to *Journal of Accounting Research* (1972): 156–182.

House, R. J. "A Path-Goal Theory of Leader Effectiveness." *Administrative Science Quarterly* (September 1971): 321–338.

House, R. J., A. C. Filley, and S. Kerr. "Relation of Leader Consideration and Initiating Structure to R.D. Subordinates' Satisfaction." *Administrative Science Quarterly* (March 1971): 19–30.

Industrial Democracy in Europe International Research Group, "Participation: Formal Rules, Influence and Involvement." *Industrial Relations* (Fall 1979): 273–294.

Jablin, F. M. "Superior's Upward Influence, Satisfaction and Openness in Superior-Subordinate Communication: A Reexamination of the 'Pelz Effect,'" *Human Communication Research* (1980): 210–220.

Jones, A. P., L. R. James, and J. R. Bruni. "Perceived Leadership Behavior and Employee Confidence in the Leader as Moderated by Job Involvement." *Journal of Applied Psychology* (1978): 146–149.

Kenis, I. "Effects of Budgetary Goal Characteristics on Managerial Attitudes and Performance." *Accounting Review* (October 1979): 707–721.

King, C. D., and M. van de Vall. *Models of Industrial Democracy*. New York: Mouton, 1978.

Locke, E. A., K. N. Shaw, L. M. Saari, and G. P. Latham. "Goal Setting and Task Performance: 1969–1980." *Psychological Bulletin* (1981).

Melman, S. "Managerial vs. Cooperation Decision in Israel." *Studies in Comparative International Development* 6 (1970–1971).

Meyer, H. H. "The Effective Superior: Some Surprising Findings." In A. J. Marrow, ed., *The Failure of Success*. New York: Amacom, 1972.

Milani, K. W. "The Relationship of Participation in Budget-Setting to Industrial Supervisor Performance and Attitudes: A Field Study." *Accounting Review* (April 1975): 274–285.

Mitchell, T. R. "Expectancy Models of Job Satisfaction, Occupational Preference, and Effort: A Theoretical, Methodological, and Empirical Appraisal." *Psychological Bulletin* (December 1974): 1053–1077.

Naylor, J. C., and D. R. Ilgen. "Goal Setting: A Theoretical Analysis of a Motivational Technology." In B. M. Staw and L. L. Cummings, eds., *Research in Organizational Behavior* 6:95–140. Greenwich, Conn.: JAI Press, 1984.

O'Reilly, C. A., and K. H. Roberts. "Supervisor Influence and Subordinate Mobility Aspirations as Moderators of Consideration and Initiating Structure." *Journal of Applied Psychology* (1978): 96–102.

Otley, David T. "Budget Use and Managerial Performance." *Journal of Accounting Research* (Spring 1978): 122–149.

Pelz, D. "Influence: A Key to Effective Leadership in the First Line Supervisor." *Personnel* (1952): 209–271.

Roberts, K. H., and C. A. O'Reilly. "Failures in Upward Communication: Three Possible Culprits." *Academy of Management Journal* (1974): 205–215.

Rockness, H. O. "Expectancy Theory in a Budgetary Setting: An Empirical Examination," *Accounting Review* (October 1977): 893–903.

Ronen, J., and J. L. Livingstone. "An Expectancy Theory Approach to the Motivational Impacts of Budgets." *Accounting Review* (October 1975): 671–685.

Searfoss, D. "Some Behavioral Aspects of Budgeting for Control: An Empirical Study." *Accounting, Organizations and Society* (November 1976): 375–385.

Searfoss, D., and R. Monczka. "Perceived Participation in the Budget Process and Motivation to Achieve the Budget." *Academy of Management Journal* (December 1973): 541–554.

Seiler, R. E., and R. W. Bartlett. "Personality Variables as Predictors of Budget Systems Characteristics." *Accounting, Organizations and Society* (December 1982): 381–403.

Stedry, A., and E. Kay. "The Effects of Goal Difficulty on Performance: A Field Experiment." *Behavioral Science* (November 1966): 459–470.

Swieringa, R. J., and R. H. Moncur. *Some Effects of Participative Budgeting on Managerial Behavior.* New York: National Association of Accountants, 1974.

Tiller, M. G. "The Dissonance Model of Participative Budgeting: An Empirical Exploration." *Journal of Accounting Research* (Autumn 1983): 581–595.

Tushman, M. L., and D. A. Nadler. "Information Processing as an Integrating Concept in Organizational Design." *Academy of Management Review* (1978): 613–624.

Vroom, V. H. *Some Personality Determinants of the Effects of Participation.* Englewood Cliffs, N.J.: Prentice-Hall, 1960.

Wahba, M. A., and R. J. House. "Expectancy Theory in Work and Motivation—Some Logical and Methodological Issues." *Human Relations* (February 1974): 121–147.

6

HUMAN RESOURCE CONSIDERATIONS IN PUBLIC ACCOUNTING FIRMS

The primary asset of a certified public accounting firm is its professional staff. The success of the firm depends on motivating them, retraining them, and keeping them satisfied. Research on human resource considerations in public accounting firms is therefore necessary in order to identify the factors that create the ideal atmosphere for members of accounting firms to function efficiently and be satisfied with their jobs. This type of research is growing and has already covered such areas as job satisfaction, organizational climate, performance evaluation, staff turnover, motivation in the accounting environment, and the personal and situational characteristics of accountants and their consequences. The purpose of the chapter is to report on this type of research, which now constitutes an important part of behavioral accounting research.

JOB SATISFACTION IN PUBLIC ACCOUNTING FIRMS

Studies on job satisfaction in all types of work environments and work groups have led to the general conclusion that an inverse relationship exists between job satisfaction and job turnover; as job satisfaction increases, turnover decreases, and as job satisfaction decreases, turnover increases.[1] Another general finding has been that job satisfaction and performance are not necessarily positively related.[2] Many studies have attempted to provide evidence on the degree of job satisfaction in public accounting firms. Using Porter and Mitchell's need-satisfaction questionnaire,[3] Strawser, Ivancevich, and Lyon investigated the job satisfaction of accountants in large and small CPA firms.[4] Their results showed that satisfaction of the need to self-actualize depended on the type of occupation and the type of firm, but that the Eight Big firms showed the highest level of satisfaction. Nevertheless, accountants working in small firms showed the highest degree of satisfaction of autonomy needs. Carpenter and Strawser examined the satisfaction levels of academic accountants.[5] Their results found that academics in small schools were the least satisfied and the most deficient in four of the six need categories studied (social, self-esteem, self-actualization, and compensation). Deficiencies in security and autonomy needs were found among accounting academicians in large schools. A comparison of the job satisfaction of industrial managers and CPAs showed that the largest perceived need deficiencies were found in the self-actualization category.[6]

Aranya, Lachman, and Armenic examined accountants' job satisfaction as a process model by examining the influences of organizational and professional commitments and of need deprivation on job satisfaction and migration intentions.[7] The results of their path analysis showed that the migration tendencies of accountants were not related to their job satisfaction or to the organizational commitment of accountants in public practice. However, migration tendencies were related to the organizational commitment of accountants in industry and government. In addition, with the exception of accountants in nonprofessional organizations, professional commitment had an effect on both job satisfaction and organizational commitment. "It suggests that the fulfillment of work needs is a determinant of both job satisfaction and commitment to the organization which allows for much fulfillment."[8] This confirmed an earlier finding that job satisfaction is affected by professional deprivation.[9]

The impact of environmental uncertainty on job satisfaction has been examined in the accounting environment. Ferris provided survey evidence showing that as the level of perceived environmental uncertainty increases, the level of job satisfaction will decrease.[10] Other important implications were drawn from the findings:

First, the presence of even moderate levels of uncertainty may be sufficient to explain, in part, the relatively high turnover rate among staff accountants. Second, if perceived uncertainty impacts job satisfaction, then it should also be expected to impact the antecedents of job satisfaction, for example, employee motivation. And, finally, perceived uncertainty may be a causal factor of diminished employee performance.[11]

Benke and Rhode investigated the job satisfaction of higher-level employees in large CPA firms with the following objectives: (1) determining possible differences between audit, tax, and management services with respect to job satisfaction, personal characteristics, and job features; and (2) predicting the job satisfaction of audit, tax, and management services using personal characteristics and job features as independent variables.[12] Findings on the first objective indicated various differences between management services specialists and audit and tax specialists as a combined group. Their findings on the second objective pointed to the possibility of predicting the job satisfaction of audit and tax specialists, but not of management services specialists. The overall results pointed to the need for large CPA firms (1) not to treat higher-level professional employees as a professional group and to use different personnel policies in the audit, tax, and management services sections; and (2) not to assume that policies aimed at increasing the level of satisfaction and reducing turnover among one kind of specialists will have no impact on the job satisfaction of other kinds of specialists.

Harrell and Stahl used McClelland's trichotomy-of-needs theory[13] to provide a conceptual explanation of the job satisfaction and work performance of CPA firm professionals.[14] The theory assumes that individuals are motivated by three needs—the need for affiliation, the need for power, and the need for achievement. Harrell and Stahl's survey of practicing CPAs in one office of a large international firm indicated that the need for power and the need for achievement were positively related to job satisfaction and to superior work performance.

ORGANIZATIONAL CLIMATE IN PUBLIC ACCOUNTING FIRMS

The organizational climate in public accounting firms is of importance because of its impact on employee attitudes and behavior. It has been investigated with regard to the accountant's organizational-professional conflict, the impact of role conflict and role ambiguity, the role of informal and nonformal communication and mentoring, the impact of the leadership style of supervisors, and the management strategy of public accounting firms.

Organizational-Professional Conflict

The relationship between organizations and their professional employees has been a subject of concern and research because of its effect on the work environment and its impact on employee attitudes and behavior. Organizations vary in the degree to which they allow professionals the opportunity to act in accordance with their professional judgment. In addition, the incompatibility of the norms and values of the profession with the organization has created a conflict in the relationship between the organization and its professional employees.[15] In the field of organizational behavior, results of research on the notion of "inherent compatibility" have been inconsistent. In accounting, the dysfunctional outcomes of professional-organizational conflict in public accounting firms have been supported in some studies[16] and deemphasized in others.[17] In the study where the conflict was supported, it was found to result in job dissatisfaction and migration.[18] Norris and Nielbuhr, however, provided results showing that accountants who reported high levels of professionalism also reported high levels of organizational commitment.[19]

In reexamining the accountant's organizational-professional conflict, Aranya and Ferris focused on the relationship between the antecedents and outcomes of organizational-professional conflict. They also examined organizational and professional commitments, perceived conflict, job satisfaction, and turnover intentions.[20] Their survey of 2,016 U.S. and Canadian accountants showed the potential for organizational-professional conflict to be greatest in nonprofessional organizations and to vary inversely with the position in the hierarchy of professional organizations. In addition, the conflict seemed to cause lower job satisfaction and higher employee-turnover intentions.

Impact of Role Conflict and Role Ambiguity

The organizational climate in public accounting firms can be affected by factors other than the organizational-professional conflict. For example, Senatra argued that perceived role conflict and role ambiguity in public accounting firms by audit seniors can have three potential consequences: job-related tension, job satisfaction, or a propensity to leave the organization.[21] Ten potential sources of role conflict and role ambiguity were identified in the organizational climate of public accounting firms: violation in chain of command, formalization of rules and procedures, emphasis on subordinate personnel development, tolerance of error, top management receptiveness, adequacy of work coordination, decision timeliness, information suppression, adequacy of authority, and adequacy of professional autonomy.[22] The results of a survey of seniors in eight offices of one Big Eight public accounting firm verified the model. The survey showed that high levels of both role conflict and role ambiguity were significantly related to high job-related tension, low job satisfaction, and a high propensity to leave the firm.

Role of Informal and Nonformal Communication and Mentoring

The organizational climate in a public accounting firm is also a function of the role of informal and nonformal communication and mentoring in coordinating and controlling members. Using a naturalistic, qualitative research methodology, Dirsmith and Covaleski confirmed (1) the existence of informal communication in public accounting firms that benefits lower-level individuals, in spite of its limited role in informing organizational members of the politics and power within the organization; and (2) the important role of nonformal communication and mentoring in the performance of audit tasks, socialization of the individual firm, instruction as to politics and power in the firm, and benefit according to the protégé, mentor, and firm.[23] Calls were also made for future research to examine the relationship among these three forms of communication. They were adequately defined as follows: ''One analogy which we feel may prove useful is that formal communications are used to convey organizational rules and laws, while nonformal communications convey and enculture people to conform to organizational norms, while informal communications instruct as to organizational and group moves."[24]

Impact of the Leadership Style of Supervisors

The problems of organizational communication in general and of supervisor-subordinate communication in particular can have an impact on the organizational climate in public accounting firms. In studies of superior-subordinate communication, researchers have focused attention on the effects that a superior's influence in the organizational hierarchy has on relationships with subordinates.[25] The nature of the accounting work environment, with its regular job interactions between superior and subordinates, suggests that a superior's influence can provide a framework for analyzing the satisfaction and motivation of public accountants as well as the firm's organizational climate. Researchers of superior-subordinate communication have studied the effects of a superior's upward influence in the organizational hierarchy on their relationship with subordinates—what has become commonly known as the Pelz effect. In his seminal study, Pelz reported the existence of a positive association between a supervisor's upward hierarchical influence and a subordinate's satisfaction with the performance of the superior, provided the supervisor also exhibited a "supportive" leadership style in interactions with the employee.[26] (See also the discussion of the Pelz effect in Chapter 5.)

Wager also explored the effects of supervisors' hierarchical influence and of leadership style on the fulfillment of their supervisory role obligations toward others lower in the organization.[27] He found results similar to Pelz's, observing that a supportive style of leadership was a more powerful variable than hierarchical influence in contributing to the fulfillment of supervisory role obligations. Wager also found that the magnitude of the moderating effect of influence varied markedly with the organizational status of the respondent: "The more organizationally marginal the status occupied by subordinates, the greater will be the pervasiveness of the effect of a supervisor's influence on his style of leadership as it bears on fulfillment of his supervisory role."[28] Other related studies have supported the Pelz effect.[29]

The uniqueness of CPA firms, in terms of their composition, organization, tasks, and purposes, creates a different type of relationship between a supervisor's upward influence and a subordinate's satisfaction with a superior and job. For example, the organizational status and autonomy of subordinates in CPA firms differ from that of individuals in the organizations that have been studied. Analyzing these phenomena in an accounting context, Belkaoui advanced the following research question: "For subordinates in a CPA firm—who perceive their supervisors as supportive or not supportive leaders—does the level of supervisor's hierarchical influence affect subordinates' intention to leave the firm, job satisfaction and level of anxiety stress?"[30] A survey of seniors and managers of two Big Eight public accounting firms located in a large metropolitan area verified the research question for senior accountants with regard to satisfaction with superiors and colleagues when the superior was viewed as having work-related influence.

Without using the Pelz effect, Pratt and Jiambalvo identified, in a field experiment, a number of leader behaviors that related, either directly or through some intermediary factors, to audit team performance (ATP).[31] They found that "in-charge auditors who were considerate to the personal needs of staff assistants, allowed staff innovation and administered frequent positive reinforcement, infrequent negative reinforcements, and complete and timely feedback supervised those audit teams rated to be most effective by audit managers."[32] In a follow-up survey, they found that leader behavior in an audit environment was related to three variables: (1) the match between the accountant-in-charge's perception of the complexity of the task assigned to the staff assistant and the staff assistant's job experience, (2) the staff assistant's intolerance of ambiguity, and (3) the accountant-in-charge's personality dominance.[33] The effects of the leader behavior (that is, of consideration and initiation structure) were also found to be contingent upon the assistant's perception of task complexity.[34]

Management Strategy of Public Accounting Firms

Like any other type of organization, the public accounting firm faces a complex and changing environment, if not a turbulent one. It needs strategy adequate to deal with such an environment. Little is known, however, about the strategies of public accounting firms. Some light has been shed by Baker's use of participant observation to investigate the management strategy of a large public accounting firm.[35] A descriptive model of its management strategy included three components: doing, representing, and being. They were defined as follows:

Doing may be defined as those activities which the firm undertakes to maintain and improve its relationship with its clients. . . . Representing may be defined as those activities which the firm undertakes to maintain and improve its relationships to outside parties other than clients. . . . Being may be defined as the image of the firm.[36]

Doing, or delivery of a tangible product, and representing, or practice development, act to create an image and a name for the firm, or being, to serve an environment composed of clients, the government, the business community, and the profession. Because of a possible conflict between the delivery of a tangible product, mandated by an economic contract with the client, and the delivery of a social value, mandated by the social contract with the government and society, Baker suggested the need for three tactical if not strategic responses, namely: the advent of audit committees, the institutionalization of peer review systems and the provision of an "audit of business" rather than an "audit of books."[37]

The management strategy of public accounting firms faces some unique conditions in the differentiated environments of audit services and management services. Project teams in both environments may have to confront different degrees of task environmental uncertainty and varying amounts of formalization of team structure. Watson investigated both research questions in an exploratory study using both a questionnaire and an interview format.[38] The results confirmed both questions, in the sense that the task environmental uncertainty was higher for management services than for auditing, and different structural relations developed in the teams. These findings are related to Sorensen's observations that there is a conflict between bureaucratism and professionalism in large CPA firms, job satisfaction is affected by professional deprivation, and migration is affected by the task of managing a hybrid professional-bureaucratic orientation.[39] The observed differences in the two functional areas of management services and auditing point to the facts that (1) the conflict between bureaucratism and professionalism can differ between the two functional areas, given the mechanistic organization of the auditing department and the organismic organization of both the auditing department and the management service function; and (2) job satisfaction and migration may differ between the two functional areas, with higher job satisfaction and lower migration in the management services area.

PERFORMANCE EVALUATION IN PUBLIC ACCOUNTING FIRMS

Performance evaluation results are used as a basis for reward systems and as a way to provide development-oriented feedback to employees.[40] In accounting research, performance evaluation is often cited as a major source of dissatisfaction by those leaving public accounting.[41] Several research studies have examined the performance evaluation question in public accounting firms.

Jiambalvo used an expectancy theory model, called an "evaluation model of directed job effort," to predict the amount of time CPAs, working as auditors, direct toward aspects of their job and their job performance.[42] The model was expressed as follows:

$$W_i = f\left[E_{si} \cdot E_{2i} \cdot E_{3i} \left(\sum_{j=1}^{m} I_j V_j \right) + IAV_i \right]$$

where

W_i = the effect directed toward activities related to evaluation dimension i

E_{si} = the expectation that effort leads to effective performance on evaluative dimension i

E_{2i} = the expectation that being effective on evaluative dimension i leads to being judged as effective on dimension i by a superior

E_{3i} = the expectation that being judged effective on evaluative dimension i contributes to a high overall evaluation of performance

I_j = the instrumentality of a high overall evaluation of performance for the attainment of job outcome j

V_j = the desirability (valence) of job outcome j

IAV_i = the intrinsic value or desirability of engaging in activities related to evaluative dimension i

The IAV variable was added following Turney's findings that it was a better predictor of job effort and performance than typical expectancy theory constructs.[43] The results of a survey using senior accountants and their audit managers verified the model by showing that it was possible to predict the amount of time CPAs directed toward various aspects of their job and their performance on job dimensions based on both their perceptions of effort-reward relationships and the intrinsic value of the activities associated with the job performance under both a multiplicative and an additive formulation.

Large CPA firms are segmented into three distinct and minimally independent functional areas: auditing, tax services, and management services. Because the task subenvironment in these firms differs with respect to their uncertainty, it follows that the behavior of the organization's members will be affected by this organizational differentiation.[44] Performance evaluation is one of the behaviors that can be affected by segmentation. From this, Jiambalvo, Watson, and Baumler advanced the following hypothesis: "That organizational differentiation impacts the decision model used by subunit members in the evaluation of personnel, in particular, the weights assigned to different evaluation categories, the consistency in the application of evaluation policies, the self-insight of decision makers and inter-rater agreement."[45] A sample of partners, managers, and session staff accountants from a large international CPA firm was asked to rate hypothetical individuals according to each of the following eight categories:

1. Willingness and ability to accept responsibility;
2. Ability to effectively utilize staff and plan work assignments;
3. Ability to identify and develop practical, workable solutions to problems;
4. Ability to win confidence and respect of clients;
5. Level of creativity exhibited in adapting to unique problems;
6. Knowledge and experience reflected in adherence to known and acceptable procedures and principles;
7. Ability and desire to work effectively with people;
8. Level of judgment exercised.[46]

As hypothesized, the results showed substantial disagreements among firm members on overall evaluations and on the importance attached to the performance evaluation categories. No differences emerged with regard to consistency or self-insight.

Wright found that engagement reviews were the primary source of information on which staff auditor salary and promotion decisions were based.[47] A follow-up experiment showed that, for the appraisal of staff auditors, seniors focused almost exclusively on examining technical skills, whereas personnel administrators called for several measures of short-run performance (for example, technical skills) and long-run performance (such as communication skills, motivation).[48]

Kida investigated two essential performance appraisal processes that occur between managers and seniors in international CPA firms, namely the determination of overall evaluations and the interpersonal characteristics of the feedback meeting.[49] Managers and seniors of international CPA firms were administered an instrument designed to capture their design strategies and review meeting perceptions. The results indicated similar weighting schemes between managers and seniors in the aggregate, but differences among individual rater's strategies. The decision strategies were affected by leadership style. Subjects with higher consideration scores placed more weight on client relations and communication skills, while those higher on initiation structure placed greater weight on technical competence. Perceived feedback characteristics, such as supportive behavior, initiation to participate, and anticipation in goal setting, were found to be related to the seniors' improved job performance. Moreover, criticism directed at certain aspects of the seniors' job was strongly correlated with improving performance.

An evaluation system can influence both turnover and quality control. Evidence has shown that dissatisfaction can result from the appraisal process and lead to staff turnover.[50] In addition, because meeting time budgets is an important factor in performance evaluation, great pressure results from the situation. Some consequences of this pressure include signing off on uncompleted audit procedures[51] and working excessive hours on personal time.[52]

Maher, Ramanathan, and Patterson and later Jiambalvo found that performance ratings were highly related to accuracy and congruence measures.[53] Accuracy, in these cases, referred to the person's ability to correctly assess the key success factors, and congruence referred to the situation where a person agreed with perceived major factors and directed work accordingly.

From these results on the appraisal process in CPA firms, and in order to improve the process, Wright proposed a behaviorally anchored rating scale (BARS).[54] Explaining the function of these scales, Wright stated: "BARS scales attempt to provide descriptions for the rater to *observe staff actions* rather than

Exhibit 6.1
Overall Behaviorally Anchored Rating Scale (BARs) for the Evaluation of Staff Auditors

PERFORMANCE DIMENSION	Critical Incidents		
	High Point Performance	Mid-Point Performance	Low-Point Performance
PART ONE: TECHNICAL AND ANALYTICAL SKILLS			
CREATIVE: innovative thought; adaptative to changing conditions; considers audit goals and alternative approaches to achieve goals.	Continually exhibits innovative thought; able to adapt very effectively to changing conditions; carefully considers audit goals and alternate approaches; sound analytical ability.	Makes limited changes to work done in prior year or does what is readily apparent; at times audit goals and/or alternate procedures not fully considered; shows some ability to adapt to changing conditions.	Mechanically follows prior year's work; exhibits little original thinking; unable to react to new or surprise events.
EFFICIENT AND ORGANIZED: completion of assignments on a timely basis and with little supervision; diligent; plans and monitors the progression of work and time incurred well.	Completes assignments on a timely basis; able to proficiently complete a task with little supervision; works diligently and pays attention to important details.	Aware of work to be done and makes reasonable attempt to attain preset time goals; able to complete task with a reasonable amount of supervision; some signs of over-auditing; beginning to organize areas into "to-do" lists.	Gets bogged down in unnecessary detail; requires excessive guidance; regularly over time budget without explanation; work is at times not done or half done; disorganized.
WORKING PAPERS: documentation, clarity, neatness, and organization; conclusions are well-supported.	Work is well-documented, clear, neat, and well-organized; conclusions are well-supported.	Working papers are satisfactory; some audit work is redundant, or repetitive explanations and conclusions are made; some papers may be disorganized; some improvement needed in clarity and neatness.	Working papers poorly documented; conclusions not properly supported; papers hard to follow, sloppy, disorganized.
KNOWLEDGE OF ACCOUNTING AND AUDITING STANDARDS/THEORY: technical foundation; application of knowledge on the job; ability to identify problem areas and weigh theory vs. practice.	Displays very strong technical foundation; able to proficiently apply knowledge on the job; willingness to research areas; ability to identify problems; can weigh theory vs. practice considerations.	Can resolve normal accounting issues; adequate technical foundation and skills; application requires some refinement; has some problems in weighing theory vs. practice; can identify major problem areas.	Displays weak accounting knowledge and/or technical ability to apply knowledge to situations; issues on an engagement; has difficulty in identifying problems and/or weighing factors of theory vs. practice.

JUDGMENT AND COMMON SENSE: able to reach logical conclusions given the information available; understands the purpose of a procedure and the framework of the overall audit ("the big picture"); understands materiality.

Possesses the ability to reach logical conclusions given the information available. Has a good understanding of the purpose of a given procedure and how it fits into the overall audit; understands materiality; asks good questions.

Generally displays sound judgment; conclusions reasonable; brings unnecessary audit steps to the attention of the senior; beginning to recognize significant interrelationships. Understands audit area worked on; has some difficulties grasping materiality; willing to ask questions.

Can't see the forest for the trees; misses key issues; reluctant to think deeply and arrive at a conclusion. Performs work without understanding purpose behind it; either asks few important questions or far too many trivial questions.

PART TWO: INTERPERSONAL SKILLS

INTERPERSONAL SKILLS: ability to get along and build a strong rapport with fellow staff and the client; a team player.

Ability to get along very well with fellow staff and the client personnel; a team player; pleasant and courteous; leaves a very positive impression.

Gets along adequately with fellow staff and client; able to avoid confrontation and maintain positive working relationship; quiet, pleasant and polite.

At times is arrogant; can alienate the client or irritate fellow staff; deals with clients in an accusatory manner; can be rude or discourteous; too shy or unassertive.

PART THREE: COMMUNICATION SKILLS

COMMUNICATION SKILLS: clear expression of ideas both orally and in writing.

Has the ability to express ideas clearly and concisely both *orally* and in *writing*; communicates well with others assigned to the engagement.

Too wordy in some cases but generally gets the idea across; written communications often not original (taken from prior working papers); could improve clarity and refinement of ideas.

Has difficulty in oral and/or written expression; illogical, unclear, or disorganized expression; spelling errors, incomplete sentences, carelessness.

PART FOUR: PROFESSIONAL CHARACTERISTICS

INITIATIVE AND AMBITION: willingness to take responsibility and put in extra effort when needed; positive and professional attitude; accepts challenges.

Willing to take responsibility and put in extra effort and time when necessary; positive and professional attitude; readily accepts the challenges ahead.

Puts in effort and time requested by in-charge; often defers final resolution of issues to the in-charge.

Negative attitude at times; complains and/or is argumentative; constructs obstacles; lacks drive; does not seek new areas of work.

MATURITY AND CONFIDENCE: good professional demeanor; responsible; able to constructively accept and learn from criticism; is confident of abilities.

Displays strong maturity and self-confidence; good professional demeanor; responsible; able to constructively accept and learn from criticism.

Generally mature and confident; adequate professional image; accepts criticism; some difficulty in learning from criticism and/or lacks confidence at times.

Has significant difficulty in accepting criticism (argumentative and defensive); lack of professional image; not responsible at times; does not defend decisions and conclusions (appears weak).

Source: Arnold Wright, "Performance Evaluation of Staff Auditors: A Behaviorally Anchored Rating Scale," *Auditing: A Journal of Practice and Theory* (Spring 1986): 104–105. Reprinted with the permission of the American Accounting Association.

forcing one to subjectively judge a person as 'excellent,' 'above average,' or 'below average.' "[55] An example of a BARS is shown in Exhibit 6.1. It presents clear critical incidents describing effective and ineffective performance.

STAFF TURNOVER IN PUBLIC ACCOUNTING FIRMS

High rates of staff turnover characterize public accounting firms.[56] About 85 percent of accounting graduates who join big CPA firms will leave within 10 years for positions in government, education, or smaller CPA firms.[57] Benke and Rhode estimated the replacement cost of an entry-level staff accountant to be in excess of $20,000.[58] For one large CPA firm with a turnover of 10,000 employees over a recent ten year period, total replacement costs would reach $200,000,000.[59] The reasons behind this high turnover need to be known, because the cost to CPA firms and to the discipline are high. Among the reasons that have been suggested are the following:

1. The turnover is due to both a failure to challenge qualified people and the easing out of unqualified people.[60]
2. The best of a lower-quality set of students are attracted to accounting; these students generally have experienced a cultural lag in the areas of education and guidance.[61] The best students opt for majors other than accounting.[62] What results is a lack of technical competence, which could explain the turnover.[63]
3. The needs of young accountants are not met by work-related activities in public accounting firms.[64] In addition, the work is tedious enough to cause turnover.[65]
4. While the views of managing partners and their professional staff are congruent on most strategic goals, the staff is asking for greater variety and better communication of performance criteria.[66]
5. An elevated personality profile as well as a preference for analytic or scientific orientations characterize a group of accountants that has remained in public accounting.[67] Therefore, personality characteristics as well as the vocational interests of entry-level staff accountants may be a strong determinant of turnover in public accounting firms.
6. The personality profiles of managers, partners, juniors, and seniors are known to differ and can result in high turnover. According to one analysis: "Those personality differences may be a partial predictor of turnover since CPA firms, like other large organizations with few permanent positions at the top and a large staff, often have personnel evaluation criteria that indicate 'if you want to be one of us, then, you should be like us—in terms of ability, interests, and personality characteristics.' "[68]
7. The turnover decision in public accounting firms may be a function of negatively valued task outcomes, the likelihood of obtaining these outcomes in one's current position, and the greater chance of realizing certain positive outcomes in alternative positions.[69]

8. A poor communication atmosphere may exist in public accounting firms not only because the relationships between supervisors and workers are imperfect but also because the staff accountants are not fully integrated into the firms and are left on their own about the job's expectations. This situation is destructive of the job performance of individuals and could explain their turnover decision.[70] The following advice has been offered:

The data analyzed represent open and legitimate concerns from a selected group of staff accountants during the first 3½ years of professional employment. Their concerns are objectively reported and do not represent what someone suspects is the cause of turnover. They are the reasons for turnover actually experienced by staff personnel. It is now up to the CPA firms to act individually to remedy their unwanted staff losses. This can be done if CPA firms can increase the positive aspects of their work environments and minimize the negative aspects.[71]

9. Satisfaction is inversely related to turnover.[72]
10. Turnover is affected by the task of managing a hybrid professional-bureaucratic orientation in public accounting firms.[73]

MOTIVATION IN AN ACCOUNTING ENVIRONMENT

The importance of motivation lies in its ability to affect performance and job satisfaction. Expectancy theory models generally have been used in research settings to study the subject of work motivation and performance.[74] Basically, the theories postulate relationships for the determination of motivation (M) and/or job performance (P). With regard to motivation, the theory holds that the motivation (M) of an individual to perform at a particular effort level (E) is a function of the algebraic sum of the products of: (1) the individual's expectancies that specific outcomes or rewards (O) will follow from exerted effort, and (2) the perceived valences of the specific rewards (V) or outcomes associated with performing at that effort level.[75] Two expectancy theory models have been formulated to express the individual's motivation. The first model holds that an individual will opt for a particular behavior and a given effort level on the basis of his or her expectancies that effort will lead to certain outcomes and the valences placed on these outcomes. In other words,

$$M = [(E \rightarrow O)\ (V)]$$

The second model includes two expectancies on the assumption that an individual usually encounters two outcomes: the actual task performance and an outcome resulting from the realization of the first outcome.[76] It holds that an individual will offer a particular behavior and effort level on the basis of (1) his or her expectancy that effort will result in task performance, and (2) his or her expectancy that accomplishment of the task will lead to a second-level outcome. In other words,

$$M = (E \rightarrow P) \, [(P \rightarrow O) \, (V)]$$

With regard to performance, expectancy theory holds that an individual's job performance (P) is a joint function of the ability (A) to perform the job, the role perceptions (R) with respect to the job, and the motivation (M) to perform the job. In other words,

$$P = f(A, R, M)$$

The function has been shown to be multiplicative or additive. Expectancy models have also been used to argue that where there is a high performance $\rightarrow$ outcomes expectancy, there should be a positive correlation between job performance and job satisfaction.[77] Known as the Lawler and Porter–Lawler job satisfaction model, it was first tested in an accounting environment by Ferris.[78] The results indicated that the expectancy models were not good predictors of audit staff performance but were good predictors of employee job satisfaction.

A valence–instrumentality–expectancy model refers to a theory of work motivation to explain either job effort or job choice.[79] Basically, it holds that the level of motivation (W) of an individual to perform at a particular effort level is a joint function of the following: V_j, the valence of the outcomes associated with the job; I_{ij}, the instrumentality of these outcomes; and E_i, the expectancies of the performance. In other words,

$$W = E_i \left(\sum_{j=1}^{n} I_{ij}V_j \right)$$

The model also holds that the utility of rewards (U_i) is a function of I_{ij} and V_j:

$$U_i = \sum_{j=1}^{n} I_{ij}V_j$$

While this model has been used in accounting to predict performance,[80] and turnover,[81] it has also been used to compare the motivational levels in Australia and the United States.[82] The results of the latter study showed that few differences existed between the groups of accountants from the two countries with regard to personal value structures, motivation levels, and perceptions of the work environment.

PERSONAL CHARACTERISTICS OF ACCOUNTANTS AND THEIR CONSEQUENCES

Evidence in the behavioral sciences indicate that the personal characteristics of individuals affect how they respond to the work environment. These characteristics include, for example, an individual's personality and personal interests[83] and an individual's feelings toward the work environment.[84] The thesis has also been tested in the accounting work environment. Research has been performed on several characteristics: the general and distinctive characteristics of those who deal with accounting, professional commitment in public accounting, career intentions, and job stress in public accounting.

The Stereotypical Accountant

Various studies have investigated many negative general characteristics that have been attributed to accountants, particularly the traits of inflexibility, introversion, quantitative thinking, and lack of interest in interpersonal relations. The stereotypical image of the accountant was confirmed in the following instances:

1. The accountant can exhibit a low level of verbal competence, prefer working with numbers, be precise and exact when it comes to detail, and avoid facing new things without being prepared for them.[85]

2. Conformity, low social interests, and a poorly developed aesthetic sensitivity characterize accountants.[86]

3. Unlike other students, accounting students prefer a moderate but stable income and aspire less to work with people and to creative work.[87]

4. Compared to teachers, they score higher in domination and esteem but lower on perception and acceptance of themselves.[88]

5. Compared to creative writing students, accounting students identify positively with their parents and have a largely accepting attitude toward authority and external regulations, as well as toward people in general.[89] This confirmed earlier positive results on a hypothesis that suggested that signs of a more rigid, fearful identification were seen in accounting students as compared to a seeking for the completion of multiple identification in creative writing students.[90] A study by Aranya, Meir, and Bar-Ilan found that accounting students tended to show stronger adherence to social values and norms than psychology students.[91] The same study found that accounting students showed vocational interests in business and organization, but not in general culture or the areas of art and entertainment.

6. Accounting subjects are primarily enterprising and social types, not the investigative type.[92] These results were partially confirmed in another study, which found, moreover, that the conventional type was dominant among sole practitioners and partners in small firms, and the enterprising type was dominant among partners in large firms.[93] These studies were investigated in the framework of Holland's theory, which (a) postulates that the individual, through his or her choice of occupation, attempts to fulfill a way of life, and (b) accounts for six types of people—realistic, investigative, artistic, social, enterprising, and conventional—and assumes there is a professional environment that corresponds to each.[94]

7.   A survey by Estes showed that, in a comparison with accountants, physicians and attorneys came from families with significantly higher socioeconomic status, and that the children of physicians entered careers with significantly higher SES scores.[95] Engineers were comparable to accountants. Estes concluded:

These results suggest that the accounting profession is, along with engineering, drawing its people more from blue collar and rural families, in contrast to other professions. This situation reflects an opportunity, in that law and medicine are apparently not competing effectively in this human resource pool. It also presents a challenge: are we recruiting an appropriate share of young people from families in the upper socioeconomic strata?[96]

The stereotypical image of accountants was, however, disconfirmed in one case by evidence that a group of accountants scored higher in friendliness, personal acceptance, and psychological sensitivity than other professional groups included in a survey.[97]

To characterize the stereotypical accountant, Aranya, Meir, and Bar-Ilan used an inclusive theory of professional stereotypes.[98] This framework was based on Holland's theory that an individual, in choosing an occupation, attempts to fulfill a way of life within the context of his or her work.[99] Vocational interests and adherence to socially accepted values were examined for both accounting and psychology students. The results showed that accounting students opted for vocational interests in business and organization but not in general culture or in the areas of art and entertainment, while psychology students opted for vocational interests in the areas of service, art and entertainment, and general culture. In addition, accounting students exhibited a stronger adherence to social norms and values as predicted by Holland's theory.

An examination of the personality profiles of juniors, seniors, managers, and partners in selected national accounting firms showed that partners were oriented toward confirming, conservative, and inflexible behavior. The other categories of accountants tended toward a behavior characterized as competitive aggressive and directed toward independence through achievement.[100] Vocational interests and organizational or professional attitudes toward public accounting were found to differ between young CPAs and partners and other CPAs with more extensive work experience.[101] In fact, a generation gap of ideals and values existed between partners and staff personnel.[102]

Professional Commitment in Public Accounting

Professional commitment in public accounting, that is, the relative strength of accountants' identification with and involvement in their profession, has been the subject of investigation. The concern with both organizational and professional commitment is important for the following reasons: better performance is obtained from highly committed employees,[103] turnover can be better predicted from the level of organizational commitment than from job satisfaction,[104] and organizational effectiveness is related to organizational commitment.[105]

Sorensen and Sorensen examined the effects of related variables, for example, holding professional versus bureaucratic orientations and values.[106] They found that conflict between professionalism and bureaucratization led to job dissatisfaction and job migration. Hastings and Hastings showed that chartered accountants in industry had lower levels of attachment to professional values than did those in public practice.[107]

Aranya, Pollock, and Armenic's model assumed that three major factors influenced professional commitment to a profession, namely organizational commitment, professional organizational conflict, and satisfaction with rewards.[108] The relationship was also assumed to be moderated by the organizational level, following Sorensen and Sorensen's findings of an increase in bureaucratic orientations and a decrease in professional orientations from lower to higher positions, junior to senior partners.[109] A survey of Canadian chartered accountants showed the primacy of organizational commitment in predicting professional commitment in all organizational levels. In addition, professional commitment was found to be negatively related to the professional organizational conflict and positively related to the satisfaction with income. In a follow-up study, Aranya and Wheeler found that the accountants' commitment to both profession and organization was essentially related to their scores as conventional and enterprising types.[110]

Career Intentions

Following McClelland's theory that individuals, consciously or unconsciously, seek an environment that is congruent with the size of their application, power, and achievement needs,[111] Harrell and Eickhoff suggested that influence-oriented auditors may be predisposed to have more positive affective responses than others to the Big Eight public accounting work environment.[112] The results of a survey verified their hypothesis by showing that influence-oriented auditors experienced higher future job satisfaction than others, greater future organizational commitment than others, and more positive Big Eight career intentions than others. In addition, they exhibited lower future levels of voluntary turnover behavior than others.

Other research studies have examined the need for achievement as a factor that could explain the career intentions of accounting students. Belkaoui examined the likelihood of an association between accounting students' need for achievement and their career aspirations. His hypotheses were that (1) a high need for achievement would be associated with a desire for mobility out of lower-status accounting positions and into higher-status positions, and (2) very low need for achievement may be associated with unrealistic career aspirations.[113] An experiment yielded results that supported the first hypothesis for both male and female subjects, and the second hypothesis for only the female group with regard to their late-career aspirations (that is, 25 years hence).

Dillard used a goal expectancy model of occupation-position choice behavior.[114] He explained the model as follows:

Stated succinctly, this model predicts that an individual makes choices based on occupation-position goals. These goals are a function of perceived rewards and punishments associated with the position, the likelihood of obtaining these outcomes, and the chances for acquiring the position. Each position alternative can be ranked in terms of expected utility, the individual's choice acquisitions may be restricted by not perceived situational, institutional, and personal constraints, but as these become evident they impact on the decision process.[115]

The model was supported by results showing that the measured occupation-position goals were significantly related to the position with the highest expected utility.

Job Stress in Public Accounting

Stress has been defined as ''a state which arises from an actual or perceived demand-capability imbalance in the organism's vital adjustment actions and which is partially manifest by a nonspecific response.''[116] It is caused by a type of stressor, ''a demand made by internal or external environment of an organism that upsets its homeostasis, restoration of which depends on nonautomatic and not readily available energy-expending action.''[117] Examples of stressors cited by Antonovosky include:

accidents and the survivors; the untoward experiences of others in social networks; the horrors of history in which we are involved; intrapsychic, unconscious conflicts and anxieties; the fear of aggression, mutilation and destruction; the events of history brought in our living rooms; the changes of the narrower world in which we live; other normative life crises—role entries and exits, inadequate socialization, underboard and overboard; the inherent conflicts in all social relations; and the gap between culturally inculcated goals and socially structured means.''[118]

Stress is no stranger to the accounting world. In fact, it could be considered an important accompaniment to accounting practices. Accounting procedures affect the perceptions of control and predictability of those who impose these procedures as well as of those who are their target.[119] Several authors have pointed to the effect of job-related stress on professional auditors.[120] Other studies have elaborated on some of the nonpersonality factors that can have an impact on stress in accounting firms, such as type and quality of supervision, promotional procedures, job autonomy, career opportunities, and social supports.[121] One study hypothesized that personality variables can also be significantly linked to job stress. It investigated four personality dispositions that are potential determinants of job-related stress: type A, control, commitment, and challenge.[122] Type A personality is characterized by a life-style of behavioral responses leaning toward extremes, such as competitiveness, hard-driving, intense striving for achievement, sense of time urgency, aggressiveness, hostility, hyperalertness, and inability to respond to bodily signals of stress.[123] Such an individual generally can not cope with job stress. Control disposition suggests that an individual tends to believe and act as if he or she is in control of events. It can reduce the effects of a stressful situation.[124] Commitment disposition implies that an individual likes to get involved with events happening to them.[125] It is a good way to cope with stress. Challenge disposition suggests that an individual prefers change to stability in working life because change offers interesting incentives to growth rather than threats to security.[126] A survey of practicing auditors indicated the existence of a positive relationship between job stress and type A personality, and a negative relationship between job stress on the one hand and control, commitment, and challenge personality dispositions on the other hand.[127] The same survey supported the presence of an inverted U relationship between stress and performance in the auditing profession. Such a relationship, called the Yerkes-Dodson law, assumes that stress in the work environment causes job performance to improve up to a point, after which a situation of stress overload can hinder performance.[128]

SOURCES OF FEEDBACK IN A CPA FIRM

Performance feedback in the work setting has been considered important to employee training, performance, motivation, and satisfaction. Research questions have primarily focused on identifying sources of feedback,[129] work as an information environment,[130] and defining the construct of feedback.[131] In assessing the importance of different potential sources of job performance information, these studies viewed the worker as an information receiver in an environment capable of providing a variety of information from different sources. They relied on either student subjects or faculty members and opened an interesting area of research into feedback sources in the work environment.

Three methods have been used to investigate the concept of feedback: knowledge of results, management appraisal, and job quality.[132] While each approach has demonstrated the importance of feedback, they have been criticized (1) for using single tasks with unidimensional feedback in the case of the knowledge-of-results approach, (2) for taking a simplistic and prescriptive stand (for example, ''feedback is important'') in the case of the management-appraisal literature, and

(3) for restricting the importance of feedback to being a component of job design and ignoring the possibility that other aspects of feedback might exist. A different research approach was used by Greller and Herold and also by Hansen and Muchinsky.[133] It relied on a deductive strategy to assess the importance of different potential sources of job performance information and viewed the worker as an information receiver in an environment containing many possible sources of feedback. In their attempt to clarify the feedback construct, Greller and Herold dimensionalized feedback according to five potential sources: company, supervisor, coworkers, task, and the self.[134] Using student subjects, their findings indicated that there was a greater reliance on intrinsic sources (that is, sources psychologically "closer" to the individual) than on more external sources of feedback, and that this reliance was reduced for referent information.[135] Hansen and Muchinsky replicated the study using faculty members as subjects and found similar results.[136] Both studies' findings may be influenced by the subjects' population and environment, because performance is experienced and measured in terms of personal creativity. They may have attached more importance to psychologically closer sources than external sources. The work environment of a CPA firm is defined in terms of firm policies, close supervision, and cooperation with coworkers, rather than in terms of personal creativity. Thus one might expect to find different results regarding the informativeness of the feedback sources examined. Accordingly, Belkaoui and Picur examined the nature of CPA work environments with regard to sources, types, and reliability of the information received.[137] Five sources of information—the formal organization, immediate supervision, coworkers, the task and personal feelings, and ideas—were rated by seniors and managers in the metropolitan offices of two Big Eight CPA firms as to their ability to provide referent and appraisal information. The study's results supported the main conclusion of earlier research that referent and appraisal information can be viewed as emanating from different sources that vary in their degree of informativeness. The most notable finding of this study was the consistent importance of the supervisor as the most reliable source of both referent and appraisal information. The findings suggested that CPA firms should develop the interpersonal skills of supervisory personnel.

CONCLUSION

Many survey and laboratory experiments have examined human resource considerations in public accounting firms. Strong results have been found mainly with regard to job dissatisfaction and high turnover. Several causes have been identified, providing the beginnings of a clear picture of what is wrong and what is right about the organizational climates of public accounting firms. Much remains to be done, as other human resource variables need to be examined.

Among these variables are absenteeism, administrative intensity, autonomy, communication, complexity, violence of conflict, coordination, departmentalization, distributive justice, effectiveness, formalization, general training, ideology, innovation, motivation, need strength, pay stratification, bases of power, power stratification, prestige stratification, productivity, routinization, size, standardization, work group cohesion, and workload in public accounting firms, to name several.[138]

NOTES

1. L. W. Porter and R. M. Steers, "Organizational Work and Personal Factors in Employee Turnover and Absenteeism," *Psychological Bulletin* (1973): 151–176.

2. E. E. Lawler, *Pay and Organizational Effectiveness: A Psychological View* (New York: McGraw-Hill, 1971); E. A. Locke, "The Nature and Causes of Job Satisfaction," in M. D. Dunnette, ed., *Handbook of Industrial and Organizational Psychology* (Chicago: Rand McNally, 1976), pp. 1297–1349.

3. L. W. Porter and V. F. Mitchell, "Comparative Study of Need Satisfaction in Military and Business Hierarchies," *Journal of Applied Psychology* (April 1967): 139–144.

4. R. H. Strawser, J. M. Ivancevich, and H. L. Lyon, "A Note on the Job Satisfaction of Accountants in Large and Small CPA Firms," *Journal of Accounting Research* (Autumn 1969): 339–345.

5. C. G. Carpenter and R. H. Strawser, "A Study of the Job Satisfaction of Academic Accountants," *Accounting Review* (July 1971): 509–518.

6. John M. Ivancevich and Robert H. Strawser, "A Comparative Analysis of the Job Satisfaction of Industrial Managers and Certified Public Accountants," *Academy of Management Journal* (March 1969): 193–203.

7. N. Aranya, R. Lachman, and J. Armenic, "Accountants' Job Satisfaction: A Path Analysis," *Accounting, Organizations and Society* (December 1982): 201–215.

8. Ibid., p. 210.

9. J. E. Sorensen, "Professional and Bureaucratic Organization in Public Accounting Firms," *Accounting Review* (July 1967): 553–565.

10. K. R. Ferris, "Perceived Uncertainty and Job Satisfaction in the Accounting Environment," *Accounting, Organizations and Society* 2, no. 1 (1977): 23–28.

11. Ibid., p. 28.

12. Ralph L. Benke, Jr., and J. G. Rhode, "The Job Satisfaction of Higher Level Employees in Large Certified Public Accounting Firms," *Accounting, Organizations and Society* (July 1980): 187–201.

13. D. C. McClelland, *Power: The Inner Experience* (New York: Irvington, 1975).

14. A. M. Harrell and M. J. Stahl, "McClelland's Trichotomy of Needs Theory and the Job Satisfaction and Work Performance of CPA Firm Professionals," *Accounting, Organizations and Society* (June 1984): 241–252.

15. P. M. Blau and W. R. Scott, *Formal Organization* (San Francisco: Chandler, 1962).

16. Sorensen, "Professional and Bureaucratic Organization in Public Accounting

Firms''; R. G. Schroeder and L. F. Imdieke, "Local-Cosmopolitan and Bureaucratic Perceptions in Public Accounting Firms," *Accounting, Organizations and Society* (1977): 39–45.

17. R. H. Hall, "Professionalization and Bureaucratization," *American Sociological Review* (February 1968): 92–104; P. D. Montagna, "Professionalization and Bureaucratization in Large Professional Organizations," *American Journal of Sociology* (September 1968): 138–145.

18. J. E. Sorensen and T. L. Sorensen, "The Conflict of Professionals in Bureaucratic Organizations," *Administrative Science Quarterly* (March 1974): 98–106.

19. D. R. Norris and R. E. Nielbuhr, "Professionalism, Organizational Commitment and Job Satisfaction in an Accounting Organization," *Accounting, Organizations and Society* (December 1983): 49–60.

20. N. Aranya and K. R. Ferris, "A Reexamination of Accountant's Organizational-Professional Conflict," *Accounting Review* (January 1984): 1–15.

21. P. T. Senatra, "Role Conflict, Role Ambiguity, and Organizational Climate in a Public Accounting Firm," *Accounting Review* (October 1980): 594–603.

22. Ibid.

23. M. W. Dirsmith and M. A. Covaleski, "Informal Communications, Nonformal Communications and Mentoring in Public Accounting Firms," *Accounting, Organizations and Society* (May 1985): 149–169.

24. Ibid., p. 166.

25. F. M. Jablin, "A Reexamination of the 'Pelz Effect,'" *Human Communication Research* (1980): 210–220.

26. D. Pelz, "Influence: A Key to Effective Leadership in the First Line Supervisor," *Personnel* (1952): 209–271.

27. L. W. Wager, "Leadership Style, Influence and Supervisory Role Obligations," *Administrative Science Quarterly* (1965): 391–420.

28. Ibid., p. 418.

29. K. H. Roberts and C. A. O'Reilly, "Failures in Upward Communication: Three Possible Culprits," *Academy of Management Journal* (1974): 205–215; A. P. Jones, L. R. James, and J. R. Bruni, "Perceived Leadership Behavior and Employee Confidence in the Leader as Moderated by Job Involvement," *Journal of Applied Psychology* (1978): 146–149; C. A. O'Reilly and K. H. Roberts, "Supervisor Influence and Subordinate Mobility Aspirations as Moderators of Consideration and Initiating Structure," *Journal of Applied Psychology* (1978): 96–102; F. M. Jablin, "Supervisor's Upward Influence, Satisfaction, and Openness in Superior-Subordinate Communication: A Reexamination of the 'Pelz Effect,'" *Human Communication Research* (1980): 210–220.

30. Ahmed Belkaoui, "Leadership Style, Dimensions of Superior's Upward Influence and Participative Budgeting" (Working paper, University of Illinois at Chicago, June 1988).

31. J. Pratt and J. Jiambalvo, "Relationships between Leader Behaviors and Audit Team Performance," *Accounting, Organizations and Society* (August 1981): 133–142.

32. Ibid., p. 139.

33. J. Pratt and J. Jiambalvo, "Determinants of Leader Behavior in an Audit Environment," *Accounting, Organizations and Society* (December 1982): 369–379.

34. J. Jiambalvo and J. Pratt, "Task Complexity and Leadership Effectiveness in CPA Firms," *Accounting Review* (October 1982): 734–750.

35. C. Richard Baker, "Management Strategy in a Large Accounting Firm," *Accounting Review* (July 1977): 576–586.

36. Ibid., pp. 579–581.

37. Ibid., pp. 582–583.

38. David J. H. Watson, "The Structure of Project Teams Facing Differentiated Environments: An Exploratory Study in Public Accounting Firms," *Accounting Review* (April 1975): 259–273.

39. Sorensen, "Professional and Bureaucratic Organization in Public Accounting Firms."

40. J. Kane and E. Lawler, "Performance Appraisal Effectiveness: Its Assessments and Determinants," *Research in Organizational Behavior* (1979): 425–478.

41. Arnold Wright, "Performance Appraisal of Staff Auditors," *CPA Journal* (November 1980): 37–43.

42. J. Jiambalvo, "Performance Evaluation and Directed Job Effort: Model Development and Analysis in a CPA Firm Setting," *Journal of Accounting Research* (Autumn 1979): 436–455.

43. J. R. Turney, "Activity Outcome Expectancies and Intrinsic Activity Values as Predictors of Several Motivation Indexes for Technical-Professionals," *Organizational Behavior and Human Performance* (February 1974): 65–82.

44. Watson, "The Structure of Project Teams Facing Differentiated Environments."

45. J. Jiambalvo, D. J. H. Watson, and J. V. Baumler, "An Examination of Performance Evaluation Decisions in CPA Firm Subunits," *Accounting, Organizations and Society* (March 1983): 13–29.

46. Ibid., pp. 18–19.

47. Wright, "Performance Appraisal of Staff Auditors."

48. Arnold Wright, "An Investigation of the Engagement Evaluation Process for Staff Auditors," *Journal of Accounting Research* (Spring 1982): 227–239.

49. T. E. Kida, "Performance Evaluation and Review Meeting Characteristics in Public Accounting Firms," *Accounting, Organizations and Society* (February 1984): 137–148.

50. J. G. Rhode, J. E. Sorensen, and E. E. Lawler III, "Sources of Professional Staff Turnover in Public Accounting Firms Revealed by the Exit Interview," *Accounting, Organizations and Society* (1977): 165–175; D. Hellriegal and G. White, "Turnover of Professionals in Public Accounting: A Comparative Analysis," *Personnel Psychology* (1973): 239–249.

51. J. Rhode, *Survey on the Influence of Selected Aspects of the Auditors' Work Environment on Professional Performance of Certified Public Accountants: A Study and Report for the Commission on Auditors' Responsibilities* (New York: AICPA, 1977).

52. S. Lightner, S. Adams, and K. Lightner, "The Influence of Situational, Ethical, and Expectancy Theory Variables on Accountants' Underreporting Behavior," *Auditing: A Journal of Practice and Theory* (Fall 1982): 1–12.

53. M. Maher, K. Ramanathan, and R. Patterson, "Preference Congruence, Information Accuracy, and Employee Performance," *Journal of Accounting Research* (Autumn 1979): 476–503; J. Jiambalvo, "Measures of Accuracy and Congruence in the Performance Evaluation of CPA Personnel: Replications and Extensions," *Journal of Accounting Research* (Spring 1982): 152–161.

54. Arnold Wright, "Performance Evaluation of Staff Auditors: A Behaviorally An-

chored Rating Scale,'' *Auditing: A Journal of Practice and Theory* (Spring 1986): 95–108.

55. Ibid., p. 97.

56. R. S. Capui, "How to Cope with the Staff Man Shortage," *Practical Accountant* (1969): 22; R. C. Ellyson and B. S. Shaw, "The Psychological Assessment and Staff Recruiting," *Journal of Accountancy* (1970): 35–42; C. Konstans and K. Ferris, "Female Turnover in Professional Accounting Firms: Some Preliminary Findings," *Michigan CPA* (Winter 1981): 11–15.

57. F. P. Kollaritsh, "Job Migration Patterns of Accounting," *Management Accounting* (September 1968): 52–55.

58. Ralph L. Benke, Jr., and J. G. Rhode, "Intent to Turnover among Higher Level Employees in Large CPA Firms," *Advances in Accounting* (1984): 157–174.

59. J. Healy, "The Drudge Is Dead," *MBA* (November 1976): 48–56.

60. J. Carey, *The CPA Plans for the Future* (New York: American Institute of Certified Public Accountants, 1965).

61. J. Ashworth, "People Who Become Accountants," *Journal of Accounting* (1968): 43–49; idem, "The Pursuit of High Quality Recruits," *Journal of Accountancy* (1969): 53–57; idem, "A Must for Effective Recruiting: Mutual Understanding between Students and the Accounting Profession," *Journal of Accountancy* (1969): 84–86.

62. F. C. Pierson, *The Education of American Businessmen* (New York: McGraw-Hill, 1959).

63. R. Cruse, "What Can the Behavioral Sciences Contribute to the Selection of CPAs," *Journal of Accountancy* (1965): 88.

64. J. Zweig, "Individualisms—A Recruiting Aid for Local Practitioners," *Journal of Accountancy* (1969): 80; C. G. Carpenter and R. H. Strawser, "Job Selection Preference of Accounting Students," *Journal of Accountancy* (1970): 84–86; V. C. Brenner, P. E. Dasher, and W. J. Grasty, "Attitude Change after College Campus Recruiting Interview," *New York Certified Public Accountant* (1971): 165.

65. P. E. Leathers, *The Staff Retention Problem in Public Accounting: Background and Questions for Discussion* (New York: American Institute of Certified Public Accountants, 1970).

66. K. V. Ramanathan, R. B. Peterson, and M. W. Maher, "Strategic Goals and Performance Criteria in CPA Firms," *Journal of Accountancy* (1976): 56–64.

67. J. G. Rhode, J. E. Sorensen, and E. E. Lawler III, "An Analysis of Personal Characteristics Related to Professional Staff Turnover in Public Accounting Firms," *Decision Sciences* (1976): 771–800.

68. Ibid., p. 773.

69. J. F. Dillard and K. R. Ferris, "Sources of Professional Staff Turnover in Public Accounting Firms: Some Further Evidence," *Accounting, Organizations and Society* (February 1980): 179–186.

70. Rhode, Sorensen, and Lawler, "Sources of Professional Staff Turnover in Public Accounting Firms Revealed by the Exit Interview."

71. Ibid., p. 174.

72. Porter and Steers, "Organizational Work and Personal Factors in Employee Turnover and Absenteeism"; M. L. Bullen and E. G. Flamholtz, "A Theoretical and Empirical Investigation of Job Satisfaction and Intended Turnover in Large CPA Firms," *Accounting, Organizations and Society* (August 1985): 287–302.

73. Sorensen, "Professional and Bureaucratic Organization in Public Accounting Firms."

74. V. H. Vroom, *Work and Motivation* (New York: John Wiley and Sons, 1964).

75. O. C. Behling, C. Schriesheim, and J. Tolliver, "Alternatives to Expectancy Theories of Work Motivation," *Decision Sciences* (January 1975): 449–461.

76. J. R. Galbraith and L. L. Cummings, "An Empirical Investigation of the Motivational Determinants of Task Performance: Interactive Effects between Instrumentality-Valence and Motivation-Ability," *Organizational Behavior and Human Performance* (1967): 237–257.

77. Lawler, *Pay and Organizational Effectiveness;* L. W. Porter and E. E. Lawler, *Managerial Attitudes and Performance* (Homewood, Ill.: Irwin, 1968).

78. K. R. Ferris, "A Test of the Expectancy Theory of Motivation in an Accounting Environment," *Accounting Review* (July 1977): 605–615.

79. T. R. Mitchell, "Expectancy Models of Job Satisfaction, Occupational Preference, and Effort: A Theoretical, Methodological, and Empirical Appraisal," *Psychological Bulletin* (December 1974): 1053–1077.

80. J. Jiambalvo, "Performance Evaluations in CPA Firms: An Empirical Test of an Evaluation Model of Directed Job Effort," *Journal of Accounting Research* (Autumn 1979): 436–455.

81. Jesse F. Dillard, "Valence–Instrumentality–Expectancy Model Validation Using Selected Accounting Groups," *Accounting, Organizations and Society* (1979): 31–38; Dillard and Ferris, "Sources of Professional Staff Turnover in Public Accounting Firms."

82. K. R. Ferris, J. F. Dillard, and L. Nethercott, "A Comparison of V–I–E Mode Predictions: A Cross National Study in Professional Accounting Firms," *Accounting, Organizations and Society* (December 1980): 361–368.

83. W. Mobley, R. Griffith, H. Hand, and B. Meglino, "Review and Conceptual Analysis of the Employee Turnover Process," *Psychological Bulletin* (1979): 493–522.

84. H. Arnold and D. Felchman, "A Multivariate Analysis of the Determinants of Turnover," *Journal of Applied Psychology* (1982): 350–360.

85. A. Maslow, *Eupsychian Management* (Homewood, Ill.: Irwin, 1965).

86. D. D. O'Dowd and P. C. Beardslee, "College Student Images of a Selected Group of Professions and Occupations" (Working paper, Wesleyan University, April 1960).

87. W. Thielen, Jr., "Recruits for Accounting: How the Class of 1961 Entered the Profession" (Unpublished report, American Institute of Certified Public Accountants, 1966).

88. J. T. Gray, "Need and Values in Three Occupations," *Personnel Guidance* (1963): 238–244.

89. S. J. Segal and R. Szabo, "Identification in Two Vocations: Accountants and Creative Writers," *Personnel and Guidance Journal* (November 1964): 252–255.

90. S. J. Segal, "A Psychoanalytic Analysis of Personality Factors in Vocational Choice," *Journal of Counseling Psychology* (1961): 202–210.

91. N. Aranya, E. I. Meir, and A. Bar-Ilan, "An Empirical Examination of the Stereotype Accountant Based on Holland's Theory," *Journal of Occupational Psychology* (1978): 139–145.

92. N. Aranya and A. Barak, "A Test of Holland's Theory in a Population of Accountants," *Journal of Vocational Behavior* (1981): 15–24.

93. N. Aranya and J. T. Wheeler, "Accountants' Personality Types and Their Commitment to Organization and Profession," *Contemporary Accounting Research* (Fall 1986): 184–199.

94. J. L. Holland, "Some Explorations of a Theory of Vocational Choice: One and Two-Year Longitudinal Studies," *Psychological Monographs* 76 (1962); idem, "Explorations of a Theory of Vocational Choice, Part I: Vocational Images and Choice," *Vocational Guidance Quarterly* (1965): 232–239; idem, "Explorations of a Theory of Vocational Choice, Part IV: A Longitudinal Study Using a Sample of Typical College Students," *Journal of Applied Psychology* (February 1968): 1–37.

95. Ralph Estes, "An Intergenerational Comparison of Socioeconomic Statistics among CPAs, Attorneys, Engineers, and Physicians," *Advances in Accounting* (1984): 3–17.

96. Ibid., p. 16.

97. T. D. DeCoster and J. G. Rhode, "The Accountant's Stereotype: Real or Imagined, Deserved or Unwarranted," *Accounting Review* (1971): 651–664.

98. Aranya, Meir, and Bar-Ilan, "An Empirical Examination of the Stereotype Accountant Based on Holland's Theory."

99. J. L. Holland, *The Psychology of Vocational Choice* (Englewood Cliffs, N.J.: Prentice-Hall, 1973).

100. DeCoster and Rhode, "The Accountant's Stereotype: Real or Imagined, Deserved or Unwarranted."

101. Sorensen, "Professional and Bureaucratic Organization in Large Accounting Firms."

102. J. E. Sorensen, J. G. Rhode, and E. E. Lawler, "The Generation Gap in Public Accounting," *Journal of Accountancy* (1973): 42–50.

103. L. R. Jauch, W. F. Gluck, and R. N. Osbom, "Organizational Loyalty, Professional Commitment, and Academic Research Productivity," *Academy of Management Journal* (June 1978): 84–92.

104. L. W. Porter, R. M. Steers, R. T. Mowday, and P. V. Boulian, "Organizational Commitment, Job Satisfaction and Turnover among Psychiatric Technicians," *Journal of Applied Psychology* (October 1974): 603–609.

105. R. N. Steers, "Antecedents and Outcomes of Organizational Commitment," *Administrative Science Quarterly* (March 1977): 46–56.

106. Sorensen and Sorensen, "The Conflict of Professionals in Bureaucratic Organizations.

107. H. Hastings and C. R. Hastings, "Role Relations and Value Adaptation: A Study of the Professional Accountant in Industry," *Sociology* (September 1970): 353–366.

108. N. Aranya, J. Pollock, and J. Armenic, "An Examination of Professional Commitment in Public Accounting," *Accounting, Organizations and Society* (December 1981): 271–280.

109. Sorensen and Sorensen, "The Conflict of Professionals in Bureaucratic Organizations."

110. Aranya and Wheeler, "Accountants' Personality Types and Their Commitment to Organization and Profession."

111. D. C. McClelland, "Is Personality Consistent?" in A. Rubin, J. Aronoff, A. Barclay, and R. Zucker, eds., *Further Explorations in Personality* (New York: John Wiley and Sons, 1981).

112. A. M. Harrell and R. Eickhoff, "Auditors' Influence-Orientation and Their Affective Responses to the 'Big Eight' Work Environment" (Manuscript, University of South Carolina, 1988).

113. Ahmed Belkaoui, "The Accounting Students' Need for Achievement and Career Aspirations: An Experiment," *Issues in Accounting Education* (Fall 1986): 197–206.

114. Jesse F. Dillard, "A Longitudinal Evaluation of an Occupational Goal-Expectancy Model in Professional Accounting Organizations," *Accounting, Organizations and Society* (February 1981): 17–26; idem, "Applicability of an Occupational Goal-Expectancy Model in Professional Accounting Organizations," *Decision Sciences* (1979): 161–176.

115. Ibid., p. 164.

116. A. Mikhail, "Stress: A Psychophysical Conception," *Journal of Human Stress* (June 1981): 9–15.

117. A. Antonovsky, *Health, Stress and Coping* (San Francisco: Jossey-Bass, 1979).

118. Ibid., p. 72.

119. K. E. Weick, "Stress in Accounting Systems," *Accounting Review* (April 1983): 350–369; Robert Libby, "Comments on Weick," *Accounting Review* (April 1983): 370–374.

120. J. Kusel and N. J. Deyonb, "Internal Auditor Burnout," *Internal Auditor* (October 1983): 22–25; K. J. Smith and M. S. Katzman, "Stress and Internal Auditors," *Accountants' Journal* (1983): 27–32; T. Helliwell, "The Wages of the Overwork-Burnout," *Chartered Accountant Magazine* (August 1982): 83–87; G. Firth, "The Impact of Size and Stress in Accounting Firms," *Chartered Accountant in Australia* (August 1982): 20–33; J. D. Kimes, "Handling Stress in the Accounting Profession," *Management Accounting* (September 1977): 17–23.

121. R. H. Strawser, J. P. Kelly, and R. Wise, "What Causes Stress for Management Accountants?" *Management Accounting* (March 1982): 32–35; R. W. Sapp and R. Seiler, "Accounting for Performance: Stressful But Satisfying," *Management Accounting* (August 1980): 29–35; C. L. Cooper and R. Payne, *Stress at Work* (London: John Wiley and Sons, 1978).

122. F. Choo, "Job Stress, Job Performance, and Auditor Personality Characteristics," *Auditing: A Journal of Practice and Theory* (Spring 1986): 17–34.

123. F. Choo, "Accountants and Occupational Stress," *Australian Accountant* (November 1982): 633–638.

124. S. Cohen, "After-Effects of Stress on Human Performance and Social Behavior: A Review of Research and Theory," *Psychological Bulletin* (July 1980): 82–108.

125. S. R. Maddi, M. Hoover, and S. C. Kobasa, "Alienation and Exploratory Behavior," *Journal of Personality and Social Psychology* (1981).

126. M. Csikszentmihalyi, *Beyond Boredom and Anxiety* (San Francisco: Jossey-Bass, 1975).

127. Choo, "Job Stress, Job Performance, and Auditor Personality Characteristics."

128. P. L. Broadhurst, "The Interaction of Task Difficulty and Motivation: The Yerkes-Dodson Law Revised," *Acta Psychologica* (1959): 321–338.

129. M. M. Greller and D. M. Herold, "Sources of Feedback: A Preliminary Investigation," *Organizational Behavior and Human Performance* (1975): 244–256.

130. L. M. Hansen and P. M. Muchinsky, "Work as an Information Environment," *Organizational Behavior and Human Performance* (1978): 47–60.

131. D. M. Herold and M. M. Greller, "Feedback: The Definition of the Construct," *Academy of Management Journal* (1977): 142–147.

132. J. Annett, *Feedback and Human Behavior* (Baltimore: Penguin, 1969); A. N. Turner and P. R. Lawrence, *Industrial Jobs and the Workers* (Boston: Harvard University Graduate School of Business Administration, 1965); J. R. Hackman and E. E. Lawler III, "Employee Reactions to Job Characteristics," *Journal of Applied Psychology* (June 1971): 259–286.

133. Greller and Herold, "Sources of Feedback"; Hansen and Muchinsky, "Work as an Information Environment."

134. Greller and Herold, "Sources of Feedback."

135. Ibid., p. 244.

136. Hansen and Muchinsky, "Work as an Information Environment."

137. Ahmed Belkaoui and R. D. Picur, "Sources of Feedback in a CPA Firm," *Journal of Business Finance and Accounting* (Summer 1987): 175–186.

138. J. L. Price and C. W. Mueller, *Handbook of Organizational Measurement* (Marshfield, Mass.: Pitman Publishing, 1986).

SELECT BIBLIOGRAPHY

Annett, J. *Feedback and Human Behavior*. Baltimore: Penguin, 1969.

Antonovsky, A. *Health, Stress and Coping*. San Francisco: Jossey-Bass, 1979.

Aranya, N., and A. Barak. "A Test of Holland's Theory in a Population of Accountants." *Journal of Vocational Behavior* (1981): 15–24.

Aranya, N., and K. R. Ferris. "A Reexamination of Accountant's Organizational-Professional Conflict." *Accounting Review* (January 1984): 1–15.

Aranya, N., and J. T. Wheeler. "Accountants' Personality Types and Their Commitment to Organization and Profession." *Contemporary Accounting Research* (Fall 1986): 184–199.

Aranya, N., R. Lachman, and J. Armenic. "Accountants' Job Satisfaction: A Path Analysis." *Accounting, Organizations and Society* (December 1982): 201–215.

Aranya, N., E. I. Meir, and A. Bar-Ilan. "An Empirical Examination of the Stereotype Accountant Based on Holland's Theory." *Journal of Occupational Psychology* (1978): 139–145.

Aranya, N., J. Pollock, and J. Armenic. "An Examination of Professional Commitment in Public Accounting." *Accounting, Organizations and Society* (December 1981): 271–280.

Arnold, H., and D. Felchman. "A Multivariate Analysis of the Determinants of Turnover." *Journal of Applied Psychology* (1982): 350–360.

Ashworth, J. "A Must for Effective Recruiting: Mutual Understanding between Students and the Accounting Profession." *Journal of Accountancy* (1969): 84–86.

————. "People Who Become Accountants." *Journal of Accounting* (1968): 43–49.

————. "The Pursuit of High Quality Recruits." *Journal of Accountancy* (1969): 53–57.

Baker, C. Richard. "Management Strategy in a Large Accounting Firm." *Accounting Review* (July 1977): 576–586.

Behling, O. C., C. Schriesheim, and J. Tolliver. "Alternatives to Expectancy Theories of Work Motivation." *Decision Sciences* (January 1975): 449–461.

Belkaoui, Ahmed. "The Accounting Students' Need for Achievement and Career Aspirations: An Experiment." *Issues in Accounting Education* (Fall 1986): 197–206.

———. "Leadership Style, Dimensions of Superior's Upward Influence and Participative Budgeting" Working paper, University of Illinois at Chicago, June 1988.

Belkaoui, Ahmed, and R. D. Picur. "Sources of Feedback in a CPA Firm." *Journal of Business Finance and Accounting* (Summer 1987): 175–186.

Benke, Ralph L., Jr., and J. G. Rhode. "Intent to Turnover among Higher Level Employees in Large CPA Firms." *Advances in Accounting* (1984): 157–174.

———. "The Job Satisfaction of Higher Level Employees in Large Certified Public Accounting Firms." *Accounting, Organizations and Society* (July 1980): 187–201.

Blau, P. M., and W. R. Scott. *Formal Organization*. San Francisco: Chandler, 1962.

Brenner, V. C., P. E. Dasher, and W. J. Grasty. "Attitude Change after College Campus Recruiting Interview." *New York Certified Public Accountant* (1971): 165.

Broadhurst, P. L. "The Interaction of Task Difficulty and Motivation: The Yerkes-Dodson Law Revised." *Acta Psychologica* (1959): 321–338.

Bullen, M. L., and E. G. Flamholtz. "A Theoretical and Empirical Investigation of Job Satisfaction and Intended Turnover in Large CPA Firms." *Accounting, Organizations and Society* (August 1985): 287–302.

Capui, R. S. "How to Cope with the Staff Man Shortage." *Practical Accountant* (1969): 22.

Carey, J. *The CPA Plans for the Future*. New York: American Institute of Certified Public Accountants, 1965.

Carpenter, C. G., and R. H. Strawser. "Job Selection Preference of Accounting Students." *Journal of Accountancy* (1970): 84–86.

———. "A Study of the Job Satisfaction of Academic Accountants." *Accounting Review* (July 1971): 509–518.

Choo, F. "Accountants and Occupational Stress." *Australian Accountant* (November 1982): 633–638.

———. "Job Stress, Job Performance, and Auditor Personality Characteristics." *Auditing: A Journal of Practice and Theory* (Spring 1986): 17–34.

Cohen, S. "After-Effects of Stress on Human Performance and Social Behavior: A Review of Research and Theory." *Psychological Bulletin* (July 1980): 82–108.

Cooper, C. L., and R. Payne. *Stress at Work*. London: John Wiley and Sons, 1978.

Cruse, R. "What Can the Behavioral Sciences Contribute to the Selection of CPAs." *Journal of Accountancy* (1965): 88.

Csikszentmihalyi, M. *Beyond Boredom and Anxiety*. San Francisco: Jossey-Bass, 1975.

DeCoster, T. D., and J. G. Rhode. "The Accountant's Stereotype: Real or Imagined, Deserved or Unwarranted." *Accounting Review* (1971): 651–664.

Dillard, Jesse F. "Applicability of an Occupational Goal-Expectancy Model in Professional Accounting Organizations." *Decision Sciences* (1979): 161–176.

———. "A Longitudinal Evaluation of an Occupational Goal-Expectancy Model in Professional Accounting Organizations." *Accounting, Organizations and Society* (February 1981): 17–26.

———. "Valence–Instrumentality–Expectancy Model Validation Using Selected Accounting Groups." *Accounting, Organizations and Society* (1979): 31–38.

Dillard, J. F., and K. R. Ferris. "Sources of Professional Staff Turnover in Public Accounting Firms: Some Further Evidence." *Accounting, Organizations and Society* (February 1980): 179–186.

Dirsmith, M. W., and M. A. Covaleski. "Informal Communications, Nonformal Communications and Mentoring in Public Accounting Firms." *Accounting, Organizations and Society* (May 1985): 149–169.

Ellyson, R. C., and B. S. Shaw. "The Psychological Assessment and Staff Recruiting." *Journal of Accountancy* (1970): 35–42.

Estes, Ralph. "An Intergenerational Comparison of Socioeconomic Statistics among CPAs, Attorneys, Engineers, and Physicians." *Advances in Accounting* (1984): 3–17.

Ferris, K. R. "Perceived Uncertainty and Job Satisfaction in the Accounting Environment." *Accounting, Organizations and Society* 2, no. 1 (1977): 23–28.

———. "A Test of the Expectancy Theory of Motivation in an Accounting Environment." *Accounting Review* (July 1977): 605–615.

Ferris, K. R., J. F. Dillard, and L. Nethercott. "A Comparison of V–I–E Mode Predictions: A Cross National Study in Professional Accounting Firms." *Accounting, Organizations and Society* (December 1980): 361–368.

Firth, G. "The Impact of Size and Stress in Accounting Firms." *Chartered Accountant in Australia* (August 1982): 20–33.

Galbraith, J. R., and L. L. Cummings. "An Empirical Investigation of the Motivational Determinants of Task Performance: Interactive Effects between Instrumentality-Valence and Motivation-Ability." *Organizational Behavior and Human Performance* (1967): 237–257.

Gray, J. T. "Need and Values in Three Occupations." *Personnel Guidance* (1963): 238–244.

Greller, M. M., and D. M. Herold. "Sources of Feedback: A Preliminary Investigation." *Organizational Behavior and Human Performance* (1975): 244–256.

Hackman, J. R., and E. E. Lawler III. "Employee Reactions to Job Characteristics." *Journal of Applied Psychology* (June 1971): 259–286.

Hall, R. H. "Professionalization and Bureaucratization." *American Sociological Review* (February 1968): 92–104.

Hansen, L. M., and P. M. Muchinsky. "Work as an Information Environment." *Organizational Behavior and Human Performance* (1978): 47–60.

Harrell, A. M., and R. Eickhoff. "Auditors' Influence-Orientation and Their Affective Responses to the 'Big Eight' Work Environment." Unpublished manuscript, University of South Carolina, 1988.

Harrell, A. M., and M. J. Stahl. "McClelland's Trichotomy of Needs Theory and the Job Satisfaction and Work Performance of CPA Firm Professionals." *Accounting, Organizations and Society* (June 1984): 241–252.

Hastings, H., and C. R. Hastings. "Role Relations and Value Adaptation: A Study of the Professional Accountant in Industry." *Sociology* (September 1970): 353–366.

Healy, J. "The Drudge Is Dead." *MBA* (November 1976): 48–56.

Helliwell, T. "The Wages of the Overwork-Burnout." *Chartered Accountant Magazine* (August 1982): 83–87.

Hellriegal, D., and G. White. "Turnover of Professionals in Public Accounting: A Comparative Analysis." *Personnel Psychology* (1973): 239–249.

Herold, D. M., and M. M. Greller. "Feedback: The Definition of the Construct." *Academy of Management Journal* (1977): 142–147.

Holland, J. L. "Explorations of a Theory of Vocational Choice, Part I: Vocational Images and Choice." *Vocational Guidance Quarterly* (1965): 232–239.

_____. "Explorations of a Theory of Vocational Choice, Part IV: A Longitudinal Study Using a Sample of Typical College Students." *Journal of Applied Psychology* (February 1968): 1–37.

_____. *The Psychology of Vocational Choice*. Englewood Cliffs, N.J.: Prentice-Hall, 1973.

_____. "Some Explorations of a Theory of Vocational Choice: One and Two-Year Longitudinal Studies." *Psychological Monographs* 76 (1962).

Ivancevich, John M., and Robert H. Strawser. "A Comparative Analysis of the Job Satisfaction of Industrial Managers and Certified Public Accountants." *Academy of Management Journal* (March 1969): 193–203.

Jablin, F. M. "A Reexamination of the 'Pelz Effect.' " *Human Communication Research* (1980): 210–220.

_____. "Supervisor's Upward Influence, Satisfaction, and Openness in Superior-Subordinate Communication: A Reexamination of the 'Pelz Effect.' " *Human Communication Research* (1980): 210–220.

Jauch, L. R., W. F. Gluck, and R. N. Osbom. "Organizational Loyalty, Professional Commitment, and Academic Research Productivity." *Academy of Management Journal* (June 1978): 84–92.

Jiambalvo, J. "Measures of Accuracy and Congruence in the Performance Evaluation of CPA Personnel: Replications and Extensions." *Journal of Accounting Research* (Spring 1982): 152–161.

_____. "Performance Evaluation and Directed Job Effort: Model Development and Analysis in a CPA Firm Setting." *Journal of Accounting Research* (Autumn 1979): 436–455.

_____. "Performance Evaluations in CPA Firms: An Empirical Test of an Evaluation Model of Directed Job Effort." *Journal of Accounting Research* (Autumn 1979): 436–455.

Jiambalvo, J., and J. Pratt. "Task Complexity and Leadership Effectiveness in CPA Firms." *Accounting Review* (October 1982): 734–750.

Jiambalvo, J., D. J. H. Watson, and J. V. Baumler. "An Examination of Performance Evaluation Decisions in CPA Firm Subunits." *Accounting, Organizations and Society* (March 1983): 13–29.

Jones, A. P., L. R. James, and J. R. Bruni. "Perceived Leadership Behavior and Employee Confidence in the Leader as Moderated by Job Involvement." *Journal of Applied Psychology* (1978): 146–149.

Kane, J., and E. Lawler. " Performance Appraisal Effectiveness: Its Assessments and Determinants." *Research in Organizational Behavior* (1979): 425–478.

Kida, T. E. "Performance Evaluation and Review Meeting Characteristics in Public

Accounting Firms." *Accounting, Organizations and Society* (February 1984): 137–148.

Kimes, J. D. "Handling Stress in the Accounting Profession." *Management Accounting* (September 1977): 17–23.

Kollaritsh, F. P. "Job Migration Patterns of Accounting." *Management Accounting* (September 1968): 52–55.

Konstans, C., and K. Ferris. "Female Turnover in Professional Accounting Firms: Some Preliminary Findings." *Michigan CPA* (Winter 1981): 11–15.

Kusel, J., and N. J. Deyonb. "Internal Auditor Burnout." *Internal Auditor* (October 1983): 22–25.

Lawler, E. E. *Pay and Organizational Effectiveness: A Psychological View.* New York: McGraw-Hill, 1971.

Leathers, P. E. *The Staff Retention Problem in Public Accounting: Background and Questions for Discussion.* New York: American Institute of Certified Public Accountants, 1970.

Libby, Robert. "Comments on Weick." *Accounting Review* (April 1983): 370–374.

Lightner, S., S. Adams, and K. Lightner. "The Influence of Situational, Ethical, and Expectancy Theory Variables on Accountants' Underreporting Behavior." *Auditing: A Journal of Practice and Theory* (Fall 1982): 1–12.

Locke, E. A. "The Nature and Causes of Job Satisfaction." In M. D. Dunnette, ed., *Handbook of Industrial and Organizational Psychology,* pp. 1297–1349. Chicago: Rand McNally, 1976.

McClelland, D. C. "Is Personality Consistent?" In A. Rubin, J. Aronoff, A. Barclay, and R. Zucker, eds., *Further Explorations in Personality.* New York: John Wiley and Sons, 1981.

————. *Power: The Inner Experience.* New York: Irvington, 1975.

Maddi, S. R., M. Hoover, and S. C. Kobasa. "Alienation and Exploratory Behavior." *Journal of Personality and Social Psychology* (1981).

Maher, M., K. Ramanathan, and R. Patterson. "Preference Congruence, Information Accuracy, and Employee Performance," *Journal of Accounting Research* (Autumn 1979): 476–503.

Maslow, A. *Eupsychian Management.* Homewood, Ill.: Irwin, 1965.

Mikhail, A. "Stress: A Psychophysical Conception." *Journal of Human Stress* (June 1981): 9–15.

Mitchell, T. R. "Expectancy Models of Job Satisfaction, Occupational Preference and Effort: A Theoretical, Methodological and Empirical Appraisal." *Psychological Bulletin* (December 1974): 1053–1077.

Mobley, W., R. Griffith, H. Hand, and B. Meglino. "Review and Conceptual Analysis of the Employee Turnover Process." *Psychological Bulletin* (1979): 493–522.

Montagna, P. D. "Professionalization and Bureaucratization in Large Professional Organizations." *American Journal of Sociology* (September 1968): 138–145.

Norris, D. R., and R. E. Nielbuhr. "Professionalism, Organizational Commitment and Job Satisfaction in an Accounting Organization." *Accounting, Organizations and Society* (December 1983): 49–60.

O'Dowd, D. D., and P. C. Beardslee. "College Student Images of a Selected Group of Professions and Occupations." Working Paper, Wesleyan University, April 1960.

O'Reilly, C. A., and K. H. Roberts. "Supervisor Influence and Subordinate Mobility Aspirations as Moderators of Consideration and Initiating Structure." *Journal of Applied Psychology* (1978): 96–102.

Pelz, D. "Influence: A Key to Effective Leadership in the First Line Supervisor." *Personnel* (1952): 209–271.

Pierson, F. C. *The Education of American Businessmen.* New York: McGraw-Hill, 1959.

Porter, L. W., and E. E. Lawler. *Managerial Attitudes and Performance.* Homewood, Ill.: Irwin, 1968.

Porter, L. W., and V. F. Mitchell. "Comparative Study of Need Satisfaction in Military and Business Hierarchies." *Journal of Applied Psychology* (April 1967): 139–144.

Porter, L. W., and R. M. Steers. "Organizational Work and Personal Factors in Employee Turnover and Absenteeism." *Psychological Bulletin* (1973): 151–176.

Porter, L. W., R. M. Steers, R. T. Mowday, and P. V. Boulian. "Organizational Commitment, Job Satisfaction and Turnover among Psychiatric Technicians." *Journal of Applied Psychology* (October 1974): 603–609.

Pratt, J., and J. Jiambalvo. "Determinants of Leader Behavior in an Audit Environment." *Accounting, Organizations and Society* (December 1982): 369–379.

————. "Relationships between Leader Behaviors and Audit Team Performance." *Accounting, Organizations and Society* (August 1981): 133–142.

Price, J. L., and C. W. Mueller. *Handbook of Organizational Measurement.* Marshfield, Mass.: Pitman Publishing, 1986.

Ramanathan, K. V., R. B. Peterson, and M. W. Maher. "Strategic Goals and Performance Criteria in CPA Firms." *Journal of Accountancy* (1976): 56–64.

Rhode, J. G. *Survey on the Influence of Selected Aspects of the Auditors' Work Environment on Professional Performance of Certified Public Accountants: A Study and Report for the Commission on Auditors' Responsibilities.* New York: AICPA, 1977.

Rhode, J. G., J. E. Sorensen, and E. E. Lawler III. "An Analysis of Personal Characteristics Related to Professional Staff Turnover in Public Accounting Firms." *Decision Sciences* (1976): 771–800.

————. "Sources of Professional Staff Turnover in Public Accounting Firms Revealed by the Exit Interview." *Accounting, Organizations and Society* (1977): 165–175.

Roberts, K. H., and C. A. O'Reilly. "Failures in Upward Communication: Three Possible Culprits." *Academy of Management Journal* (1974): 205–215.

Sapp, R. W., and R. Seiler. "Accounting for Performance: Stressful But Satisfying." *Management Accounting* (August 1980): 29–35.

Schroeder, R. G., and L. F. Imdieke. "Local-Cosmopolitan and Bureaucratic Perceptions in Public Accounting Firms." *Accounting, Organizations and Society* (1977): 39–45.

Segal, S. J. "A Psychoanalytic Analysis of Personality Factors in Vocational Choice." *Journal of Counseling Psychology* (1961): 202–210.

Segal, S. J., and R. Szabo. "Identification in Two Vocations: Accountants and Creative Writers." *Personnel and Guidance Journal* (November 1964): 252–255.

Senatra, P. T. "Role Conflict, Role Ambiguity, and Organizational Climate in a Public Accounting Firm." *Accounting Review* (October 1980): 594–603.

Smith, K. J., and M. S. Katzman. "Stress and Internal Auditors." *Accountants' Journal* (1983): 27–32.

Sorensen, J. E. "Professional and Bureaucratic Organization in Public Accounting Firms." *Accounting Review* (July 1967): 553–565.

Sorensen, J. E., and T. L. Sorensen. "The Conflict of Professionals in Bureaucratic Organizations." *Administrative Science Quarterly* (March 1974): 98–106.

Sorensen, J. E., J. G. Rhode, and E. E. Lawler. "The Generation Gap in Public Accounting." *Journal of Accountancy* (1973): 42–50.

Steers, R. N. "Antecedents and Outcomes of Organizational Commitment." *Administrative Science Quarterly* (March 1977): 46–56.

Strawser, R. H., J. M. Ivancevich, and H. L. Lyon. "A Note on the Job Satisfaction of Accountants in Large and Small CPA Firms." *Journal of Accounting Research* (Autumn 1969): 339–345.

Strawser, R. H., J. P. Kelly, and R. Wise. "What Causes Stress for Management Accountants?" *Management Accounting* (March 1982): 32–35.

Thielen, W., Jr. "Recruits for Accounting: How the Class of 1961 Entered the Profession." Unpublished report, American Institute of Certified Public Accountants, 1966.

Turner, A. N., and P. R. Lawrence. *Industrial Jobs and the Workers.* Boston: Harvard University Graduate School of Business Administration, 1965.

Turney, J. R. "Activity Outcome Expectancies and Intrinsic Activity Values as Predictors of Several Motivation Indexes for Technical-Professionals." *Organizational Behavior and Human Performance* (February 1974): 65–82.

Vroom, V. H. *Work and Motivation.* New York: John Wiley and Sons, 1964.

Wager, L. W. "Leadership Style, Influence and Supervisory Role Obligations." *Administrative Science Quarterly* (1965): 391–420.

Watson, David J. H. "The Structure of Project Teams Facing Differentiated Environments: An Exploratory Study in Public Accounting Firms." *Accounting Review* (April 1975): 259–273.

Weick, K. E. "Stress in Accounting Systems." *Accounting Review* (April 1983): 350–369.

Wright, Arnold. "An Investigation of the Engagement Evaluation Process for Staff Auditors." *Journal of Accounting Research* (Spring 1982): 227–239.

———. "Performance Appraisal of Staff Auditors." *CPA Journal* (November 1980): 37–43.

———. "Performance Evaluation of Staff Auditors: A Behaviorally Anchored Rating Scale." *Auditing: A Journal of Practice and Theory* (Spring 1986): 95–108.

Zweig, J. "Individualisms—A Recruiting Aid for Local Practitioners." *Journal of Accountancy* (1969): 80.

7

CULTURAL DETERMINISM IN ACCOUNTING

A growing body of research supports the idea that there exists a cultural determinism in accounting, whereby a country's culture determines its choice of accounting techniques and the perception of related phenomena and attitudes. This new endeavor takes a cross-cultural perspective on management known as comparative management research. The objective of this chapter is to cover the development and scope of comparative management research and its potential impact on accounting practice and research.

THE CONCEPT OF CULTURE

Societies present similarities and differences in their cultural patterns. A culture shapes and is shaped by its people. As an interpretive tool, a culture can constrain people into a less than objective understanding of other cultures. As Triandis has pointed out, people from other cultures tend to appear strange, peculiar, or often crazy.[1] In a sense, culture controls human behavior in nonrational and persistent ways.[2]

The concept of culture is illusive; no consensus exists on its definition. In their review of how the concept of culture has been used in the past 150 years, Kroeber and Kluckhohn proposed the following definition:

Culture consists of patterns, explicit and implicit, of and for behavior acquired and transmitted by symbols, constituting the distinctive achievements of human groups, including their embodiments in artifacts; the essential core of culture consists of traditional (i.e., historically derived and selected) ideas and especially their attached values; culture systems may on the one hand be considered as products of action, on the other as conditioning elements of future action.[3]

The distinctive achievements that constitute culture include both the physical objects (or physical culture) made by humans and subjective objects (or subjective culture), which are the subjective responses to what humans have made. Triandis elaborated on this last concept as follows:

Subjective culture refers to variables that are attributes of the cognitive structures of groups of people. The *analysis* of subjective culture refers to variables extracted from consistencies in their responses and results in a kind of "map" drawn by a scientist which outlines the subjective culture of a particular group. In short, when we observe consistent responses to classes of stimuli that have some quality in common, we assume that some "mediators" (attitudes, norms, values, etc.) are responsible for their consistencies. It is the cognitive structures which "mediate" between stimuli and responses in different cultural settings that we wish to study.[4]

Culture is also not a monolithic concept.[5] Anthropological concepts of culture have led to the use of many different metaphors for varied purposes in organizational research. Malinowski's functionalism, with its view of culture as an instrument that serves human biological and psychological needs, motivated cross-cultural, or comparative, management research.[6] Radcliffe-Brown's structuralism, with its view of culture as an adaptive regulatory mechanism that unites individuals in social structures, motivated research on corporate culture.[7] Goodenough's ethnoscience, with its view of culture as a system of shared cognition in which the human mind generates culture by means of a finite number of rules, motivated research on organizational cognition.[8] Geertz's symbolic anthropology, with its view that culture is a system of shared symbols and meanings and that symbolic action needs to be interpreted, read, or deciphered in order to be understood, motivated research on organizational symbolism.[9] Finally, Levi-Strauss's structuralism, with its view of culture as a projection of the mind's universal unconscious infrastructure, motivated research on unconscious processes and organization.[10]

CROSS-CULTURAL RESEARCH AND COMPARATIVE MANAGEMENT

The basic objective of cross-cultural research is to test the universality of psychological laws in order to understand whatever cultural differences are observed. Berry provided the following explanation:

Cross-cultural psychology seeks to comprehend the systematic covariation between cultural and behavioral variables. Included within the term *cultural* are ecological and societal variables, and within the term *behavioral* are inferred variables. Thus the purpose is to understand how two systems, at the levels of group- and individual-analyses, relate to each other. Ideally, of course, more than covariation is sought; under some conditions *causal* relations may be inferred as well.[11]

Cross-cultural research was, in fact, started by cultural anthropologists, but it gradually attracted the interest of other social scientists and international business researchers in particular. Comparative management is therefore a subject of cross-cultural research that aims at understanding the cultural environments of international business. Issues in comparative management that have been examined to date include: attitude change; attitudes and values; conflict resolution and ethnocentricity; decision making and bargaining; economics; education, creativity, and intelligence; efficiency and productivity; international business; interpersonal behavior; labor; language and communication; leadership; management development; motivation and achievement; national character and stereotypes; occupational prestige; organizational structure; perception; personality; personnel selection and testing; satisfaction; social and technical change; and training for cross-cultural contacts.[12] These variables, generally as dependent variables, are supposed to be influenced by culture, the independent variable.

Three approaches characterize comparative management research: the universalist approach, the value systems approach, and the cultural cluster approach. The universalist, or cultural universals, approach aims to find the circumstances common to all cultures. In an article first published in 1952, anthropologist Clyde Kluckhohn argued for such an approach:

In principle . . . there is a generalized framework that underlies the more apparent and striking facts of cultural relativity. All cultures constitute so many somewhat distinctive answers to essentially the same questions posed by human biology and by the generalities of the human situation. . . . Every society's patterns for living must provide approved and sanctioned ways of dealing with such universal circumstances as the existence of two sexes; the helplessness of infants; the need for satisfaction of the elementary biological requirements such as food, warmth, and sex; the presence of individuals of different ages and of different physical and other capacities.[13]

Murdock has provided an exhaustive list of "cultural universals."[14] This approach obviously stresses the similarities rather than the differences among cultures and has limited impact on comparative management research.

Another approach classifies cultures according to differences in their value systems. People of a culture, faced with basic human problems, develop value systems to define how the problems can best be solved. A precise anthropological definition of value was proposed by Kluckhohn: "A value is a conception, explicit or implicit, distinctive of an individual or characteristic of a group, of the desirable which influences the selection from available modes, means and ends of actions."[15] A definition that runs through contemporary theoretical approaches to values was proposed by McLaughlin:

Values (1) are not directly observable, (2) have cognitive, affective, and connotative elements, (3) do not operate independently of the biological organization or social field. . . . Values are conceived of as (4) referring to standards of the desirable rather than to the desired, (5) hierarchically organized in the personality system, and (6) relevant to actual behavior as a function of personal commitment and situational factors.[16]

Cross-cultural research has shown that value systems differ from one culture to another and that "value profits" can be developed for various cultures. Several instruments still in use have been used for the task, including the following:

1. Allport, Vernon, and Lindzey's values, which classify human ideas and activities as theoretical, economic, aesthetic, political, and religious.[17]

2. Morris's ways to live, which measure values as philosophical orientations about ways to live.[18]

3. Kluckhohn and Strodtbeck's value theory, which focuses on existential and evaluative beliefs.[19]

4. Sarnoff's human value index, which views values as "values of aggrandizement"— reflected in wealth, prestige, and power—and as "values of realization"—reflected in humanitarian, egalitarian, aesthetic, and intellectual areas.[20]

5. Rokeach's value survey, which classifies eighteen values as terminal and eighteen values as instrumental.

The value systems approach led to results supporting the existence of different cultural value systems that have impact on behavior.[21]

Finally, the systems approach to comparative management research focuses on the systems and subsystems that define a given culture. For example, Harris and Moran identified eight such subsystems: kinship, education, economy, politics, religion, association, health, and recreation.[22] Others have attempted to cluster countries on attitudinal dimensions by defining the country rather than the culture as the unit of analysis. One review of the literature identified eight cluster studies.[23] These included Haire, Ghiselli, and Porter; Sirota and Greenwood; Ronen and Kraut; Hofstede; Griffith, Horn, DeNisi, and Kirchner; Hofstede; Redding; and Badawy.[24]

The objective of these clustering studies was to show that certain aspects of employee attitude and behavior can be generalized to a particular society and that the differences between these aspects can be explained by cultural or national differences. Several variables were examined in these studies: work goal importance; need deficiency, fulfillment, and job satisfaction; managerial and organizational variables; and work role and interpersonal orientation. The writers tended to cluster geographically, linguistically, and religiously, as well as on the basis of technological development. These clusters, when synthesized, included the Anglo cluster, the Germanic and Nordic cluster, the Latin European cluster, the Latin American cluster, the Near Eastern cluster, the Far Eastern cluster, and the Arab cluster. Some of the clusters were, however, ill-defined in these studies. Despite the limitations inherent to any type of cross-cultural research, the clustering approach provided a worthwhile step toward theoretical development. As stated by Ronen and Shenkar:

The clusters produced in the present synthesis can be used as a general framework of reference for theoreticians and practitioners. Researchers in the future should put these clusters to continuous empirical testing. They should be concerned, however, not only with the predictive qualities of clustering, but also with its promotion of theoretical development. Rather than just inquire about the nature of differences in employee work goals, future researchers should proceed to investigate the underlying cultural and social traits that may produce these differences.[25]

APPROACHES TO RESEARCHING CROSS-CULTURAL MANAGEMENT ISSUES

Cross-cultural management studies have been found to vary in their assumptions about universality, their ways of dealing with similarities and differences, and their methodologies used. In a methodological review of the literature, Adler delineated six approaches to researching cross-cultural management issues:

1. The *parochial* approach, which focuses on one country, resulting in single-country studies.

2. The *ethnocentric* approach, which replicates one-country research in foreign countries, resulting in second-culture replication studies.

3. The *polycentric* approach, which conducts research in foreign countries, resulting in studies conducted in many cultures.

4. The *comparative* approach, which focuses on differences in various cultures, resulting in studies contrasting organizations across cultures.

5. The *geocentric* approach, which investigates organizations operating in more than one culture, resulting in international management studies.

6. The *synergistic* approach, which focuses on creating universality, resulting in cross-cultural management studies.[26]

METHODOLOGIES IN RESEARCHING CROSS-CULTURAL MANAGEMENT ISSUES

Two typologies have been used to classify and analyze international business and comparative management research. Schöllhammer referred to five approaches: conceptualizing, synthesizing, descriptive, analytical-interpretive, and generalizing-normative.[27] Boddewyn and Nath referred to three categories: descriptive, conceptual, and hypothesis-testing.[28] Each of Boddewyn and Nath's methodologies are examined next.

Descriptive Studies

The descriptive studies in cross-cultural management have generally been exploratory in nature and have relied on specific data collection methods such as interviews, case-collection, and survey techniques. They have tended to report the results of studies that focus on a particular research question. These questions have dealt with matters such as (1) financial issues, for example the use of corporate finance techniques, financial control systems, or capital budgeting techniques; (2) personnel issues, for instance the selection, compensation, and development of international executives, job satisfaction of managers, or such topics as managerial attitudes, leadership, and motivation in organizations; and (3) other functional area issues, namely marketing, production, or accounting. The findings of these studies are rarely generalizable and are constrained by various limitations. Witness the following comment:

A critical analysis of a large number of empirical research studies in international business that can be placed into the "descriptive" category leads one to the conclusion that these studies are generally one-dimensional, i.e., narrow in scope, and they tend to be based on a relatively small sample from which the *empirical data* are derived. In addition, the information in most cases is gathered by means of questionnaire surveys among a randomly selected sample. In general, these descriptive studies are not directed toward the refutation or confirmation of specific hypotheses and thus their potential contribution to theory development is impaired.[29]

Conceptual Studies

Conceptual studies have aimed at deductively building a conceptual framework and/or a model of comparative management. The first example of a conceptual study was provided by Harbison and Myers's attempt to construct a framework for comparing management in the industrial world.[30] Their analysis compared managers from three dimensions: (1) management as a resource, and the extent of its use; (2) management as a system of authority (dictational, paternalistic, constitutional, or democratic); and (3) management as a class or elite (patrimonial, political, or professional). The situations of twelve countries were compared using secondary sources and interviews.

The second example of a conceptual study was provided by Farmer and Richman's conceptual model of comparative management.[31] The model postulated that external constraints (educational, sociological, legal, political, and economic) *affect* elements of the management process (planning, organizing, staffing, directing, controlling, and policy making), which also *affect* management and managerial effectiveness, therefore *determining* firm efficiency and system efficiency.

Another example, provided by Perlmutter, classified multinational corporations, on the basis of the attitudes taken by their top management toward multinational business policies, as ethnocentric (home-country oriented), polycentric (host-country oriented) or geocentric (world-oriented).[32] He deduced that performance evaluation in a centralized ethnocentric firm will be tightly controlled by the parent company while in a decentralized polycentric or geocentric company it will be less controlled by the parent company. Perlmutter also found that more conflict situations arise in ethnocentric and polycentric cases than in geocentric cases, which led to a maximization of organizational effectiveness in the geocentric cases.

A fourth example, provided by Negandhi and Prasad, viewed management and enterprise effectiveness (the effectiveness of the economic system as a whole) as the result of specific management practices (planning, organizing, staffing, motivation and directing, and controlling), which in turn are considered to be determined by both management philosophy (management attitudes toward employees, consumers, suppliers, stockholders, government, and community) and environmental factors (socioeconomic, educational, political, legal, and cultural).[33] When applying the model to American subsidiaries in Argentina, Brazil, India, the Philippines, and Uruguay, along with local firms, Negandhi and Prasad found that managers in American subsidiaries were more likely to debate than managers in locally owned firms, and that there were few differences in their managerial styles or effectiveness.[34] To test the Farmer and Richman model against that of Negandhi and Prasad, a study by Kelley and Worthley compared similarities and differences in the managerial attitudes of Japanese, Caucasian American, and Japanese-American managers working in financial institutions, given previous research by Kitano suggesting an attachment to Japanese attitudes and values by Japanese-Americans in Hawaii.[35] Their findings supported Farmer and Richman's thesis on the role of culture in shaping managerial attitudes. Their findings, however, do not mean that managerial philosophy is not an important variable. In fact, it may act as an important independent variable in the role of culture in shaping managerial attitudes. Ronan emphasized the point as follows:

We suggest that managerial philosophy may be important and that philosophy and culture may not necessarily coincide. To the extent that philosophy fits well into the prevailing culture, both variables should yield similar behavioral consequences. To the extent that philosophy does not fit in with the prevailing culture, the impact of culture may diminish. Culture may be the primary variable from a theoretical standpoint, but its impact depends on precisely this fit. The Farmer and Richman and Negandhi and Prasad model may thus *complement* each other—the relative importance of either model may be expected to vary from country to country.[36]

Hypothesis-Testing Studies

These studies were first structured around specific hypotheses then conducted after the securing of adequate data to test whether what was postulated was, in fact, true. They can be classified as either (1) analytical-interpretive studies aimed at classifying, explaining, and evaluating new general knowledge given established hypotheses and existing, related research findings, or (2) generalizing-normative studies aimed at drawing generalizations from empirical results. An evaluation of these studies resulted in the following conclusions:

1. The cross-cultural comparisons led to the development of some conceptual models.
2. Comparative management research highlighted the role of the environment.
3. Most studies of foreign management systems (or parts thereof) were not explicitly comparative.
4. There was also an uneven coverage of actors, processes, structures, and functions in the comparative studies of management systems.
5. A lack of rigor characterized many of the studies.
6. The research provided some valid generalizations although findings were apt to be more tentative and suggestive than conclusive.[37]

Methodological problems have also been raised. For example, Berrien pointed to four of them: the comparability of respondents or subject samples, the ethnic influences on research questions, the comparability of research instruments, and the circumstances under which ethnically detached or culturally bound interpretations can be justified.[38] Ronen pointed to ten factors that could affect the international validity of the experimental results in cross-cultural research: emic versus etic distinction, problems of instrumentation—construction and validation, data collection techniques, sampling design issues, data analysis, problems of translation/stimulus equivalence, static group comparisons, lack of knowledge of others' way of seeing things, problems of resolving contradictory findings, and administrative problems.[39]

To avoid some of these problems Berrien proposed a superego cross-cultural research and stated the following:

The best cross-cultural research is that which 1) engages the collaborative efforts of two or more investigators of different countries, who are 2) strongly supported by institutions in their respected countries, to 3) address researchable problems of a common concern not only to the science of psychology, but 4) relevant to the social problems of our time. Such collaborative enterprises would begin with 5) the joint definition of problems, 6) employ comparable methods, 7) pool data that would be "owned" by the collaborators jointly who are free to 8) report their own interpretations to their own constituents, but 9) are obligated to strive for interpretations acceptable to a world community of scholars.[40]

Other shortcomings of cross-cultural research include:

1. The absence of a theoretical base;
2. The presence of ethnocentrism;

3. Heavy reliance on convenience samples;

4. Over-emphasis on cultural variance;

5. Studies limited to one nation rather than being truly comparative;

6. Problems of linguistic meanings, failing to take into account the limitation of language in conveying equivalent meanings in two or more languages;

7. The assumption that important factors in one nation have equal value in another nation;

8. The use of a single research method in general questionnaires;

9. The limitations of cross sectional studies, providing an image of reality that is confined to one point in time;

10. The lack of data to support conclusions;

11. The bias toward studying large corporations;

12. The rare instances of using samples of employees and managers across hierarchical levels across nations;

13. The failure to state and test a priori hypotheses;

14. The over-emphasis on studying attitudes rather than behavior;

15. The unbalance in terms of areas of the world studies, with critical ignorance of the third world;

16. The failure to articulate cultural and other explanations.[41]

ACCOUNTING RESEARCH OF RELEVANCE TO CROSS-CULTURAL RESEARCH

Culture has been considered to be an important environmental factor impacting upon the accounting system of a country.[42] It has also been argued that (1) accounting is, in fact, determined by culture,[43] and (2) the lack of consensus across different countries on what constitutes proper accounting methods is the result of their purpose being cultural not technical.[44] These arguments point to a cultural determinism in accounting whereby the culture of a given country determines the choice of its accounting techniques and the perception of its various accounting phenomena. Several studies have examined the cultural determinism thesis both conceptually and empirically.

Conceptual Examination of the Cultural Determinism Thesis

Conceptual examination of cultural determinism in accounting stems from cultural anthropology. Jaggi examined the impact of the cultural environment and individual orientations on information disclosures.[45] He argued that the value orientations of managers, products of the cultural environment, have an important influence on financial disclosures. The differences in the value orientation of individuals examined by Parsons and Shils were used to identify the varied patterns of value orientations of individuals between countries.[46] Basically, the cultural background of an individual affects his or her choice between *universalism*, a value orientation toward institutionalized obligations to society, and *particularism*, a value orientation toward institutionalized obligations of friendship. Countries that exhibit complex technology, emphasize individual independence and mobility, and value competition and achieved status tend to adopt a universalistic value orientation. Countries that are less technical, less scientific, and less urban tend to adopt a particularistic value orientation. Extending the impact of these values to the type of disclosures, Jaggi argued that managers' value orientations will influence disclosure decisions to reflect management's commitment to, or repudiation of, disclosure of adequate and accurate information:

Managers with a universalistic value orientation are likely to be deeply committed to disclosing relatively reliable information compared to those with a particularistic orientation. . . .

Managers with a particularistic value orientation will have different types of attitudes. They are not likely to realize their obligation to outsiders or to society. Instead their obligations will primarily relate to family members owning and managing the firm.[47]

Following Jaggi's contribution, various attempts were made to identify a set of specific societal values or cultural factors that influence accounting practices. Arpan and Radebaugh identified conservatism, secrecy, attitudes toward business, and attitudes toward the accounting profession as cultural factors that can influence accounting practices.[48] Gray developed a model linking cultural dimensions to four value dimensions of the accounting subculture: professionalism, uniformity, conservatism, and secrecy.[49] The cultural dimensions were those proposed by Hofstede: individualism versus collectivism, large versus small power-distance, strong versus weak uncertainty-avoidance, and masculinity versus femininity.[50]

The individualism versus collectivism dimension represents the degree of integration a society maintains among its members, or the relationship between an individual and his or her fellow individuals. While individualists are expected to take care of themselves and their immediate families, only collectivists are expected to remain emotionally integrated into in-groups, which protect them in exchange for unquestioning loyalty.

Large versus small power-distance has to do with the extent to which members of a society accept an unequal distribution of power in institutions and organizations. In large power-distance societies, people tend to accept a hierarchical order, whereas in small power-distance societies, people tend to look for equality and demand justification for any existing power inequalities.

Strong versus weak uncertainty-avoidance expresses the degree to which the members of a society feel uncomfortable with uncertainty and ambiguity. In strong uncertainty-avoidance societies, people do not tolerate ambiguity and try to control it at all costs, whereas in weak uncertainty-avoidance societies, people are more tolerant of ambiguity and simply live with it.

The masculinity versus femininity dimension represents the nature of the social divisions of sex roles. Masculine roles imply a preference for achievement, assertiveness, making money, sympathy for the strong, and so on. Feminine roles imply a preference for warm relationships, modesty, care for the weak, preservation of the environment, and quality of life, among other things.

Building on the presumed relationships between societal values (proposed by Hofstede) and the accounting subculture (proposed by Gray), Perera and Mathews formulated the following hypothesis:

1. The greater the individualism and the smaller the uncertainty avoidance within a society *then* the greater the professionalism (or the smaller the uniformity) exhibited within an accounting sub-culture.

corollary

2. The less the individualism and the greater the uncertainty avoidance within a society the less the professionalism (or the greater the uniformity) exhibited within an accounting sub-culture.

3. The greater the uncertainty avoidance and the less the individualism within a society then the greater the conservatism exhibited within an accounting sub-culture.

corollary

4. The smaller the uncertainty avoidance and the greater the individualism within a society *then* the smaller the conservatism exhibited within an accounting sub-culture.

5. The greater the uncertainty avoidance and the less the individualism within a society *then* the greater the secrecy exhibited within an accounting sub-culture.

corollary

6. The smaller the uncertainty avoidance and the greater the individualism within a society *then* the smaller the secrecy exhibited within an accounting sub-culture.[51]

Empirical Examination of the Cultural Determinism Thesis

Accounting research relevant to cultural determinism in accounting is in its infancy. One anthropological study explored the degree to which accounting systems influence perception of opportunities by comparing the local view of business possibilities derived from the native system of accounting in Cuanago, a Tarascan village in Mexico, with more formal accounting methods.[52] In his study, Acheson found that the native accounting system, a crude cash-flow-based system, did not permanently block responsiveness to opportunities where they existed. However, it confused the view of opportunities, leading to many poor business decisions, and hence played a critical role in influencing further business decisions.

Many other accounting issues have been examined to test the cultural determinism thesis in accounting. First, the issue of whether the same accounting information can be perceived differently by different cultural groups was examined by Chevalier.[53] The perceptions of French Canadians and English Canadians were found not to differ with regard to the importance of conventional published financial information. French Canadians had been expected to place more importance on additional and nonconventional information such as data on human resources, earnings forecasts, and management philosophy.

Chevalier's subjects were largely students from the Francophone and Anglophone sections of Canada. Other groups examined, however, included investors and financial analysts from diverse cultural settings. Chang and Most investigated the uses of financial statements by individual investors, institutional investors, and financial analysts from three countries—the United States, the United Kingdom, and New Zealand—all of which have large capital markets and well-organized stock exchanges that tend to function in a similar manner.[54] The results showed a strong belief in the importance of corporate annual reports as a source of information for investment decisions and a stronger belief that the most important parts of the corporate annual report pertained to financial data. The study also examined the composition of the three financial user groups and found that institutional investors and financial analysts comprised homogeneous groups while individual investors were a diverse group.

Because the decisions of most investors in any country are greatly influenced by the opinions of financial analysts, Belkaoui, Kahl, and Peyrard examined the different needs of financial analysts in Canada, the United States, and Europe.[55] Any differences in perception were hypothesized to be primarily due to differences in the European and North American methods of investing. The European approach has been more debt-oriented, with analysis concentrated on the balance sheet. In brief, the method requires the preparation of three reports: the profit and loss account, the financing table, and the balance sheet. These reports are presented in vertical form to highlight a set of totals and subtotals deemed to be of interest to financial analysts. The reports offer a convenient means of achieving comparisons of European accounting information. In contrast, the North American method is oriented more toward equity investment, the income statement, and corporate earning power.

As expected, the study demonstrated a high degree of consensus among North American financial analysts on the informational items of value to equity investors, but there was quite a divergence of opinion when the North Americans were compared with their European counterparts. This difference was attributed to institutional differences in the accounting and investment environments of Europe and North America, as well as to differences in outlook, with Europeans more interested in balance sheet information while North Americans tended to be more concerned about the income statement.

While all the above studies investigated the cultural determinism thesis as it affects the choice of accounting techniques internationally, Belkaoui investigated its impact on the degree of professional self-regulation.[56] More specifically, the four dimensions of individualism, power-distance, uncertainty-avoidance, and masculinity were investigated in terms of their impact on the degree of professional self-regulation of the accounting profession internationally. The results of the empirical study showed that the degree of professional self-regulation in accounting internationally is negatively influenced by the uncertainty-avoidance and individualism dimensions and positively affected by the masculinity dimension. Basically, societies where people tolerate ambiguity are collectivist in their relations with others, show a preference for competitiveness, achievement motivation, assertiveness, and the enjoyment of material success, and have ideal conditions for professional self-regulation.

Finally, Soeters and Schreuder used Hofstede's value survey model to investigate the interaction between national and organizational culture on accounting firms within a particular country (the Netherlands).[57] Three local offices of international Big Eight accounting firms, all having strong U.S. orientations in their organizational philosophies and policies, and three Dutch firms were chosen. The results showed that for two of Hofstede's four cultural dimensions—uncertainty-avoidance and masculinity—U.S. culture had significant effects on the organizational culture of the Big Eight firms.

ACCOUNTING RESEARCH OF RELEVANCE TO THE COGNITIVE VIEW OF CULTURE

The branch of cognitive anthropology known as ethnoscience can be used to explicate the cultural determinism thesis in accounting. Ethnoscience views culture as a system of shared cognition or a system of knowledge and beliefs: "a unique system for perceiving and organizing material phenomena, things, events, behaviors and emotions."[58] It is generated by the human mind "by means of a finite number of rules or means of unconscious logic."[59]

Using the cognitive emphasis, national cultures act as networks of subjective meanings or shared frames of reference that members of each culture share to varying degrees and that, to an external observer, appear to function in a rule-like or grammar-like manner. Relating this to accounting and the cultural determinism thesis, it can be stated that cultural groups in accounting create different cognitions or systems of knowledge for intracultural and/or intercultural communications. These, in turn, lead to a different understanding of accounting and social relationships. This led Belkaoui and Picur to test the following hypothesis:

"The perceptions of accounting concepts, as measured by individual weights assigned by users to the dimensions of a common perceptual space, are a function of cultural group affiliation."[60]

Accordingly, perceptions of a selected set of accounting concepts were subjected to analysis using two separate multidimensional scaling techniques to evaluate the intercultural perceptual differences of three cultural groups, made up of Canadian, American, and British partners and managers of a single international Big Eight accounting firm. The cultural determinism thesis provided the research hypothesis on the relationship between cultural membership and concept perception. The multidimensional scaling techniques were applied to the matrix of subjects' similarity judgments on pairs of concepts, thus enabling the identification of three dimensions. The dimensions were labeled conjunctive, relational, and disjunctive, and assumed to be related to the criteria employed by the subjects in their similarity rankings. An analysis of variance of individual saliences on each dimension provided evidence of cultural determinism for the three dimensions. These findings supported the contention that accountants from different cultural groups have different cognition or systems for perceiving and organizing accounting knowledge in general, and different concept perception in particular.

CONCLUSION

Cultural determinism research in accounting is in its initial phases. The existing empirical findings point to culture as an important determinant of perceptions, attitudes, and behavior internationally. Future research should expand the analysis to the various auditing and accounting tasks that comprise the accounting craft and investigate how they are affected by national, organizational, and occupational cultures.

NOTES

1. Harry C. Triandis, *Interpersonal Behavior* (Monterey, Calif.: Brooks/Cole, 1977).

2. G. Hofstede, *Culture's Consequences: International Differences in Work Related Values* (Beverly Hills, Calif.: Sage, 1980); E. T. Hall, *The Silent Language* (Greenwich, Conn.: Fawcett, 1959).

3. A. L. Kroeber and Clyde Kluckhohn, *Culture: A Critical Review of Concepts and Definitions* (Cambridge, Mass.: Peabody Museum, 1952), p. 81.

4. Harry C. Triandis, *The Analysis of Subjective Culture* (New York: John Wiley and Sons, 1972), p. 3.

5. M. H. B. Perera and M. R. Mathews, "The Interrelationship of Culture and Accounting with Particular Reference to Social Accounting" (Discussion paper no. 59, Department of Accounting and Finance, Massey University, New Zealand, 1987).

6. B. Malinowski, *A Scientific Theory of Culture* (Chapel Hill: University of North Carolina Press, 1944).

7. A. R. Radcliffe-Brown, *Structure and Function in Primitive Society* (New York: Free Press, 1968).

8. Ward H. Goodenough, *Culture, Language and Society* (Reading, Mass.: Addison-Wesley, 1971).

9. Clifford Geertz, *The Interpretation of Culture* (New York: Basic Books, 1973).

10. Claude Levi-Strauss, *Structural Anthropology* (Chicago: University of Chicago Press, 1983).

11. J. Berry, "An Ecological Approach to Cross-Cultural Psychology," *Netherlands Journal of Psychology* 30 (1973): 379–392.

12. Karlene H. Roberts, "On Looking at an Elephant," *Psychological Bulletin* 74, no. 5 (1970): 329.

13. Clyde Kluckhohn, "Universal Categories of Culture," in S. Tax, ed., *Anthropology Today* (Chicago: University of Chicago Press, 1962), pp. 317–318.

14. G. P. Murdock, "Common Denominator of Cultures," in R. Linton, ed., *The Science of Man in the World Crisis* (New York: Columbia University Press, 1945), pp. 12–142.

15. C. Kluckhohn, "Values and Value-Orientations in the Theory of Actions: An Exploration in Definition and Classification," in Talcott Parsons and Edward A. Shils, eds., *Towards a General Theory of Action* (Cambridge, Mass.: Harvard University Press, 1951), p. 395.

16. G. McLaughlin, "Values in Behavioral Science," *Journal of Religion and Health* (1965).

17. G. W. Allport, P. E. Vernon, and G. Lindzey, *A Study of Values* (Boston: Houghton Mifflin, 1960).

18. C. Morris, *Varieties of Human Value* (Chicago: University of Chicago Press, 1956).

19. F. R. Kluckhohn and F. Strodtbeck, *Variations in Value Orientations* (Westport, Conn.: Greenwood Press, 1961).

20. I. Sarnoff, *Society with Tears* (Secaucus, N.J.: Citadel Press, 1960).

21. J. Rokeach, *The Nature of Human Values* (New York: Free Press, 1973).

22. P. R. Harris and R. T. Moran, *Managing Cultural Differences* (Houston: Gulf Publishing, 1974).

23. S. Ronen and O. Shenkar, "Clustering Countries on Attitudinal Dimensions: A Review and Synthesis," *Academy of Management Review* 10, no. 3 (1985): 435–454.

24. M. Haire, E. E. Ghiselli, and L. W. Porter, *Managerial Thinking: An International Study* (New York: John Wiley and Sons, 1966); D. Sirota and J. M. Greenwood, "Understand Your Overseas Work Force," *Harvard Business Review* 49, no. 1 (1971): 53–60; S. Ronen and A. I. Kraut, "Similarities among Countries Based on Employee Work Values and Attitudes," *Columbia Journal of World Business* 12, no. 2 (1977): 89–96; G. Hofstede, "Nationality and Espoused Values of Managers," *Journal of Applied Psychology* 61, no. 2 (1976): 148–155; R. W. Griffith, P. W. Horn, A. DeNisi, and W. Kirchner, "A Multivariate of Managerial Attitudes, Beliefs and Behavior in England and France" (Paper presented at the 40th Annual Meeting of the Academy of Management, Detroit, August 1980); Hofstede, *Culture's Consequences;* S. G. Redding, "Some Perceptions of Psychological Needs among Managers in South-East Asia" (Paper presented at the Third International Conference at the International Association for Cross-Cultural Psychology, Tilburg, Holland, July 1976); M. R. Badawy, "Managerial Attitudes and

Need Orientations of Mid Eastern Executives: An Empirical Cross-Cultural Analysis'' (Proceedings of the 39th Annual Meeting of the Academy of Management, Atlanta, (August 1979).

25. Ronen and Shenkar, ''Clustering Countries on Attitudinal Dimensions,'' p. 453.

26. Nancy Adler, ''A Typology of Management Studies Involving Culture,'' *Journal of International Business Studies* (Fall 1983): 29–47.

27. Hans Schöllhammer, ''Strategies and Methodologies in International Business and Comparative Management Research,'' *Management International Review* (1973): 6–32.

28. J. Boddewyn and R. Nath, ''Comparative Management Studies: An Assessment,'' *Management International Review* 10 (1970): 3–11.

29. Schöllhammer, ''Strategies and Methodologies in International Business and Comparative Management Research,'' p. 6.

30. F. Harbison and C. A. Myers, *Management in the Industrial World* (New York: McGraw-Hill, 1959).

31. Richard N. Farmer and Barry M. Richman, ''A Model for Research in Comparative Management,'' *California Management Review* (Winter 1964): 55–68; Richard N. Farmer and Barry M. Richman, *Comparative Management and Economic Progress* (Homewood, Ill.: R. D. Irwin, 1965).

32. Howard V. Perlmutter, ''The Tortuous Evolution of the Multinational Corporation,'' *Columbia Journal of World Business* (January–February 1969): 9–18.

33. Anant R. Negandhi and S. Benjamin Prasad, *Comparative Management* (New York: Appleton-Century, 1971).

34. Ibid.

35. L. Kelley and R. Worthley, ''The Role of Culture in Comparative Management: A Cross-Cultural Perspective,'' *Academy of Management Journal* 24, no. 1 (1981): 164–173; H. Kitano, *Japanese-Americans: Evolution of a Subculture* (New York: Prentice-Hall, 1968).

36. S. Ronen, *Comparative and Multinational Management* (New York: John Wiley and Sons, 1986).

37. Boddewyn and Nath, ''Comparative Management Studies,'' pp. 5–8.

38. F. Kenneth Berrien, ''Methodological and Related Problems in Cross-Cultural Research,'' *International Journal of Psychology* 2 (1967): 33–43.

39. S. Ronen, *Comparative and Multinational Management*, p. 47.

40. F. Kenneth Berrien, ''A Super-Ego for Cross-Cultural Research,'' *International Journal of Psychology* 5 (1970): 33–34.

41. Richard Peterson, ''Future Directions in Comparative Management Research: Where We Have Been and Where We Should Be Going,'' *International Management Newsletter* (Fall 1986): 6–8.

42. Ahmed Belkaoui, *International Accounting* (Westport, Conn.: Greenwood Press, 1985).

43. William J. Violet, ''The Development of International Accounting Standards: An Anthropological Perspective,'' *International Journal of Accounting Education and Research* (Spring 1983).

44. G. Hofstede, ''The Ritual Nature of Accounting Systems'' (Paper presented at EIASM Workshop on Accounting and Culture, Amsterdam, June 1985).

45. B. L. Jaggi, ''Impact of the Cultural Environment on Financial Disclosure,'' *International Journal of Accounting Education and Research* 16, no. 2 (1982): 75–84.

46. Talcott Parsons and Edward A. Shils, eds., *Towards a General Theory of Action* (Cambridge, Mass.: Harvard University Press, 1951).

47. Jaggi, "Impact of the Cultural Environment on Financial Disclosure," p. 81.

48. J. S. Arpan and L. H. Radebaugh, *International Accounting and Multinational Enterprises* (New York: John Wiley and Sons, 1985).

49. S. J. Gray, "Cultural Influences and the International Classification of Accounting Systems" (Paper presented at EIASM Workshop on Accounting and Culture, Amsterdam, June 1985).

50. Hofstede, *Culture's Consequences.*

51. M. H. B. Perera and M. R. Mathews, "The Interrelationship of Culture and Accounting with Particular Reference to Social Accounting."

52. J. Acheson, "Accounting Concepts and Economic Opportunities in a Tarascan Village: Emic and Etic Views," *Human Organization* (Spring 1979): 83–91.

53. G. Chevalier, "Should Accounting Practices Be Universal?" *CA Magazine* (July 1977): 47–50.

54. L. S. Chang and K. S. Most, "An International Comparison of Investor Uses of Financial Statements," *International Journal of Accounting Education and Research* (Fall 1981): 43–60.

55. A. Belkaoui, A. Kahl, and J. Peyrard, "Information Needs of Financial Analysts: An International Comparison," *International Journal of Accounting Education and Research* (Fall 1977): 19–27.

56. Ahmed Belkaoui, "Cultural Determinism and Professional Self-Regulation in Accounting" (Manuscript, University of Illinois at Chicago, 1989).

57. Joseph Soeters and Hein Schreuder, "Interactions between National and Organizational Cultures in Accounting Firms," *Accounting, Organizations and Society* 13, no. 1 (1988): 75–85.

58. Ino Rossi and Edwin O'Higgins, "The Development of Theories of Culture," in Ino Rossi, ed., *People in Culture* (New York: Praeger, 1980), p. 63.

59. Ibid., pp. 63–64.

60. Ahmed Belkaoui and Ronald D. Picur, "Cultural Determinism and the Perception of Accounting Concepts" (Manuscript, University of Illinois at Chicago, 1989).

SELECT BIBLIOGRAPHY

Acheson, J. "Accounting Concepts and Economic Opportunities in a Tarascan Village: Emic and Etic Views." *Human Organization* (Spring 1979): 83–91.

Adler, Nancy. "A Typology of Management Studies Involving Culture." *Journal of International Business Studies* (Fall 1983): 29–47.

Allport, G. W., P. E. Vernon, and G. Lindzey. *A Study of Values.* Boston: Houghton Mifflin, 1960.

Arpan, J. S., and L. H. Radebaugh. *International Accounting and Multinational Enterprises.* New York: John Wiley and Sons, 1985.

Badawy, M. R. "Managerial Attitudes and Need Orientations of Mid Eastern Executives: An Empirical Cross-Cultural Analysis." Proceedings of the 39th Annual Meeting of the Academy of Management, Atlanta, August 1979.

Belkaoui, Ahmed. "Cultural Determinism and Professional Self-Regulation in Accounting." Manuscript, University of Illinois at Chicago, 1989.

_____. *International Accounting*. Westport, Conn.: Greenwood Press, 1985.

Belkaoui, Ahmed and Ronald D. Picur. "Cultural Determinism and the Perception of Accounting Concepts." Manuscript, University of Illinois at Chicago, 1989.

Belkaoui, A., A. Kahl, and J. Peyrard. "Information Needs of Financial Analysts: An International Comparison." *International Journal of Accounting Education and Research* (Fall 1977): 19–27.

Berrien, F. Kenneth. "Methodological and Related Problems in Cross-Cultural Research." *International Journal of Psychology* 2 (1967): 33–43.

Berry, J. "An Ecological Approach to Cross-Cultural Psychology." *Netherlands Journal of Psychology* 30 (1973): 379–392.

Boddewyn, J., and R. Nath. "Comparative Management Studies: An Assessment." *Management International Review* 10 (1970): 3–11.

Chang, L. S., and K. S. Most. "An International Comparison of Investor Uses of Financial Statements." *International Journal of Accounting Education and Research* (Fall 1981): 43–60.

Chevalier, G. "Should Accounting Practices Be Universal?" *CA Magazine* (July 1977): 47–50.

Farmer, Richard N., and Barry M. Richman. *Comparative Management and Economic Progress*. Homewood, Ill.: R. D. Irwin, 1965.

_____. "A Model for Research in Comparative Management," *California Management Review* (Winter 1964): 55–68.

Geertz, Clifford. *The Interpretation of Culture*. New York: Basic Books, 1973.

Goodenough, Ward H. *Culture, Language and Society*. Reading, Mass.: Addison-Wesley, 1971.

Gray, S. J. "Cultural Influences and the International Classification of Accounting Systems." Paper presented at EIASM Workshop on Accounting and Culture, Amsterdam, June 1985.

Griffith, R. W., P. W. Horn, A. DeNisi, and W. Kirchner. "A Multivariate of Managerial Attitudes, Beliefs and Behavior in England and France." Paper presented at the 40th Annual Meeting of the Academy of Management, Detroit, August 1980.

Haire, M., E. E. Ghiselli, and L. W. Porter. *Managerial Thinking: An International Study*. New York: John Wiley and Sons, 1966.

Hall, E. T. *The Silent Language*. Greenwich, Conn: Fawcett, 1959.

Harbison, F., and C. A. Myers. *Management in the Industrial World*. New York: McGraw-Hill, 1959.

Harris, P. R., and R. T. Moran. *Managing Cultural Differences*. Houston: Gulf Publishing, 1974.

Hofstede, G. *Culture's Consequences: International Differences in Work Related Values*. Beverly Hills, Calif.: Sage, 1980.

_____. "Nationality and Espoused Values of Managers." *Journal of Applied Psychology* 61, no. 2 (1976): 148–155.

_____. "The Ritual Nature of Accounting Systems." Paper presented at EIASM Workshop on Accounting and Culture, Amsterdam, June 1985.

Jaggi, B. L. "Impact of the Cultural Environment on Financial Disclosure." *International Journal of Accounting Education and Research* 16, no. 2 (1982): 75–84.

Kelley, L., and R. Worthley. "The Role of Culture in Comparative Management: A

Cross-Cultural Perspective." *Academy of Management Journal* 24, no. 1 (1981): 164–173.

Kitano, H. *Japanese-Americans: Evolution of a Subculture.* New York: Prentice-Hall, 1968.

Kluckhohn, Clyde. "Universal Categories of Culture." In S. Tax, ed., *Anthropology Today.* Chicago: University of Chicago Press, 1962.

————. "Values and Value-Orientations in the Theory of Actions: An Exploration in Definition and Classification." In Talcott Parsons and Edward A. Shils, eds., *Towards a General Theory of Action.* Cambridge, Mass.: Harvard University Press, 1951.

Kluckhohn, F. R., and F. Strodtbeck. *Variations in Value Orientations.* Westport, Conn.: Greenwood Press, 1961.

Kroeber, A. L., and Clyde Kluckhohn. *Culture: A Critical Review of Concepts and Definitions.* Cambridge, Mass.: Peabody Museum, 1952.

Levi-Strauss, Claude. *Structural Anthropology.* Chicago: University of Chicago Press, 1983.

McLaughlin, G. "Values in Behavioral Science." *Journal of Religion and Health* (1965).

Malinowski, B. *A Scientific Theory of Culture.* Chapel Hill: University of North Carolina Press, 1944.

Morris, C. *Varieties of Human Value.* Chicago: University of Chicago Press, 1956.

Murdock, G. P. "Common Denominator of Cultures." In R. Linton, ed., *The Science of Man in the World Crises,* pp. 12–142. New York: Columbia University Press, 1945.

Negandhi, Anant R., and S. Benjamin Prasad. *Comparative Management.* New York: Appleton-Century, 1971.

Parsons, Talcott, and Edward A. Shils, eds. *Towards a General Theory of Action.* Cambridge, Mass.: Harvard University Press, 1951.

Perera, M. H. B., and M. R. Mathews. "The Interrelationship of Culture and Accounting with Particular Reference to Social Accounting." Discussion paper no. 59, Department of Accounting and Finance, Massey University, New Zealand, 1987.

Perlmutter, Howard V. "The Tortuous Evolution of the Multinational Corporation." *Columbia Journal of World Business* (January–February 1969): 9–18.

Peterson, Richard. "Future Directions in Comparative Management Research: Where We Have Been and Where We Should Be Going." *International Management Newsletter* (Fall 1986): 6–8.

Radcliffe-Brown, A. R. *Structure and Function in Primitive Society.* New York: Free Press, 1968.

Redding, S. G. "Some Perceptions of Psychological Needs among Managers in South-East Asia." Paper presented at the Third International Conference at the International Association for Cross-Cultural Psychology, Tilburg, Holland, July 1976.

Roberts, Karlene H. "On Looking at an Elephant." *Psychological Bulletin* 74, no. 5 (1970).

Rokeach, J. *The Nature of Human Values.* New York: Free Press, 1973.

Ronen, S. *Comparative and Multinational Management.* New York: John Wiley and Sons, 1986.

Ronen, S., and A. I. Kraut. "Similarities among Countries Based on Employee Work Values and Attitudes." *Columbia Journal of World Business* 12, no. 2 (1977): 89–96.

Ronen, S., and O. Shenkar. "Clustering Countries on Attitudinal Dimensions: A Review and Synthesis." *Academy of Management Review* 10, no. 3 (1985): 435–454.

Rossi, Ino, and Edwin O'Higgins. "The Development of Theories of Culture." In Ino Rossi, ed. *People in Culture*. New York: Praeger, 1980.

Sarnoff, I. *Society with Tears*. Secaucus, N.J.: Citadel Press, 1960.

Schöllhammer, Hans. "Strategies and Methodologies in International Business and Comparative Management Research." *Management International Review* (1973): 6–32.

Sirota, D., and J. M. Greenwood. "Understand Your Overseas Work Force." *Harvard Business Review* 49, no. 1 (1971): 53–60.

Soeters, Joseph, and Hein Schreuder. "Interactions between National and Organizational Cultures in Accounting Firms." *Accounting, Organizations and Society* 13, no. 1 (1988): 75–85.

Triandis, Harry C. *The Analysis of Subjective Culture*. New York: John Wiley and Sons, 1972.

———. *Interpersonal Behavior*. Monterey, Calif.: Brooks/Cole, 1977.

Violet, William J. "The Development of International Accounting Standards: An Anthropological Perspective." *International Journal of Accounting Education and Research* (Spring 1983).

INDEX

About the Author

AHMED BELKAOUI is Professor of Accounting at the University of Illinois at Chicago and is a recognized authority on accounting. He has served as a consultant to corporations, institutions, and governments throughout the world. Among his recent books are *Industrial Bonds and the Rating Process*, *International Accounting*, *Socio-Economic Accounting*, *Public Policy and the Problems and Practices of Accounting*, and *The Learning Curve* (all published by Quorum Books). He is the author of more than 70 articles and reviews.